The Nature of Vermont

The Nature of Vermont

Introduction and Guide to a
New England Environment

by Charles W. Johnson

The University Press of New England
Hanover, New Hampshire and
London, England, 1980

The University Press of New England

Hanover, New Hampshire and London, England

Brandeis University

Clark University

Dartmouth College

University of New Hampshire

University of Rhode Island

Tufts University

University of Vermont

Page 48. Udall, Stewart L. 1963. *The Quiet Crisis*. Avon Books, New York.
Copyright 1963 by Stewart L. Udall. Reprinted by permission of Holt, Rinehart,
and Winston. All rights reserved.

Page 53. Bradbury, Ray. 1957.*Dandelion Wine*. Doubleday & Company, New York.
Copyright 1957 by Ray Bradbury. Reprinted by permission of the Harold Matson
Company, Inc. All rights reserved.

Page 77. Forbush, Edward H. and May, John R. 1939.*A Natural History of
American Birds of East and Central North America*. Houghton Mifflin Company,
Boston. Copyright 1939 by Houghton Mifflin Company. Reprinted by
permission.

Page 115. Densmore, Frances. 1910. "My Love Has Departed." Smithsonian
Institution Bureau of American Ethnology *Bulletin* 45 (Chippewa Music),
Washington, D.C. Reprinted by permission of the Smithsonian Institution Press.

Page 158. Trippensee, Reuben. 1953. *Wildlife Management*, Volume 2.
McGraw-Hill Book Company, New York. Copyright 1953 by McGraw-Hill Book
Company. Used with the permission of McGraw-Hill Book Company.

Page 179. *The Poems* of Dylan Thomas. New Directions Publishing Corp., New
York. Copyright 1946 by New Directions Publishing Corporation. Reprinted by
permission of New Directions.

Page 203. Barnstone, Willis. 1965.*Sappho*. Anchor Books, Garden City, N.Y.
Copyright 1965 by Willis Barnstone. Reprinted by permission of Doubleday and
Co.

Credits for illustrative material appear at the end of the book, page 278.

To my mother and father.
You opened my eyes
the first time.

Acknowledgments

My first debt is to the Vermont Department of Forests, Parks, and Recreation for allowing me the time to work on this book. I am grateful especially for the support and encouragement I received from Rodney Barber, Director of Parks, Robert DeForge, Park Operations Chief, and James Wilkinson, former Commissioner of Forests, Parks, and Recreation.

Friends, fellow workers, colleagues in the academic community, and family members have all been invaluable in untold ways. I would like to extend the deepest appreciation to my mother, Margaret Hunter Johnson, and to Gale Lawrence for the special effort they put into reviewing the manuscript. Both writers themselves, they were unselfish in sharing their skills with me and they encouraged me through both compliments and suggestions for improvement. Also, the guidance of Hub Vogelmann was welcome and valuable; he has been a source of inspiration for me as for so many others.

Other reviewers offered counsel in their particular fields of expertise, and to the following I owe a great deal: Ross Bell, Robert Candy, Benjamin Day, William Countryman, John Hall, Thomas Hudspeth, Angelo Incerpi, Stephen Loring, Giovanna Neudorfer, Charles Ratté, Robert Spear, James Stewart, Peter Thomas, James Wilkinson and Ian Worley. Several others read the first drafts of the book and gave me an early indication of how it was "coming across," and for their part in the completion of the work I would like to thank Rodney Barber, Robert DeForge, Brian Vachon, Jean Vissering, and Anne Winchester.

I pass on praise and gratitude to the people who contributed the various illustrative materials of the book, components that are essential companions to the written text. Among her many talents, Ann Pesiri shows here her fine, sensitive drawings. Jean Vissering provided the maps and diagrams, representing many hours taken from her free time. Numerous photographers were most gracious in donating their art, especially Robert Candy and John Hall.

Many organizations were generous in supplying photographs, maps, references, and other aids, and to them I extend appreciation: the Harvard University Forest, the Office of the Vermont State Geologist, the University of Vermont, the Vermont Department of Forests, Parks, and Recreation, the Vermont Fish and Game Department, the Planning Division of the Vermont Agency of Environmental Conservation, the Vermont Historical

Society, the Vermont State Planning Office, and the Vermont Travel Division.

The many drafts of the manuscript took a great deal of time, forbearance of my near-illegible handwriting, and sacrifice on the part of Etta Gibson and Kathy Wheeler. Ann Boutin, Hope Davey, and Janet Greaves were also of great help as critical deadlines approached.

I have seen that most authors need images of inspiration, both past and present, upon which to look as they labor through the writing of a book. I have been lucky to have had several such sources. John Olsen, though long deceased, remains one of the most shining of my boyhood idols—his great sea still rolls within me. With a love of nature that permeates their knowledge of it, Robert Spear and Hub Vogelmann have in many ways been standards to guide my way of thinking. And in the background always have been my family, offering a foundation to rest upon: my aunt, Marjorie Plamenatz, is a kindred spirit and cherished friend; my parents are supports far beyond being parents; and the love, patience, and encouragement of my wife, Joanna, were the ties that bound the whole thing together.

Finally, to my young sons I tender both thanks and regret. To Hunter, I hope that one day, in your own way and time, you may share in the world I talk about. To Brendan and Graylyn, I know your joys outdoors are the real answers, and for every baseball game or hiking trip missed, I'm sorry—I never realized this would take so long. I'll make it up.

Preface

The image people have of Vermont is not beyond its reality. The descriptions of wild beauty interspersed with the purity of northern–New England villages need not be exaggerated. Residents of the state have always been proud of these attributes and are protective of their territory, and for outsiders who visit at any time of year, Vermont is a release from the intensity and sameness that grip many other parts of America.

Vermont doesn't have the vast wildernesses of a Minnesota or Alaska. It doesn't have the ten-thousand-foot peaks of the Sierras or open skies of prairies. Vermont is modestly grand, a softness over old ruggedness, blessed with diversity of land and wildlife. Within this small state lives an extraordinary array of plants and animals, and the reasons for this variety are many. Vermont lies within biological transition zones, from the southern deciduous forests to the northern boreal forests, from the eastern Atlantic region to the Midwest. Being so positioned, it has biological representatives from each area. It has a variety of landscapes—mountains, rivers, bogs, lakes, marshes, forests— and the unique associations of each. It lives under the stark polarities of the seasons. It has changed under the different uses to which humans have put it.

The landscape and natural resources here are tremendously important to Vermonters, in both economic and aesthetic terms. These are around us always and much of our income is in some way tied to them. Visitors come many miles to share in this special beauty. Residents and visitors alike are excited and curious about the state: its history, geology, plants, and wildlife, and people's relationship to them through the ages. For the student with time and means to research these topics, a wealth of information can be pieced together. But for the average person, there are few sources that give a panoramic view, that make sense of the diversity of Vermont.

For the latter group, this book is intended. It is neither a field guide nor a complete inventory of the flora and fauna of the state. Rather, it is an introduction to the nature of a state, placed into comprehensible components that reflect its natural character. It is history, natural history, and general discovery brought together in one package, to be opened by any interested person.

A book may be a disembodied teacher if it doesn't allow the reader direct contact with the subject matter. Anyone reading this book can get a mental picture of Vermont, but really to see, feel, and understand the words, one must experience the reality. Thus the book first looks at the state from a distance and then, after taking the reader closer, points the way for people to explore what has been discussed. Each chapter has a corresponding section in the appendix that lists areas of importance where the reader can inspect examples first hand.

Finally, this book is an attempt to capture some of the dynamics of ever-changing natural systems and to relate them to the present scenery. Some questions will be answered, many will go unanswered, and new ones will be posed. But time cannot be frozen, and this account will be outdated as soon as it is published. That is the point exactly: the book becomes what it is treating—embodying change, it serves as a catalyst for further exploration and reaction, rather than as an end in itself.

Contents

Introduction

As we hike on one of Vermont's wooded trails, or swim in one of its lakes, or simply gaze at its mountains, most of us are impressed with the solidity of what we see. We tend to assume that what is before us has been there forever. And many hope that it will continue in its natural beauty forever hence.

But we should stop and consider. No place on earth ever really stands still. The relentless actions of erosion and deposition, the massive movements of continents, the changes of climates and seasons, the interplay of living and nonliving things—all have shaped this world. And they continue to shape it.

By and large, this work proceeds slowly and imperceptibly. But over time—whether the ticking of minutes or the vast stretches measured by millions of years—the earth, landforms, and oceans change. Today's scenery is not the first or the final picture. We are seeing only the latest frame in the film of evolution, a movie that has no end.

Geological processes have set the stage and largely dictated what fragile beings can live on and in the soil, in the earth's thin skin of atmosphere, and in the waters of oceans, rivers, and lakes. Yet living things, too, modify the environment in which they live. And one most recent arrival, a phenomenon of nature, has superimposed changes on those built by eons of physical, chemical, and biological forces: humankind.

This species has had an inordinate effect on the world, not so much as a biological animal as in its power, multiplied by great numbers and extended by machines. The human strength and influence go far beyond the immediate area or nearby region or even country. They affect the world.

So as we serenely sit and absorb the moment's beauty, we should be mindful of what has taken place to bring it to us, from long ago to the recent past. It may be hard to visualize at times, or even to accept. But understanding the way Vermont has come to us is an important part of understanding its nature today.

I The Setting

Only that day dawns to which we
are awake. There is more day to dawn.
The sun is but a morning star.

−Henry David Thoreau, *Walden* (1854)

1

To Move the World

The Bedrock

The hills, mountains, and valleys of Vermont are familiar to many through words and photographs; they are an inseparable part of life here. Their origins, however, are not easy to depict. In addition, there are other geological formations in the state that are not so well known but which are vital clues to Vermont's earlier form.

For example, 500-million-year-old fossils of coral, the oldest in the world, and other organisms occur in limestone up and down the length of Lake Champlain. Since coral is an animal community of shallow tropical oceans, and limestone is a rock of marine origin, it is difficult to imagine how such organisms came to be in the interior of New England, some 200 miles from the ocean, in a climate that is far from tropical. Also, running north-

Vermont Fossils. These fossils are from the 500-million-year-old limestones of Button Island, a small natural area off Button Bay State Park. On the left is the sea snail *Maclurites;* on the right a chunk of the coral reef that makes up the island. These fossils indicate the long-ago existence here of a warm, shallow sea.

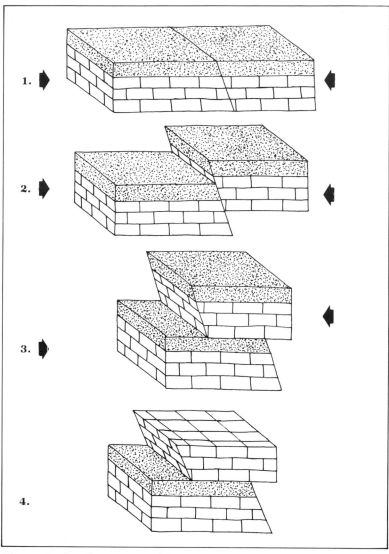

Thrust Fault. The process of formation of this landform is shown diagrammatically. (1) Pressure from the sides (due to plate tectonics) causes a great fracture in the bedrock. The bedrock has distinct layers of younger rock on top of older. In western Vermont shale often lies on top of dolostone, easily seen as black on top of white. (2) With increasing pressure, the section of land on the right slides up the slope of the fracture. (3) Finally the entire right section is pushed completely on top of the left. (4) With erosion over time the younger top layer of shale is lost, exposing the next layer of older and more resistant dolostone. In a few places the entire sequence is exposed and shows dolostone on top of shale on top of dolostone. A famous such place is Lone Rock Point just north of Burlington Bay (see Appendix I).

south in the western part of the state, for almost its entire length, are great thrust faults, where huge chunks of land have been heaved up on top of themselves. These were made by tremendous pressures from the side, but what those pressures were and where they came from remained for many years a mystery.

Until very recently, geologists could offer no convincing theories or mechanisms to account for the raising of mountains, the thrust-faulting of blocks of land, or the presence of coral thousands of miles from where it should be. All were explained in a circular reasoning: "Mountains owe their origin to mountain-building processes . . . Thrust faults are caused by great stresses at right angles to the fault line . . . Coral indicates that this area was once under a warm ocean . . ." The underlying questions *why?* and *how?* went unanswered.

In the late 1960s geologists and geophysicists came up with a revolutionary theory that began to give the answers. From a series of discoveries a grand and world-encompassing model was constructed that could explain mountains, earthquakes, volcanoes, thrust faults, and out-of-place fossils, all in the same breath. The theory had actually been proposed as early as 1915, but owing to the lack of solid evidence, it was never widely supported in scientific circles. The evidence has now come in, however, and it is still coming. The model of continental drift, or plate tectonics, is having an overwhelming impact on the earth sciences—and all natural sciences, as well.

Based on much corroborating evidence, the theory describes several global activities:

• The earth's crust is not an unbroken sphere, but rather is made of several enormous "plates," which are moving (drifting) relative to one another. The plates are solid, but float in a semi-solid mobile zone far below the surface.
• Continents on the plates are made mostly of granite, whereas ocean basins are of a darker, denser rock, basalt. A plate may be made of continental crust only, ocean crust only, or both.
• As they drift, plates collide, separate, or slip parallel to one another, resulting in great disturbances deep within the earth.
• Where plates meet or separate, tremendous forces release untold amounts of energy. Where they meet, the plates are either "consumed" in abyssal trenches or crumpled up into mountains. Where they separate, new oceanic crust is added, in the form of midocean ridges: the new crust wells up as molten rock, mounds out on both sides, and solidifies. This perceptible addition of ocean crust, producing oceanic volcanoes that are relatively close to the earth's surface, bears witness to the movement of the plates. It also explains why the oldest ocean crust is much younger than the oldest continental crust—the continental crust is neither created nor destroyed, whereas ocean crust is continually being both created and destroyed.

• Where continental crust meets ocean crust, the denser basalt of the ocean plunges beneath the lighter continental granite, creating deep ocean trenches, volcanoes, and earthquakes. This also results in the rumpling up of the continental crust — the process known as mountain building. (Where two continents collide, neither goes under the other and even higher mountains arise. This is what happened when India and Asia collided: the Himalayas became the world's greatest mountain range.)

• North and Central America and half of the North Atlantic Ocean are part of the so-called North American Plate. New ocean crust is being added at the Mid-Atlantic Ridge, and the entire plate is moving westward at a rate of 4 to 8 centimeters per year.

• The San Andreas Fault in California represents the zone where the North American Plate is slipping along and colliding with the northward-moving Pacific Plate. The regular, often intense, earth-

Plate Tectonics. The earth divided into its component plates, upon which the continents ride. The arrows indicate the direction in which the plates are currently moving. Oceanic crust is being added at the mido-cean ridges and consumed in the deep trenches (subduction zones). Transform faults are in those areas where two plates are sliding next to each other, such as the San Andreas Fault in California.

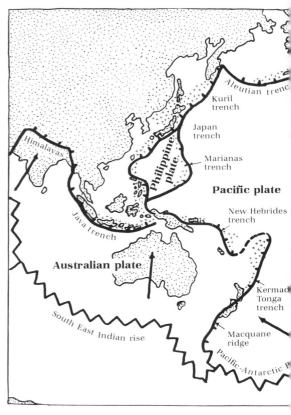

quakes along this line are a side effect of the prodigious forces in action. The Sierra and Rocky Mountain ranges are also a product of these two plates' activities; they are still being built.

• Since the North American Plate is moving west, the net result is that the Atlantic Ocean is getting larger while the Pacific is shrinking. Over a few years this amounts to but a minuscule change, but over millions of years it may involve thousands of miles.

Scientists estimate the earth to be about 4½ billion years old, but the oldest seafloor rock in the Atlantic is only about 200 million years old. As one might expect, the youngest Atlantic rock is at the Mid-Atlantic Ridge and the oldest is at the continental margins on either side of the ocean. These facts, combined with the measured rate and direction of plate movements, are evidence of a time 200 million years ago when the Atlantic

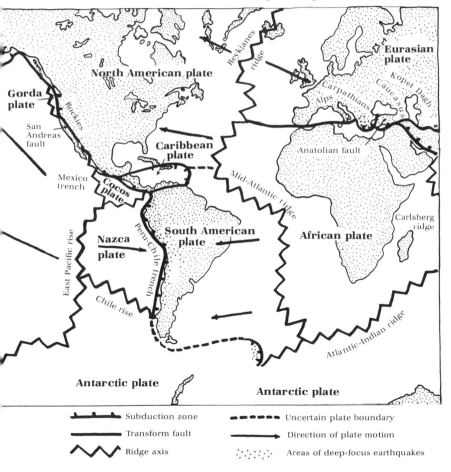

Geologic Timetable

Era and Period	Began—Years Before Present	Vermont and Regional Events	World Events— Plate Tectonics
Cenozoic Era			
	0-2,000	Cooling trend.	
	4,000- 6,000	Warming trend (hypsithermal interval). Rise of Indian cultures.	Many large Ice Age mammals become extinct.
	10,000	Last glacier leaves Vermont.	
Quaternary	3 million	Continental glaciers begin. (Ice Age)	Origin of human beings.
Tertiary	65 million		Himalayas born (25 million years ago). Mammals at maximum. Rocky Mountains born (75 million years ago).
Mesozoic Era			
Cretaceous	136 million	Younger igneous intrusions, monadnocks formed.	Dinosaurs become extinct. Origin of birds. Origin of mammals.
Jurassic	195 million	Ancient Appalachians continue to be eroded, exposing present system.	Breakup of Pangaea, North America begins to move west.
Triassic	225 million		Rise of dinosaurs.
Paleozoic Era			
Permian	280 million		Origin of reptiles.
Pennsylvanian	320 million		Vast swamps—origin of modern coal.
Mississippian	345 million	Older igneous intrusions.	Continents collide, Pangaea formed.
Devonian	395 million		Origin of amphibians.
Silurian	440 million	Formation of ancient Appalachian and Green Mountains.	Origin of fish. First vertebrates.
Ordovician	500 million	Corals and other marine life in warm ocean.	Continents begin to converge. No land life.
Cambrian	570 million		
Precambrian Era			
	4.5 billion	Archaic Appalachian system(s) created and eroded away. Adirondacks formed first time.	Archaic plate convergences and separations. Oldest fossils (3 billion years old). Oldest rocks (3.7 billion years old).

Ocean did not exist. Europe, North Africa, and North America were fused as one. In fact, all the present continents were together then, in one vast landmass called Pangaea. Since then, the continents have been shifting around, separating, colliding, arriving at their present configurations and locations.

Since mountain building occurs in the areas of plate collision, the Green Mountains of Vermont seem way out of place, far from the West Coast, where such activity is now under way. But geological research has uncovered an even more complex history of the earth than the activity of 200 million years ago, which helps to explain the origin of our landscape. Evidently, long before even Pangaea existed North America was separated from

Present Continents

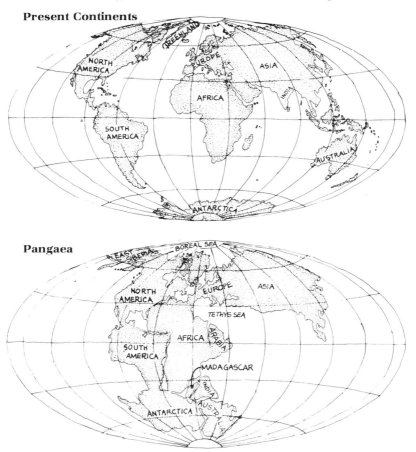

Pangaea

Pangaea. The supercontinent Pangaea as it probably looked 200 million years ago, before it broke apart into the present-day continents, depicted above. Note that the area that is now Vermont was positioned nearer the equator, next to Africa and not far from Europe.

Origin of the Appalachian Mountains. The diagrams illustrate the probable origin of the Appalachian Mountain system, including the Green Mountains of Vermont. It is a complicated and not as yet fully deciphered history.

There apparently have been at least three Appalachian systems in this region of the continent. The earliest we have evidence of was formed nearly 900 million years ago, when the continents collided and formed a supercontinent that predated Pangaea by some 700 million years.

(1, 2) Following those events the continents broke apart and began moving away from each other. Over millions of years the original Appalachians were worn away by erosive forces and the sediments carried down to and deposited in the widening sea—the ancestral ocean before our present Atlantic.

(3) About 500 million years ago the continents stopped moving apart, the midocean ridge ceased producing new seafloor, and a new boundary between the plates was established just east of present-day North America. The continents then began to converge, with the creation of a deep ocean trench and volcanoes where the plates were colliding—with oceanic crust plunging beneath the uprising North America. The sediments deposited in the ocean from the previous mountain range were then squeezed into metamorphic rock of a new mountain system.

(4) Ultimately, the continents met again to create Pangaea. It had taken 125 million years for the ancient ocean to close; it would then take another 175 million years for Pangaea to break apart to form our present continents. The making of Pangaea resulted in the massive uplifting of a second Appalachian system.

(5) About 200 million years ago Pangaea began to break apart, with a new Atlantic Ocean being born between North America and Europe-Africa; this was to widen to become our modern Atlantic. As the continents moved apart, erosion once again wore them down and the rivers carried the material to the ocean. In these last 200 million years, the second Appalachian system has probably been reduced to at least half its original height.

(6) The present picture. The modern (third) Appalachians, including the Green Mountains, although but foothills of the second range, stand above it, as the eroded remains of the earlier system now lie as ocean sediment composing the continental shelf. The earliest Appalachian system is preserved as a core, which outcrops in various places in the East.

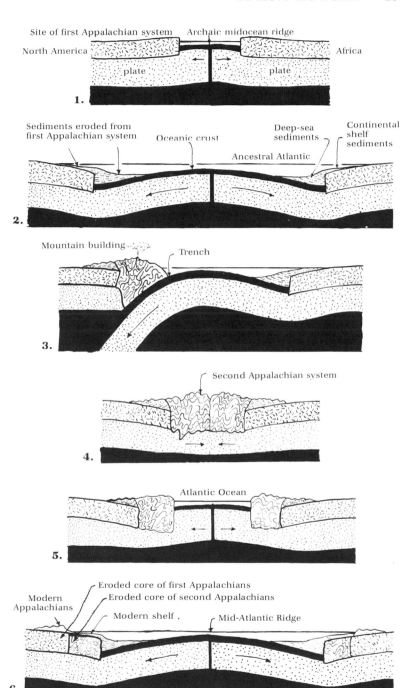

Europe and Africa by a previous Atlantic Ocean. At that time, the North American, Eurasian, and African plates were moving apart in the same direction in which they are traveling today. But sometime more than 500 million years ago the plates stopped this movement and began to converge at a new boundary between the North American and Eurasian-African plates, established just east of our present-day Appalachian Mountain system.

The continents apparently came together over a long period of time, and mountains, perhaps rivaling the present Himalayas, were built. Pangaea was thus born, to exist for more than 175 million years, from the time the earlier Atlantic Ocean closed (about 375 million years ago) to when it broke through again, as the present Atlantic. With the breakup of Pangaea, the process once again reversed itself and the separate continents began the voyage they are on to this day. In the early breakup of the supercontinent, the North American Plate continent apparently ripped off some land that was part of modern Africa—a piece that is now part of southern New England.

The Appalachian Mountains (of which the Green Mountains of Vermont are a northern extension), born 500 million years ago, have been worn away by wind, water, rock particles, and ice. In certain places here, the bedrock core of some of the oldest rock on earth is exposed. By sophisticated techniques, scientists have determined this core rock to be about 900 million years old. It is thought to be the remnant of a previous mountain range that was built when the North American and Eurasian Plates collided in a much earlier time, millions, perhaps even a billion years before the formation of Pangaea. This ancient rock can be seen cropping out in several places in the southern half of Vermont, along the Green Mountain ridges; Killington and Pico peaks are probably the most conspicuous and well-known areas where this rock is exposed.

However, as old as these rocks are, they are not anywhere near the oldest in the world. If one stands on the summits of the Green Mountains, or in the Champlain Valley, and looks west to the Adirondacks, one then sees the most ancient rocks of all. Some of these, largely granite, patriarchs have been around for more than 3 billion years. They are part of an extensive continental "shield" that has resisted the earth's ravages over unfathomable time.

The Appalachians we see today were formed out of the eroded sediments of the previous mountains that were carried by rivers and streams into the coastal ocean, forming a continental shelf. This vast shelf was compressed, changed, and pushed up as the plates came together more than 375 million years ago and Pangaea was created. The shelf sediments, under the enormous pressures and high temperatures accompanying plate collision and mountain building, were changed into rock: they were transformed into various kinds of metamorphic rock—their geological classification—the kind so familiar to us in the Green Mountains and Appalachians today.

The ancient area that was to become Vermont was apparently part of the continental shelf stretching out into the ocean. Lateral pressures from plate collisions caused not only the folding and rising of the Green Mountains, but also the "snapping" of land where thrust faults appear, especially near Lake Champlain.

The presence of coral in Vermont can be explained by plate tectonics in the repositioning of continents over a vast period of time. At the time these corals were living, the entire region was situated nearer the equator; subsequent plate movements brought the land north into a colder climate. The continental shelf on which they grew has been transformed into limestone in the Champlain Valley and into mountains farther to the east.

Though the study of plate tectonics is in its infancy, it is becoming a great unifying principle in science and an important way for us to make sense of the complexity around us. It has already helped to explain some of Vermont.

The Glaciers Pass

In 1848 workmen were excavating a new railroad bed near Mount Holly, in south central Vermont, when they unearthed large and strange bones. These were later studied by the famous Harvard zoologist and geologist Louis Agassiz, and were determined to be of a woolly mammoth, an elephant that lived in Arctic regions through the time of glaciation. Some scientists believe the bones were probably of a mastodon rather than a mammoth; mastodons lived in the scrubby spruce-fir forests of the north, whereas mammoths stayed more in the open tundra regions. Regardless, remains of both kinds of elephant were subsequently found in the American Northeast, proof that both had lived in the region at one time. The presence of the Vermont animal, buried in the earth, could mean but one thing: Vermont had a different look—owing to a different, colder climate—long ago, when these beasts were roaming the territory.

A year later, in 1849, other fossil bones were discovered in a railroad-bed excavation near Charlotte, on Lake Champlain. First thought to be of a horse, they were later determined to be of a small whale, also an extinct species but closely related to some whales that live today in Arctic waters. Along with this skeleton were found shells of clams and oysters, the same kind that now live in a cold marine environment. These facts suggest that indeed the whale lived in a cold ocean. But what ocean, and how did the whale get there?

These two mammal species, whale and ancient elephant, could not have come from the time of Pangaea or the ancient Atlantic, since no mammals had at that point even appeared on earth. There must have been a later restructuring of topography to account for them. These stories bring us to another great geological event that has profoundly affected Vermont: the Ice Age, the time of glaciation during the Pleistocene epoch, lasting from 3 million to 10,000 years ago.

The prehistoric existence of glaciers has been established from the glacial remnants that survive in the Arctic, Antarctica, Alaska, Greenland, Switzerland, Austria, and Scandinavia. But only in the mid-1800s did powerful evidence indicate that glaciers once covered most of North America, including the northern half of what is now the United States. Foremost among proponents of the new and hotly debated theory of continental glaciation was the same Louis Agassiz mentioned above. Largely to him do we owe this landmark concept, now almost universally accepted as fact.

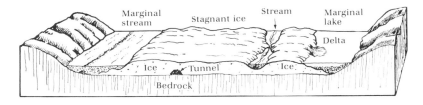

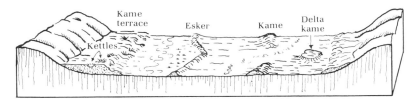

Glacial Features of the Landscape. Many of Vermont's physical features are products of the activity of glaciers. The upper picture shows the landscape while the Ice Age glaciers were present; the lower, depicting the same landscape, shows the modern results of that presence. Kames are large banks of sand and gravel that collected between the melting edges of two glaciers; the broader kame terraces occurred between the side of a hill or mountain and a melting edge. Eskers are long, tall, sinuous mounds of similar composition that collected within "tunnels" melting inside the ice sheet, where long cracks allowed water to enter and flow. Kettles are ponds in the till (glacially deposited clay, sand, gravel, boulders) created when huge blocks of ice became separated from the receding glacier, were trapped, and melted. Deltas may be formed either off the land in a river, or off the glacier, as meltwaters carry rocks, sand, and clay out into a lake or pond, building a wide fan-shaped terrace, called a delta kame.

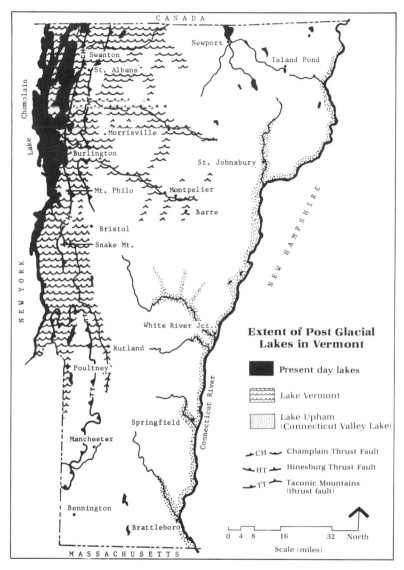

Postglacial Lakes (about 10,000 years ago). The extent of Lake Vermont on the western side of the state and Lake Upham, on the east, in relation to present-day Lake Champlain and the Connecticut River. Lake Vermont reached up the flanks of the Green Mountains and into the major east-west river valleys. Lake Upham, a long, narrow lake, was actually a swelling of the Connecticut River, which had been dammed by a large obstruction south, in Connecticut. Note the locations of the various thrust faults on the western side of the state, which were caused by lateral forces resulting from plate movements. Many high places along those thrust faults were left as islands during the period of Lake Vermont; Mount Philo and Snake Mountain are good examples.

For us, the Arctic and even Vermont in winter may be cold indeed. But in the past 3 million years there have been even colder times, when the average yearly temperature was 5 to 25 degrees Fahrenheit lower than today's. Now, continental glaciers exist only in Greenland and Antarctica, but at that earlier time they covered both poles and extended down into what are now temperate regions of the continents. They were so extensive that it is estimated that enough water was bound in glacial ice to lower the sea level worldwide by 475 feet. Even today, with Greenland's ice cap up to 10,000 feet thick and Antarctica's 3 miles in places, about 77 percent of all the fresh water in the world is in continental glaciers, or 2.5 percent of all water on earth, including oceans.

Ice is normally thought of as a solid, and indeed on a glacial surface it may be brittle. But under the tremendous pressures within a glacial mass it becomes more mobile, exhibiting a slow, fluidlike movement. The glacier indeed "flows" from north to south (in the Northern Hemisphere) in slow motion, yet with great abrasive powers.

As they moved over the land, the glaciers reworked it in two different ways: first by eroding or gouging out existing formations, and then by transporting and depositing the eroded materials. This jumble of rocks, pebbles, sand, and clay—called till—was deposited in Vermont in various fashions. Some was forcibly plastered on the bedrock surfaces to form a relatively hard coating; some was merely dumped as the glacier melted, left in loose piles, mounds, or sheets, depending on the glacier's subsequent movements. These formations are called moraines. Where the till accumulates when the glacier reaches its farthest point, the formation is a terminal moraine; we have no terminal moraines of the last continental glacier in Vermont, but two extraordinary examples farther south are Long Island and Cape Cod (Martha's Vineyard and Nantucket are terminal moraines of an earlier glacier). If the glacier recedes for a period of time and then stops, it piles up another bank of till, called a recessional moraine. But if the glacier melts back quickly, these "hills" do not have time to form and the till spreads out like a blanket over the land, creating ground moraines. This kind of till is what we see as the predominant subsoil of Vermont.

The subsoil of sand, gravel, and boulders is what the glaciers left behind. But the work they did in Vermont when they were active is also obvious. Though the mountains, gaps, and valleys were here long before the Ice Age, the glaciers reshaped them— scouring and rounding off the peaks, broadening and smoothing the valleys, widening the gaps to notches. The reshaped land and the rubble of till blocked former drainages, resulting in the creation of most of our ponds, lakes, bogs, and streams. Huge boulders (*erratics*) stand isolated in the most unlikely places, such as open fields and on the tops of mountains; these rocks were carried by the glaciers, occasionally over hundreds of miles, and then left behind when the ice receded. Sometimes the rock type of the erratic is quite different from that upon which it rests, and if these erratics were carried any distance from the parent material and in substantial numbers, geologists can trace the path the glacier took by mapping the erratics. Boulders that originated at Mount Ascutney, near Windsor, have been strewn well into Massachusetts and together make up the well-known "Mount Ascutney Train," which delineates exceptionally clearly the course of the last glacier. In addition, deep grooves and scratches in the bedrock show where erratics and other coarse materials were dragged over the landscape, and these grooves (*striae*) also help geologists record the direction glaciers took in their passage over the land.

But all was not ice and cold in times past. Interestingly, periods of glaciation alternated with long warmer intervals, often lasting hundreds of thousands of years, which caused the glaciers to retreat and expose bare ground. For the last 10,000 years or so we have been in an interglacial period, and at one stretch during this time, about 4,000 to 6,000 years ago, the climate was very much warmer than today's. This hypsithermal interval, or climatic optimum, had great influence not only on Vermont's vegetation, but also on human development, as we shall see later.

At least four glaciers have covered Vermont over the past 3 million years, but the last is the one we know most about, since it left the clearest signs and trails, as well as having obliterated the bulk of the evidence of the previous glaciers. This last is known as the Wisconsin glaciation and was at its maximum development in the northern United States about 18,000 years ago. In the East it reached as far south as the Long Island region before retreating; it left Vermont about 10,000 years ago.

Both the mammoth of Mount Holly and the whale of Charlotte are direct testimony to the existence of the glaciers. It is likely that the north-ranging mammoth populations moved steadily south ahead of the advancing glacier, and returned back north when it receded. The mammoth found here was undoubtedly only one of many that roamed over Vermont in the preglacial and early postglacial times, feeding on the tundra lichens and facing the arrows and spears of Paleolithic Indians.

The whale, however, gives no clue to other geologic events associated with the glaciers. Long before the Wisconsin glacier descended upon Vermont, the Champlain Valley had been in existence. It has been suggested that it was created when a long, massive block of bedrock dropped down between the Adirondack Mountains and the Green Mountains more than 300 million years ago; this deformation probably was due to crustal movement associated with plate collisions. The glaciers greatly modified the valley, and rivers have since brought down much silt and clay from higher adjoining areas to fill in hundreds of feet on the bottom. Millions of years after the valley's creation the Wisconsin glacier filled it. But in its retreat, about 12,500 years ago, the glacier cleared the Burlington area, the valley became exposed, all drainage to the north was blocked by ice, and the water melting from the glacier created a freshwater lake (called Lake Vermont), much larger than the present Lake Champlain. Lake Vermont extended up into the foothills of the Green Mountains, leaving such peaks as Mount Philo as islands and covering the lower hills and islands we see today. (A comparable lake was formed on the eastern side of Vermont and the western side of New Hampshire by the damming of the Connecticut River. This "Lake Upham" reached as far west as Randolph and north to St. Johnsbury, Vermont.)

The sheer weight of the ice had depressed the land 500 to 600 feet, so that Lake Vermont actually drained south into what is now the Hudson Valley. At the same time, the sea level was more than 400 feet lower than it is today, owing to water locked up as glacial ice. But as the ice melted, the land began to "spring back" and the oceans to rise. However, the oceans rose faster than the land rebounded, and salt water backed into the St. Lawrence River Valley and eventually crept around the southern and eastern edges of the shrinking glacier, and finally into Vermont. Lake Vermont became diluted with sea water and changed into the "Champlain Sea," as we have named it, an estuary of the ocean with about half its salinity.

During a later colder period the glacier advanced once more, re-creating a second Lake Vermont, then withdrew to allow formation of a second Champlain Sea. At last, some 10,000 years ago, the glacier withdrew for good. The land, relieved of its burden, rose high enough to block off the Atlantic Ocean. The southern Champlain basin, having been uncovered earlier than the northern, rose higher, giving a tilt north to the entire valley. This resulted in drainage to the north into the Richelieu River, which is the case today.

In one of the two Champlain Seas the whale must have lived, having traveled there from the ocean. It is undoubtedly one of many whales, which, after death, was buried in the sediments brought down by the rivers, only to become located on dry land when the Champlain Sea dropped to the present level of Lake Champlain.

We have many other reminders of this former "sea." Several species of fish today in Lake Champlain are ancestors of modern saltwater species. An Atlantic-coast dune plant, beach heath, is clinging to existence at a location near the shores of Lake Champlain. The sediments at such places as Sand Bar State Park, the Missisquoi River delta, and Button Bay State Park have the same blue clay that enveloped the Charlotte whale. Marine beach gravel lies at the foot of Mount Philo.

In the long view of geologic history, the glacier's presence was just a short while ago, and our closeness in time to it is still clear in many respects. We can measure the land's rebounding from its relieved stress, even though it be only a centimeter or two per year. The landforms and waters plainly show much of what the glacier did, and, as we shall see later, we know it erased former vegetation and associated wildlife, but in withdrawing it opened the way for new colonizations.

These are only some of the records of the glacier's passing—both living and nonliving records—and what it left behind has helped to make Vermont. We know that the glacier did come and go. But no one can say for sure that it has gone for good.

Physiographic Regions of Vermont

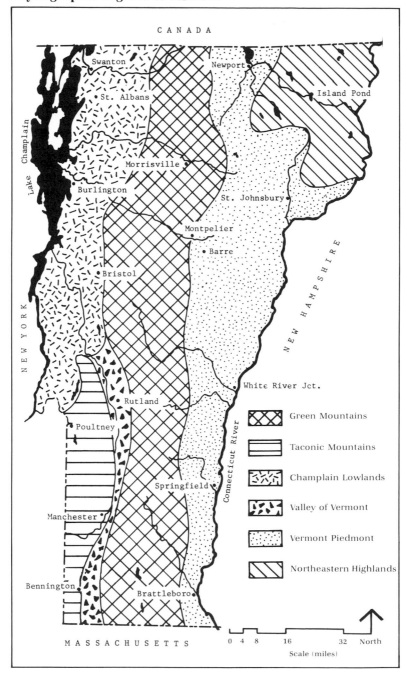

CANADA

Swanton

Newport

St. Albans

Island Pond

Lake Champlain

Morrisville

Burlington

St. Johnsbury

Montpelier

Barre

Bristol

NEW HAMPSHIRE

NEW YORK

White River Jct.

Rutland

Green Mountains

Poultney

Taconic Mountains

Connecticut River

Champlain Lowlands

Springfield

Valley of Vermont

Manchester

Vermont Piedmont

Northeastern Highlands

Bennington

Brattleboro

MASSACHUSETTS

0 4 8   16   32   North

Scale (miles)

2

Physiographic Regions of Vermont

The geologic processes of plate tectonics and glaciation have shaped the foundation of Vermont and made or affected most of the landforms we see today. Of course, a closer look at the state's 9,609 square miles yields more details of those and other events, most of which have sooner or later to do with rocks.

Geologists classify rocks in three categories, according to their manner of origin. Vermont has good examples of all three.

1. *Igneous rocks,* from molten material (*magma*), cooling and solidifying either at or below the earth's surface.

2. *Sedimentary rocks,* eroded from other rocks, the particles compacted and cemented, or chemically combined, under pressure from above or the sides.

3. *Metamorphic rocks,* "changed" from preexisting sedimentary, igneous rocks, or metamorphic rocks by intense pressure and heat associated with plate tectonics or other crustal movements.

Obviously, the three types are so closely related that they can be diagrammatically represented in the "rock cycle":

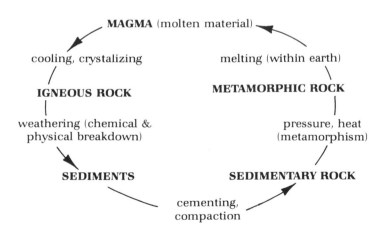

This is a simplified picture, as there are many crossovers and shortcuts.

Though the list of the kinds of rocks in each category is long, a few common ones in Vermont illustrate the processes in action.

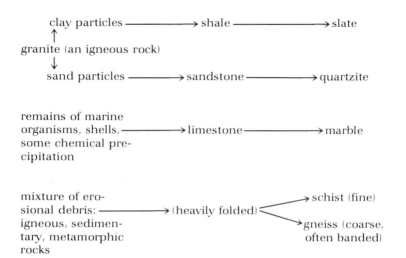

Source Material	Sedimentary Rocks	Metamorphic Rocks

clay particles ⟶ shale ⟶ slate
↑
granite (an igneous rock)
↓
sand particles ⟶ sandstone ⟶ quartzite

remains of marine
organisms, shells, ⟶ limestone ⟶ marble
some chemical pre-
cipitation

mixture of ero-   ⟶ schist (fine)
sional debris: ⟶ (heavily folded)⟨
igneous, sedimen-   ⟶ gneiss (coarse,
tary, metamorphic   often banded)
rocks

It is now believed that the great pressures and heat associated with plate collisions are responsible for the widespread regional metamorphism in mountain building. Fossils are usually destroyed by metamorphism, so any that may have existed in the mountains, which are regions of heavy metamorphism, are no longer evident. Fortunately, the limestone of the Champlain Valley somehow escaped this metamorphism, so that we have a fine record of fossil history there.

The three basic rock types differ from one another in many respects—physical appearance, resistance to erosion, the kinds of minerals they release upon weathering, and so on. Their presence in a region may be reflected in any number of ways, whether directly, as a scenic feature, or indirectly, as indicated by the kinds of plants growing on or near them.

For purposes of characterizing the state's regional differences, geographers and geologists often divide Vermont into six zones, called physiographic regions, each of which has a distinctive combination of topography, climate, and vegetation. These differences are largely attributable to geologic features (both bedrock and surface deposits) and latitude.

Granite Quarry, Barre. Extracting a famous natural resource of Vermont. The granite here was deposited as molten rock in huge subsurface spaces in the already formed surrounding bedrock. This quarry, belonging to the Rock of Ages Corporation, is the largest in the world, more than 350 feet deep. It is made wider at the top than the bottom to prevent the walls from collapsing inward.

The Green Mountains

This chain runs north-south the length of Vermont. It is part of the very long Appalachian Mountain system that extends from Alabama to the Gaspé Peninsula, in Canada, where it plummets into the St. Lawrence River Valley. In fact, as the supercontinent Pangaea is reconstructed, the Appalachian system continues even farther, lining up perfectly with the Caledonian range of Scotland and Scandinavia, and exhibiting the same folding patterns and rock types as its European relatives.

The Green Mountains are 160 miles long and fairly uniform in width, 21 miles at the Canadian border and 36 at the Massachusetts line. They are the dominant feature of Vermont, and until the automobile brought momentous road improvements, they presented a real obstacle to east-west travel and communication. When Zadock Thompson, a nineteenth-century naturalist and historian, referred in 1853 to "going over the mountain," he meant a very difficult journey. This barrier blocked more than human beings, as we shall see later, in that it prevented populations of plants and animals from mixing freely throughout the state, thus setting up different botanical and zoological zones on either side of the mountains.

The highest peaks in Vermont are in the Green Mountain range. Mount Mansfield is the tallest, at 4,393 feet, followed in order by Killington Peak, Mount Ellen, and Camel's Hump. The substance of the Green Mountains is by and large metamorphic rock. Most abundant is the schist form, with its green-gray color and often wavy appearance, due to heavy folding. It is exposed on the higher summits and in many outcroppings throughout the region. Just east of the backbone of the Green Mountains are parallel subsidiary ranges: north of the Winooski River Valley are the Lowell and Worcester ranges, south of it is the Northfield range.

In addition to the dominant metamorphic rocks, important igneous mineral deposits occur in the Green Mountains, especially on the eastern flanks, and help make the range an economically important region. Talc and asbestos are quarried here in such quantities as to put Vermont high on the list of total United States production.

The Green Mountains to some extent influence the climate of the whole state. They are high enough to intercept the prevailing west winds, forcing them to move up and then over, which cools the air masses and causes them to release precipitation regularly throughout the year, as rain in summer, snow in winter. In the mountains themselves are recorded the greatest snowfall and overall wetness—and on north-facing slopes, the shortest growing season, coldest temperatures, heaviest precipitation, and severest winter weather—of any place in the state.

The Taconic Mountains

The Taconic range runs from near Lake Bomoseen 75 miles south to the Massachusetts line, and west from the Valley of Vermont to the New York line. They are low, rounded, mature mountains, and strange as it sounds, they appear to be upside down. That is, whereas in the usual sequence of rock deposition younger layers lie on top of older, in the Taconics just the reverse is true. A puzzle, indeed.

The Taconics are about the same age as the Green Mountains—perhaps slightly older—but the bedrock of the Taconics is unlike that of the Green Mountains or any area north, west, or south of them. Near the surface they are mostly a mixture of shale and slate, and have a geologic affinity with the area southeast of the Green Mountains. This affinity has led geologists to speculate that the Taconics were originally thrust over from somewhere east of the area that was to become the Green Mountains. The clay-based shales and slates indicate that the original material of the Taconics was deep-ocean sediment beyond the continental shelf, the fine particles of which drifted far out to sea from the rivers that emptied into it. Plate collisions thrust huge chunks of this land on top of itself, and eons of time have eroded away the topmost layers of shale, revealing the older stratum of limestone. Below this limestone, however, is another layer of shale. Therefore since the uppermost layers of shale have disappeared, the mountains give the illusion of being upside down.

As the Taconics were being thrust up and over the Green Mountains, the latter were also being built, both processes, presumably, due to plate collisions. As the Green Mountains rose higher, the Taconics were continually pushed westward until they slumped down the western flank of the Greens. Subsequent drainage between the two ranges became established, and ancient rivers cut the Valley of Vermont deep and wide between them.

The Taconics are the slate-producing center of Vermont. Quarries, both active and inactive, are spotted all over this region, especially near Lakes Bomoseen and St. Catherine; the area around Poultney is perhaps the most productive still being mined. Indeed, the slate here is famous the world over, and in total United States production Vermont is second only to Pennsylvania. Much marble has been quarried here, too, especially in the vicinity of Proctor.

The Valley of Vermont

The Valley of Vermont is a narrow strip of land nestled between the Green Mountains to the east and the Taconic Mountains to the west. It is about 85 miles long, reaching from Massachusetts to near Brandon. It varies in width from a few hundred yards near Emerald Lake to 8 miles in the Bennington area. U.S. Route 7 travels straight through the Valley, testifying to its flatness.

The Valley is underlaid by sedimentary and metamorphic rock. The bulk of the rock, however, is of a different kind from that in the mountains. Much of it is limestone, the sedimentary rock of oceanic origin, and marble, its metamorphosed counterpart. The surrounding area is famous for its marble, producing some of the finest in the world. The calcium-rich environment of the Valley fosters an interesting flora; many species here are unusual calciphilic ("calcium-loving") plants, not found with such frequency at low elevations elsewhere in the state.

Because of its flatness and fertility, this region is heavily agricultural, with few forested areas remaining.

The Valley of Vermont. Just north of Emerald Lake State Park, in southern Vermont, the Valley of Vermont narrows to a few hundred yards. On the left the Taconics descend sharply, while on the right the Green Mountains loom up. See text for explanation of the relationship of these two ranges.

The Champlain Lowlands

Lake Champlain, its basin and islands, the rivers that drain into it, and the neighboring wetlands make up the complex character of the Champlain Lowlands. This region is cradled by the Adirondack Mountains to the west and the Green Mountains to the east. Its greatest width is 20 miles, but it narrows to about 5 miles in the southern end, at the Taconics. It is about 109 miles long. The focal point, Lake Champlain, is, after the Great Lakes, the largest lake in the United States, being 109 miles long and 11 miles across at its widest, and comprising 440 square miles.

Owing to the protection offered by mountain ranges on three sides and to the moderating effect of Lake Champlain, the climate in this region is the mildest in the state: the frost-free season is longer, the precipitation less, and the temperatures not so extreme as in the other regions.

Stump Fences. The large remains of white pines that were cut down, these stumps were pulled by horses out of the fields and left as effective fences. They give an indication of the formerly wooded appearance of the landscape. This fence is near Addison, in the Champlain Valley.

This area is important geologically not only for the stories it tells in thrust faults, fossils, and glacial evidences, but also for its clay soils and flat topography, which are further testimony to the Ice Age: thick silt and clay deposits brought down year after year by rivers to the large ancient Lake Vermont, after the glacier had left the area.

This is a fertile region. Human inhabitants have transformed it into one of the prime agricultural domains of the state. The white-pine forests that originally grew here in great abundance were clear-cut, their stumps pulled out by horses and drawn to the field edges, where they made the tangled fences still occasionally seen today. Animal inhabitants make the large marshes at the union of flatland, major tributaries, and Lake Champlain important breeding, spawning, and nesting grounds for multitudes of species; these are also major oases for migrating waterfowl, which stop to feed and rest during their treks up and down the continent.

The Vermont Piedmont

Piedmont literally means "foot-mountain" or "foot-hill," and that is exactly what the Vermont Piedmont comprises: foothills of the Green Mountains, running the length of the state just east of the higher range. Extensive erosion has removed much of the metamorphic and sedimentary rocks that were originally here, and what remains is a mixture of limestone, schist, and granite. Generally, the landscape is mellow, with gentle hills, broad valleys, and quiet lakes.

An occasional higher peak emerges from the Piedmont's topography. But these are mountains of a different origin from those described earlier. They are monadnocks (named after New Hampshire's famous mountain), or mounds of resistant rock that have been exposed after the softer outer "coats" of metamorphic rock have been eroded away all around them. Such granite peaks as Mount Ascutney and Burke Mountain, both more than 3,000 feet high, were once hidden below the surface of the land, to be exposed only after the land surrounding them was carried away. These mountains, then, serve as a measuring stick of the quantity of land eroded in the region.

Monadnocks are large-scale *intrusions* of younger rock into preexisting rocks, having squeezed into cracks, pockets, or caverns in a molten state, then solidifying. Most monadnocks are much younger than the host rock into which they have flowed. This is illustrated in the Vermont Piedmont by Mount Ascutney, which is only about 120 millions years old, or three to four times younger than the bedrock around it.

Other kinds of geologic intrusions here are of substantial

economic importance. Great volumes of granite are quarried in East Barre; some of the quarries here are the largest anywhere, and Vermont granite is world-famous. Veins of copper ore were once mined heavily in the area around Vershire and Strafford, but have since been abandoned.

Because the region is in the lee of the Green Mountains, its climate is generally less severe than in some other places in the state. But a great deal of regional variation is experienced in cold pockets and valleys up and down its length. Lakes are a frequent and attractive resource of the Piedmont drawing many visitors every year.

The Northeastern Highlands ("The Northeast Kingdom")

The Northeastern Highlands are the wild corner of Vermont, totaling more than 600 square miles. The region is different from any other part of the state in that it is in fact an extension of the White Mountains of New Hampshire and Maine, and the Whites are not at all like the Green Mountains.

Like one immense monadnock, the White Mountains origi-nated as a huge subsurface reservoir of magma. As this molten material slowly cooled, it eventually formed granite. The surface

Mount Ascutney. This peak is a monadnock of igneous rock, deposited more than 120 million years ago in an underground "cavern," and left exposed after the surrounding Piedmont area was eroded away. The last glacier plucked rocks from the mountain and carried them south into Massachusetts — this line of strewn rocks, called the Mount Ascutney Train, is an important indica-tor of the direction of glacial advance in this part of the country.

has long since been worn away and the light-colored granite mountains stand out clearly. The White Mountains and the granite peaks of the Northeastern Highlands are both relatively young, being 135 million to 180 million years old.

In the Northeastern Highlands—commonly called the Northeast Kindgom—schists, other metamorphic rocks, and glacial till hide some of this ancestral relationship to the White Mountains, but large areas of igneous rock do outcrop throughout the region. Indeed, an older name of the Northeastern Highlands is the Granite Hills.

The area has some very thick glacial deposits, which are the result, it is believed, of repeated local advances and recessions — "stutters," as one author has called them. This is most evident in the fields and forests (Maidstone State Forest has striking examples) and as indicated by the many ponds, bogs, and black-spruce swamps.

Owing to the northerly location and the absence of any softening effect from a large body of water, this region's climate ranks second in severity only to some high peaks and north slopes of the Green Mountains.

3

Before We Came

The passage of the glaciers over Vermont eradicated the former forests here. Down to Long Island Sound, across Pennsylvania, Ohio, Indiana, Illinois, and farther west everything was crushed under the enormous ice sheets. No soil to warm in the sun. No spring flowers, or trees to color the fall. No mammals, no birds. It was, in effect, a biological desert.

Mostly through analysis of pollen grains preserved in bogs, scientists have been able to reconstruct a picture of what our land looked like long ago. Even 200 million years before the Ice Age, a great broad-leaved (deciduous) forest spread over most of North America, including Alaska and Greenland, as well. It is likely that this forest also covered much of the entire land mass of Pangaea. Experts believe that the Great Smoky Mountains of North Carolina and Tennessee are the place of origin of *all* modern deciduous forests in the eastern half of the United States. These mountains—especially a small ancient, undisturbed section within them called the "cove forest"— contain the greatest variety of deciduous-tree species on the continent. More than 45 species grow there: tulip poplar, maples, beech, white ash, basswood, oaks, and other, less important trees are amassed in this patriarch of forests. From this focal region, the deciduous forest of North America radiated out to other regions. But with the shifting of continents, the raising of mountains, the disruption of tracts of land, the formation of oceans, and later changes wrought by the Ice Age, the picture changed dramatically. The vast forest system was wiped out in some areas and reshaped in others, and the Smoky Mountain cove forest was left as a fraction of a once grander forest.

As continents and sections of continents acquired increasingly different environmental characteristics, their forests changed in response. In any given region, the more stringent conditions demanded by new topographies, climates, and soils meant that not all the species of the original continental forest could survive. Replacing the complex and uniform Eastern Deciduous Forest formation of the Smokies were simplified local "associations," dominated by one or two species.

For example, on dry, glaciated sites in the Midwest, species of oak and hickory dominate in the oak-hickory association. Northward, the deciduous forest in Minnesota and Wisconsin

The Virgin Forest. A small tract of virgin forest at Gifford Woods State Park, not far from Rutland, is a sample of what the presettlement hardwood forests must have looked like. Here a large sugar maple is part of a mixed forest that includes beech, hemlock, yellow birch, elm, and basswood. Although the understory is quite open, the rich and deep soils support a variety of woodland wild flowers and ferns. Some trees here have been dated as being more than 400 years old.

belongs to the maple-basswood association, and in glaciated regions of southern New England and New York the beech-maple association exists. In the Northeast, in areas where deciduous forest manages to grow, it belongs mostly to the hemlock—northern-hardwood association, typically consisting of a mixture of sugar maple, beech, yellow birch, basswood, red oak, white ash, and hemlock (a coniferous, or softwood, member). But regardless of the variations across the continent, the reservoir from which all deciduous-tree species come is the archaic forest of the Great Smoky Mountains.

The northern forests, however, have a deeper green than the forests elsewhere: over much of this area grow conifers—evergreen, cone-bearing trees with needles—the trees that point to a different direction for their origin.

As the glaciers advanced, native plants were wiped out, either bulldozed to destruction or forced to "emigrate" south, ahead of the formidable ice. In that emigration the zonation of plants was kept intact, maintaining pace with the southern advance of the glacier. Nearest the glacier, where the harshest conditions existed, only the small, hardy tundra plants could survive. Farther away, where the ice had not yet touched but the climate had become more severe, grew the cold-resistant coniferous trees (spruce and fir particularly) of the boreal forest. Even farther south, deciduous trees such as beech and sugar maple remained unaffected, though their relatives to the north had been obliterated.

This zonation is generally what we see today, but shifted back, so that the tundra is now 1,000 miles to the north of Vermont. Each zone, with its own identity and associated animal communities, is called a biome; those mentioned here—tundra, boreal forest, and deciduous forest—are only three among many worldwide.

After the glacier had reached its southern extreme and then retreated under a warming climate, the stripped land of the north became once again ice-free: living things could, after a long absence, begin to reclaim something of their former place. The tundra crept north, eventually to be replaced by the conifers, which in turn gave way to the broad-leaved trees. Yet it was not a total return to the way things were.

The deciduous forest could only go so high in the mountains; the climate, even with the glacier gone, still determined its upper limit. Where these trees had trouble surviving in the higher elevations they could no longer compete with conifers, so that the boreal forest remained intact. Similarly, higher to the peaks of many mountains only the tundra persisted in the harshest conditions, at sites with the shallowest and poorest of soils.

Today, with the glacier shrunk to only an Arctic ice cap, most of the tundra extends in a wide swath across northern Canada. The boreal forest is a broad belt below that, reaching down to southern Canada, and the realm of the deciduous forests extends below the boreal over much of the eastern United States.

But Vermont has reminders of a long-ago world before all these changes took place. Tundra still lives on several peaks in the Northeast, in Vermont on two. These "islands" of only scant acres are hundreds of miles from the family that spawned them. Yet, because the climate in their locations mimics the Arctic, they are able to persist. Other rare plants of an Arctic heritage cling to steep, cold, inaccessible cliffs in a few places in the state, and the boreal forest of spruce and fir remains on many mountainsides above the hardwoods and in much of the Northeastern Highlands as the dominant forest type.

Bogs, too, are a memento of the Ice Age. In fact, bogs have kept a record of what happened after the glacier created them. In their partially preserved organic matter are pollen grains from species of plants that grew in the area at any given time in the past. Just from these pollen grains specialists can identify many ancient plants. In addition, using radiocarbon dating techniques, they can determine the approximate age of the peat level in which the grains are found. Changes in the forest over time are read from the layers of pollen: the deepest layers are from the most distant past since glaciation, the surface layers are from the present. Thus, which plants grew when can be fairly precisely ascertained. Bogs in Vermont usually show a sequence from bare bottom, to arctic-tundra species, to spruce and fir, to white pine, to northern hardwoods. In most general terms and brought to its ultimate expression, this has been the evolution of our forests since glaciation. Obviously, however, the evolution is not so simple as this; some forests have never achieved this bog "conclusion," and others have gone beyond it. Moreover, some bogs report on other things: they tell us, for example, that 4,000 to 6,000 years ago our climate must have been much milder than before or since, because trees and other plants of a more southern distribution shed their pollen there.

The forests of Vermont, then, reflect their different prehistoric origins: southern, northern, a mixing of the two. We are standing amidst them and looking at just one expression, the present one, of a landscape that is continuously changing, responding to whatever the climate—and geologic forces— dictate. Through the miracles of science we are able to trace

Vegetation Regions of Vermont

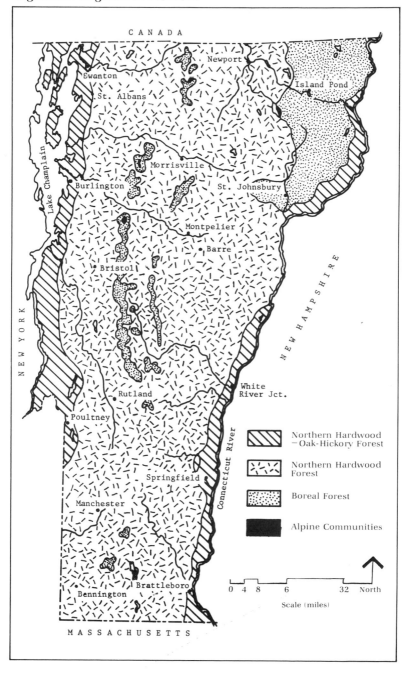

something of our past, and have come to realize the magnitude of the power of the natural systems: many of the world's greatest changes came about independent of the human hand.

4

People Arrive in Vermont

With respect to the face of the country [Vermont] . . . I know of no country that abounds in a greater diversity of hill and dale, but I must add that those hills are in general capable of being converted into arable ground, and that the most craggy mountain, if cleared, would provide tolerable pasturage.
—Ira Allen (1798)

We have now felled forest enough everywhere, in many districts far too much. Let us restore this one element of material life to its normal proportions, and devise means for maintaining the permanence of its relations to the fields, the meadows, and the pastures, to the rain and the dews of heaven, to the springs and rivulets with which it waters the earth.
—George Perkins Marsh (1864)

The men who wrote these words are both famous Vermonters, but each lived in a very different time. They speak from two different viewpoints, one looking ahead at an untouched territory, the other looking back at the damage white inhabitants had done in their brief residency in the state. From the time of one to that of the other we can see the first stirring of a conscience about the land, the very beginning of a conservation ethic.

But, backing up, we should trace some of the history of Indians in Vermont, and how white Americans came to take over the land and waters, and how their struggles directed the course of the state.

Once it was generally thought that to the Indians Vermont was a no-man's-land, that they migrated through the area, hunted, fished, and warred here, but never chose to settle in these wild lands. However, relatively recent archaeological discoveries, although few, have shown otherwise. Indeed, Indians did live here for thousands of years before the arrival of white settlers, and their changing cultures reflected the changes in the environment from the Ice Age to modern times.

The first Vermonters were small bands of hunters and food-gatherers whom anthropologists call the Paleo-Indians. These original inhabitants lived during the dying stages of the last glacier and later—roughly between 12,000 and 9,500 years ago—in the Champlain Lowlands, and in all likelihood in the Connecticut River Valley, as well. This was the period when herds of caribou and mammoths ranged over the tundra plains, mastodons and other large plant-eating animals browsed in the scrubby spruce-fir forests, and seals, walruses, and whales swam in the newly formed Champlain Sea. The Paleo-Indians probably hunted these large mammals as their main food supply.

We have little more than fragmentary evidence of the presence of the Paleo-Indians in Vermont, which comes from only fourteen sites. Bands of probably twenty-five to thirty-five individuals apparently roved from place to place, following the movements of the animal herds and making use of available foods in season, but leaving little in the way of artifacts. At a single campsite on a hill above the Missisquoi River near Highgate and scattered elsewhere have been found the occasional fluted stone spearhead and knife, the only clues we have to these Indians' long-ago presence in Vermont.

Centuries passed, and the climate slowly warmed. The land changed under the different conditions and brought a new kind of vegetation to the state. The large animals of the cold northern regions disappeared, many of which became extinct. And the Indians, too, under all these environmental changes developed new ways of living, more in tune with the landscape of this warmer period—the so-called hypsithermal interval, or climatic optimum. Some of the evidence that Indians shifted to new ways of life is in the different types of spearheads that have been found in conjunction with other artifacts that speak of a culture that was more than simply nomadic.

Gradually the environment evolved that characterizes Vermont today, with its complement of modern flora and fauna. This time of change for human beings here is called the Archaic Period; it lasted from about 9,500 to 3,000 years ago. The new name does not necessarily imply an influx of people into Vermont, but rather a change in the inhabitants' life-style that accompanied the changes in climate and vegetation. The Archaic Indians were exceptionally fine hunters and food gatherers, but they seemed to do their foraging in rather well defined territories (even if those territories were large), as opposed to the earlier Indians, who roamed much further. In the Champlain Valley and elsewhere they fished, collected wild plant foods, and hunted deer, bear, and small game of the forests. Life revolved around the seasons, and the people accordingly shifted locations to where the food was: spring and summer lake fishing gave way to fall and winter hunting in the woodlands. But all the while, these people gathered wild foodstuffs—nuts, tubers, roots, eggs, berries, and the untold assortment of wild leaves—and it is with the Archaic Indians that we have the first indications of the storing of food throughout the winter, thus implying the quasi settlement of people in an area.

The Archaic Indians prospered in the Champlain Valley, and their population expanded. But other changes were in the making. To the south and west of Vemont dramatic discoveries were revolutionizing the lives of the people there. From the lower Mississippi Valley had spread a radical new idea: agriculture. With the shift from hunting and subsistence food gathering to farming, the former small seminomadic bands were supplanted in time by socially stratified villages and chiefdoms.

Because of Vermont's relatively harsh terrain and climate, agriculture among the Indians probably played a lesser role here than in some other areas of the country. Nevertheless, both the rise of social orders, including elaborate burial cults, in the Ohio Valley and the widespread exchange of ideas via trading networks influenced the Vermont Indians. Archaeologists recognize a shift in living patterns by the appearance of pottery, agricultural implements, cultivated grains, and exotic stone tools that were also used in ceremonial activities and indicate a more developed social order. This period is called the Woodland Period and lasted from about 3,000 to three to four hundred years ago, or just prior to the whites' first view of Vermont.

The Woodland culture in its later stages apparently diverged into five language families, which were separated regionally. The two that figure importantly in Vermont prehistory were Algonquian, whose speakers lived in the Northeast and the Atlantic Coast territory, and Iroquoian, whose speakers inhabited the region around Lakes Erie and Ontario, and perhaps farther south. Many North American tribes spoke Algonquian dialects; the Abnaki tribe was the one that lived in western Vermont, furnishing many of its legends and place names, and it has numerous descendants today.

To date, very little is known about the late prehistoric period in Vermont, enough only to realize that the Champlain Lowlands region was a zone of great conflict among Indians of the Algonquian and Iroquoian language families. It is apparent that the Iroquois moved into the Champlain Valley from the west, attempted to settle in this Algonkian stronghold, and had brief, but serious, confrontations with the natives there. In fact, the immigration of Iroquois into Vermont may have had disastrous consequences for the Abnakis; facing this more warlike and highly organized group, the Abnakis probably abandoned their borders and moved to supposed safety north and east. But the battles went on, and the Abnakis may have continued moving back and forth in this region until well into the twentieth century.

About 650 prehistoric Indian sites are known in Vermont, covering the span of the Paleo-Indian to the late-Woodland stages. Although the major concentrations of Indians appear to have been in the Champlain Lowlands and Connecticut River Valley, further excavations will undoubtedly reveal sites in more upland areas.

The French explorer Samuel de Champlain is credited as the first white man to see the land of Vermont, on July 4, 1609, as he sailed down the lake that now bears his name. He traveled with a group of sixty Algonkian Indians on that trip, and when they reached the area of Crown Point, New York, they encountered the Iroquois enemy. In the ensuing battle the Iroqouis were defeated—an event that was to set the stage for many years of bitter fighting between Indian and Indian, and Indian and white man, in what are collectively called the French and Indian Wars.

This was the time of colonization of the New World. The French had secured the northern and the English the southern New England regions. In the attempts of each to expand their territories, Vermont became a middle ground in the French-English conflicts. In these wars the French had more or less allied themselves with the Algonkian groups and the English with the Iroquoian: in their lust for land the Europeans put to use the animosities of these Indian natives to achieve their own ends.

After about sixty-five years of fighting, the French were finally defeated, a victory by the British that some historians feel was due ultimately to the vengeful Iroquois. At this point—1763—the white settlement of Vermont began in earnest. For the English settlers the menace of enemies had been largely removed, land was available and cheap, and the potential of undeveloped territory beckoned migrants from southern New England. In the twenty-eight years from 1763 to 1791 Vermont went from a wilderness to statehood, from a population of 300 to 85,000. A phenomenal development indeed.

The white settlers lived far differently from the Indians, and they brought great and quick changes to land and wildlife. Certainly the Indians had modified the environment to suit their needs, including burning forests to enrich the soil, stimulate new plant growth for game, and open areas for crops. But the Indians were relatively few and their methods of plant and animal husbandry were crude, so that their impact on the land was considerably less than what was to follow.

Nevertheless, even before full-scale settlement by white

people, severe inroads on Vermont's—and the whole country's—natural resources had begun. Buyers from the European fur companies had induced the Indians to trap vast quantities of mammals to supply the foreign markets with beaver, bear, marten, fisher, lynx, and otter pelts for fashionable clothing. It was only much later, after Vermont's statehood, that the whites moved into the forests as trappers, and only after many of the valuable furbearers there had already been sorely depleted or virtually killed off.

The very heavy, unregulated year-round trapping, by both Indians and whites, was only part of a longer process in which people doing different kinds of work had affected the land in various ways. With white settlers came yet another mode of life and a new kind of relationship with the earth. The settlers were farmers, bringing with them their own agricultural outlook on land use. They saw in Vermont great potential (once the land was cleared and worked, according to age-old custom), for frontier farming methods—planting the same crop in a field year after year, regardless of slope, without fertilization—had exhausted soils farther south. So the farmers in looking for fresh land came to Vermont, despite the hardships of climate and terrain.

The farms of the 1700s were small and self-sufficient. Wood, cleared to make way for fields, was a by-product of their existence, supplying the raw material for houses, furniture, tools, utensils, and heating. Yet so great was the quantity of trees that most of the wood was burned simply to remove it. In addition, the woods posed a threat to the settlers, who were afraid of the attacking Indians or wild animals that might be lurking there. As a result, the forests were opened up and pushed back, to allow room for farmland and to dispel real (or imagined) fears.

By 1810 Vermont's population had grown to 218,000 and the land clearing continued up the mountains, down the valleys. The farming was mostly mixed grain and livestock, with the steeper, rocky slopes going into pastures and the richer lowlands into cultivated fields. The burning of felled trees also continued, and this too yielded products: great quantities of potash, an excellent early fertilizer and raw material for soap, were among Vermont's earliest export items, and the forests later furnished charcoal, fuel for the furnaces of the nation's new industrialization.

The felled trees were also the start of a vigorous logging industry that followed in the footsteps of settlement, concentrating on the stately white pines that grew abundantly in the Northeast. The early industry, though active, remained small, however, since most of Vermont's timber was inaccessible. Rivers and lakes were the sole means of transportation to mills and markets, so only the forests near waterways were cut. The Connecticut River was a major funnel for logs cut in Vermont and New Hampshire and floated down to mills in the area and farther south.

Too soon it became clear to farmers who worked the Vermont hillsides that the land was more suited to merino sheep than to cattle or plow, so that sheep farming quickly replaced grain and beef farming as the dominant agriculture in the state. Also, by 1840 the national demand for wool was at a peak, and the Vermont sheep business boomed. Meanwhile, the cutting of the forests continued, greatly accelerated by the coming of the railroad and its penetration into the remote timberlands.

Then in the 1850s Vermont's economic growth met with a sudden reversal, most strikingly in the sheep farming, which fell as quickly as it had risen to prominence. All types of farming now dwindled, and families began to abandon their land and homes. It happened so fast that their leaving has often been referred to as an exodus.

A number of causes were responsible. The same agricultural methods that had impoverished soils in southern New England had not changed here. The expanding logging industry had moved deep into the untouched forests and cut practically everything—but taking only what was marketable—then left when the trees were gone. Under the combined effects of farming and heavy logging, 70 to 75 percent of Vermont by the 1850s was open land, in the form of clear-cut areas, pastures, or croplands, and the hills and mountains, stripped of their protective trees, could no longer hold on to the soil—the streams and rivers became muddy with the runoff. The ill-farmed land became harder to work and less productive, or else simply washed away in the rivers. Hunting and trapping continued unabated, with few conservation laws and little or no enforcement of those that existed. Wildlife of the forests grew scarce, and fish that depended on clear, cold streams diminished or vanished completely.

The Green Mountains of Vermont, in short, had become a biological wasteland, offering little for people to live upon—a dramatic change from the bounty of a century earlier.

At the same time, new forms of transportation were giving access to unexploited lands elsewhere: the railroads and the Erie Canal provided cheap and easy ways out to the fresh and wonderfully fertile plains of the Midwest and West. There, the soils were boulderless, black, deep, and free for the settling. Sheep and cattle could graze by the thousands on what seemed like limitless acres of grass. There, new forests stood tall for the saw and ax. The flat lands could be easily worked with the newly developed agricultural machines, which were useless on the rocky slopes of Vermont (a new steel plow adapted to the thick sods of the prairie was invented in Illinois by a displaced Vermonter, John Deere—the founder of a now huge corporation).

Other social forces depleted the resources of the state. The growing industrialization of the nation offered new and lucrative jobs in the cities, and young people eagerly left the grind of farming for higher-paying work, work that appeared more glamorous. Then in 1861 the Civil War began, and nearly 35,000 men volunteered and left Vermont.

Thus, industrialism, new trades, westward expansion of a

1.

Changes in the New England Landscape. This series of diromas at the Harvard University Forest in Petersham, Massachusetts, depicts the changes in New England's appearance from the time before white settlement through the 1930s. All the scenes show the same spot. (1) The virgin forest of 1700: This mixed hardwood-softwood forest is what white settlers saw when they first came to the region. (2) 1740: The white settlers began to carve their small subsistence farms out of the forests. These pioneers cut the trees to make way for crops and pastureland, using the wood for a variety of purposes. (3) 1830: Land clearing at its most intense in New England. More than 75 percent of the region had been cleared of trees, and sheep and dairy farming predominated. (4) 1850: Suddenly the Vermont farmers abandoned their homes and land to look for work elsewhere in the developing nation, especially the rich soils of the Midwest. White pines then began to grow in the untended open spaces. (5) 1910: The reclamation of the land by trees. The white pines that had grown back in were then ready to harvest. When these pines were clearcut, the understory hardwood saplings and seedlings were left to grow. (6) 1915: The hardwoods take over. These trees, in the absence of competition from the pines, grew unabated and provided much food and low growth for many kinds of wildlife. (7) 1930: The hardwoods have grown to merchantable size and Vermont is heavily forested again. This forest developed into the one we live and work in today.

2.

3.

4.

5.

6.

7.

developing country, and a war drew people away from Vermont. New hardships awaited the emigrants, but even so, the lures of the outside world were bright. To the pioneer farmer and to the logger, especially, these opportunities must have seemed a blessing after the rocky, barren hills of Vermont.

Those people who stayed behind were left the legacy of impoverishment. The toll had been heavy: nonexistent or poor markets for their products, abandoned farms, plundered forests, rivers clouded with mud, many native species of fish and wildlife gone or on the verge of extinction.

In those days *conservation* had little of the meaning we give it today, and the act was rarely practiced. For the majority of people, there always seemed other places to go when the resources disappeared, better lands waiting and unending. But a few were troubled by what they saw and lived with. One of them, a Vermonter named George Perkins Marsh, became the spokesman for a rising land consciousness and expressed the new philosophy in his now famous book *Man and Nature*, published in 1864.

Marsh was a brand of Renaissance man, a philosopher, scientist, lawyer, naturalist, and linguist, with a knowledge of more than twenty languages. But he was also a product of rural Vermont, and carried with him all his life a deep love and special concern for his native state. As U.S. Secretary of the Interior Stewart Udall wrote of him in 1963:

> Science-minded and skeptical, the young New Englander rejected the easy idea that any resource could be exploited without concern for the future. Soil had a precarious purchase on the Green Mountain slopes. As a sheep raiser, lumber dealer and farmer, Marsh saw the damage done to the valleys of Vermont by land misuse. Overgrazing and overcutting were eroding hillsides; rivers overflowed; wood-growing waned; and as the woods were logged out, Burlington, once a lumber boom town, was forced to import timber from Canada to keep its mills and factories from closing down. Men were working against themselves, and by 1840 much of the Green Mountain country was already an exhibit of improvident land management. Not even in the cotton and tobacco belt were soils exhausted faster and forests mangled more thoroughly than on the hillsides of Vermont.

With his intellectual capabilities, George Perkins Marsh synthesized a conservation ethic that was to make a lasting impression on the country. He urged people to realize that our resources are not infinite and that nature works with countless interdependencies. He called for management of lands and wildlife with reason, prudence, and scientific knowledge. He knew that humankind must work with and within nature, not against it or outside of it.

Marsh was to give great impetus to the study and practice of forestry in the United States and to the wider arena of conservation as a whole. *Man and Nature* has become a landmark in the history of American conservation, being the first fully conceptualized expression of what we now call, variously, "the land ethic" or "conservation conscience." This monumental plea for resource management, growing out of scientific investigation, is what thousands of foresters and wildlife biologists today are working to satisfy: Marsh's book of 1864 is still the idea behind the act.

Out of the fields of the mid-1800s grew another forest, following the predictable sequence of plants from field to shrubby meadow to young forest—the stages of "secondary succession." White pine, one of the major pioneer species of tree in this part of the country, grew in profusion in the fields and logged-over areas. (In smaller quantities, paper birch, gray birch, and quaking aspen colonized other sites, often following the burning of the old forest.)

The pines grew densely, shielding the ground and excluding other trees. For many years they prevailed, until they were tall enough and had thinned themselves enough to offer growing space and light below for other trees. Since white pine is a pioneer species, intolerant of shade, it did not seed or sprout under itself. Instead, the more shade-tolerant hardwoods, such as sugar maple and beech, grew in the understory. The white pine had sealed its fate; hardwoods would be the future generation.

Fifty years or so went by. By the end of the century the pines were large enough to cut, and cut they were, in great numbers. Since clear-cutting was the accepted, easiest, and cheapest way to harvest the pines, the younger hardwoods previously sheltered were suddenly open to the sky and sun. But since they were not of marketable size they were, when not cleared away with the pines, left uncut.

These uncut young hardwoods now had a free rein to grow—and even those that were cut soon sprouted from the stump or root, as red maple and beech will do so readily. By the 1930s many had grown to be suitable for lumber. But lumbering had come a long way in all the years it had taken these trees to reach this size: the applied science of forestry now governed the industry. With the lessons of indiscriminate logging still strong in memory, twentieth-century professionals approached the forest differently from their predecessors of the 1800s. They

selected the trees they wanted and left the rest of the forest to
grow and supply trees for the future. They began to manage the
forest, to maintain its integrity and encourage its productivity.
They knew that this resource could be treated like a golden-egg-
laying goose that is kept alive.

Vermont today—a mixture of public and private lands;
modest dairy and hay farms; villages, towns, small cities; industry, tourism, and roads to almost everywhere; and populated by
close to half a million people—is 75 percent forest. This is a
complete reversal from a hundred years ago. The forest is, however, quite different from the one the white settlers encountered;
and so long as we claim it for our needs and recreation, it will
never be that kind again. But what the forest is now and what it
represents are significant in other ways: it teaches us historical
lessons in conservation, serving as a record of land use—and
abuse—in our state. We have come a long way since 1850 and the

Modern Logging. New forestry techniques deal with a vital Vermont product.
One of the more recent developments is the harvesting of whole trees: the
machine depicted here can take trees up to 18 inches in diameter, snip them
off at the base, and lay them in bunches to be skidded out. This form of logging
is being conducted on a limited basis and is being closely studied for its
applicability to Vermont's terrain.

first vision of George Perkins Marsh, but there is much need for even greater conservation efforts, much still to do to improve and maintain our beautiful landscape.

The human being is a latecomer in the evolution of the world, and the culture of modern Americans is but a flicker in that process. Nevertheless, in our brief dominion we have severely altered the landscape it took heaven and earth a near-eternity to form. In Vermont it is possible to study part of our history in the record of the land: how it has responded to our actions. But we must remember that we have not yet done with weighing the balance. We can only hope that we will tip it gently in the right direction.

II   Down a Mountain, Across the Forest

From a long time ago, when he dreamed as a boy, he remembered the sound. Beautiful creatures leaping under the sky, gone through brush, under trees, away, and only the soft echo their running left behind.

—Ray Bradbury, *Dandelion Wine* (1957)

5

Alpine Communities

True alpine areas, where the conditions and vegetation are Arctic-like, are few and small in Vermont. They include two different kinds of places: small tundra areas on the summits of only two high peaks, and a few cliffs where the ecosystems differ from tundra. Both kinds of alpine areas in Vermont are clinging to a precarious existence.

The largest expanse of tundra in the state—close to 250 acres—occurs on the long ridge of Mount Mansfield. The summit of Camel's Hump, 15 miles south of Mount Mansfield along the main ridge of the Green Mountains, supports the only other tundra, of but 10 acres. Although true Arctic tundra is one of the largest vegetation zones on the North American continent, the Arctic-like areas of Vermont should be considered endangered communities, since almost all the plants there are either threatened with extinction or else extremely rare. Ironically, these regions are probably among the most appreciated places in the state, visited by thousands upon thousands of people, who come to look at the views or else hike across the areas. It is this very appreciation that may kill off the tundra plants.

The extremely harsh climate on the tops of these mountains has been a condition the tundra vegetation has dealt with successfully for 10,000 years. But though they are biologically tough, the plants are extremely sensitive to physical disturbance. In addition, soils here are thin, and thus easily compacted by footsteps. Damage done is not quickly repaired, for alpine life processes are slow and painstaking. Many of the tens of thousands of visitors and hikers who come to the mountains are unaware of what the tundra really is and what it can suffer underfoot. They walk through what appears to them to be fields of grass, but which are actually communities of tundra species. Quite unintentionally, they compact the thin soils by their footsteps and crush the small, tender plants. Once the plants die, the bare soil quickly slides off the peak with the driving rains, opening the colony to erosion and permanent loss. To deal with these problems, special ranger-naturalists patrol Vermont's two alpine summits, protecting these special and irreplaceable communities by means of education of the visiting public.

Where the arctic plants live in these mountainous regions the climate is much like that of the true Arctic, far to the north.

Tundra. Hikers on the summit of Mount Mansfield, more than 4,000 feet up. The 250 acres above tree line is the largest alpine tundra area in Vermont, with many rare and endangered plants growing among the rocks. Ranger-naturalists patrol the summit in summer, helping visitors and, by alerting them to the fragility of the environment, protecting the critical plant communities.

The frost-free growing season is only 90 days or shorter. The sun beats down directly, the winds whip across steadily. The year-round temperatures are colder than at lower elevations (the highest recorded temperature to date on Mount Mansfield is 85 degrees Fahrenheit). The soils are sparse, acidic, sterile, and prone to erosion on the steep slopes. Though water is plentiful from frequent rain, snow, and clouds, most of it the plants cannot make use of, since quick runoff and high soil acidity render it unavailable to them. Thus, these 4,000-foot peaks are near-deserts. Nevertheless, the plants that do exist above the tree line are prepared to survive these arctic conditions.

Plants

The alpine plants are low-lying and creeping, taking advantage of the more protected recesses where the winds cannot tear at them. Most are evergreen, perennial, and early bloomers, all adaptations that permit them to "get under way" as early in the spring as possible and not waste precious time or energy in such a short season. Most are able to retain water or restrict its loss much in the way desert plants do; in fact, many superficially resemble desert succulents. Mountain cranberry, for example, has thick, fleshy leaves coated with wax, which effectively store water and reduce evaporation. Alpine bilberry, a close relative of the blueberries, has hard, leathery leaves that in another way resist water loss. Many of the plants—such as mountain sandwort, Bigelow's sedge, and black crowberry—grow in dense mats and have tiny, narrow leaves: these colonies soak up water like a sponge, at the same time offering little total leaf surface exposed to the sun and wind.

The complexion of the tundra changes with small variations in terrain and exposure. Moreover, the microclimate (the climate immediately surrounding the individual plant) may be strikingly different from that of the general region, contributing to the local differences in tundra vegetation.

On the gently sloping but windswept western exposures, heath plants predominate, with alpine bilberry and mountain cranberry especially abundant. Alpine sedges and grasses occupy the colder, northwestern localities, appearing like lawns or meadows: the dominant plant in such meadows is Bigelow's sedge. Scattered in rock crevices, gravelly soils, and other pockets are the three-toothed cinquefoil, the late-blooming mountain sandwort, and a nonflowering plant, fir club moss. A few tiny bogs fill in wet depressions on Mount Mansfield and contain many of the same plant species found in bogs at much lower elevations.

Animals

Except for insects, which swarm in great variety over the alpine summits on summer days, animals are few. Even among insects, the vast majority are more common to fields lower down—rising wind currents apparently blow them up the mountains to these "meadows." A few, however, are true tundra inhabitants. One species of ground beetle, *Nebria suturalis*, is found only above 4,000 feet in mountains, and in Vermont is restricted to a few *yards* on Mount Mansfield.

The occasional tundra mammal is small and secretive, in-habiting, tunnels through the vegetation. In a study of small mammals on Camel's Hump a researcher found only three species above the tree line: the hardy boreal red-backed vole, the deer mouse, and the meadow vole. The red-backed vole is a mouselike rodent that one would expect in the tundra, since all across the continent it lives in wet, northern environments and high elevations—it is even known to breed under snow. The deer mouse is a widespread, adaptable seed eater, and so is not a surprise in the mountains. The presence of the meadow vole is somewhat perplexing, however, because it is normally a field mammal of low elevations and not even found in the forests of Camel's Hump. It is likely that it reached the mountaintop follow-ing a fire that cleared a path through the forest by which the vole reached the summit.

No mammal is exclusive to these tundra regions. All live at lower elevations and some, such as the meadow vole, are more accustomed to grasslands than to tundra. An infrequent visitor such as the snowshoe hare wanders in to nibble on leaves and twigs, or to take the seeds and berries as they ripen.

Birds

Even the more mobile birds are scarce on Vermont's alpine peaks.

Both Mount Mansfield and Camel's Hump have small flocks of nesting ravens, which remain through the winter. This large scavenging bird, native to the Arctic from Greenland to Alaska, is impressive in its size, shining coat of black, and graceful riding of the air above the mountains. It is heard often in flight around the mountain, with a sonorous, metallic "grawk-grawk." Most hikers to these regions have seen ravens, but few people have managed a glimpse of their nests, tucked in the ledges or in the crowns of the denser, trackless forest below.

The dark-eyed junco and white-throated sparrow are small seed-eating finches that nest directly among the tundra plants, but migrate south before winter sets in. Hikers often see their young hopping about the rocks or attempting to fly from some low perch nearby.

In addition, the peaks are good places to watch for hawks, especially during the fall migration period, from late August to

Smugglers Notch. These rock profiles called The Hunter and His Dog, form part of scenic Smugglers Notch, near Mount Mansfield. Here the steep, moist cliffs harbor many arctic species of plants, most of which are rare worldwide and in Vermont to be found in only one or two places.

early November. Though these mountaintops do not rival other more famous places in New England and the East as vantage points for the hawk spectacle, they do let one observe these fascinating and graceful birds as they glide and fly south, flashing parallel to the ranges or spiraling up the thermal currents.

Cliff Flora

Tucked in the nooks and crannies of a very few cliffs in Vermont are plants of Arctic origin, but different from those found in the tundra. Though the climatic conditions on cliffs are similar in some respects to those of the tundra, critical topographical differences help account for the two distinct biological communities. In summer, the rocky slopes, being mostly in shadow, are cool, and they are also moist, owing to their exposure to the elements and water that percolates down from higher points and through the rock cracks. In winter, snow does not cover the vertical faces of the cliffs, so many of the plants are exposed to ice and extremely cold temperatures, even lower than those in the open but snow-blanketed tundra.

Such mysterious and seldom seen botanical species as purple mountain-saxifrage and the carnivorous butterwort (whose small, sticky leaves attract and snare insects for food) cling to the rocks of Smugglers Notch, near Mount Mansfield. Mount Pisgah, beside Lake Willoughby, also harbors many alpine cliff plants, some the same as found at Smugglers Notch, but others that are unique to it. Like the tundra species, the cliff plants have evolved to cope with the stringent conditions imposed by these forbidding formations and climate. But unlike the tundra, the community here seems to be relatively safe from human interference, since only skilled rock climbers (and the most ardent naturalists!) come close to their shelterd homes.

6

Coniferous Forests

Stretching across North America, Europe, and Russia is an immense forest of evergreens—coniferous trees, which are also called softwoods, because their wood is generally not so hard as that of broad-leaved trees. It is a forest primarily of spruce and fir, and is quite similar the world over. In North America this circumboreal forest occurs between the tundra to the north and the prairies and broad-leaved (deciduous) forest to the south. It comes into Vermont, but its distribution here is controlled by two factors: latitude and altitude.

As a forest of lower elevations, the true coniferous forest occupies much of Vermont's Northeastern Highlands and the northern portions of the Piedmont, a good deal of which is swampy or boggy. These regions have much in common with New Hampshire and Maine—as well as the obvious affinity with Canada—even more in common than with other low-elevation areas of Vermont. Its isolation from the rest of the state is well expressed in "the Northeast Kingdom."

The coniferous forest reaches farther down the state, but at higher elevations in the mountains—this "Appalachian Extension" continues all the way south to the Great Smoky Mountains, though it climbs progressively higher in the warmer climates. The coniferous forest begins at about 3,000 feet in central Vermont but in North Carolina it starts at 5,500 feet; roughly 1,000 feet of altitude bring the same biological changes as 500 to 600 miles of latitude.

This forest has several pseudonyms: the Canadian zone, boreal forest, spruce-fir forest, north woods, and, in Russian, *taiga.* Except for less piercing winds (and it does provide winter shelter for many woodland animals), its climate is not noticeably milder than that of the tundra. The growing season is still short, precipitation as rain or snow is still great and spread throughout the year, and the temperatures are still low in winter (in summer, however, they can be higher than in the tundra). Soils, too, are sandy-gravelly and acidic. And the soil minerals are leached out with the waters that continually gravitate down through the earth's porous spaces. It is truly a subarctic environment, and the kinds and numbers of plants here reflect this sterility.

Plants

In the higher mountains in Vermont the boreal forest extends up to the tree line, or about 4,000 feet. As elevation increases, the spruces and firs become progressively smaller, more twisted, and stunted. At tree line they may be only a foot or two high, prostrate, and looking more like shrubs than trees. This stage, in which the branches are contorted and pruned by wind and ice, is known by the German word *Krummholz*, meaning crooked wood.

At the lower limits of Vermont's alpine boreal forest and at the state's more southern latitudes at elevations between 2,400 and 3,000 feet, white pine enters with increasing frequency and sometimes grows as pure stands. White-pine forests are boreal in many characteristics — such as the kinds of birds and plants that

The Northeast Kingdom. The glacially formed ponds and lakes are nestled in the wide valleys, while the spruce-fir forest cloaks the land. This is in Vermont's boreal-forest realm. Norton Pond is at the top of the photograph.

accompany them—but they are not usually classified as boreal forest, which is technically defined by the predominance of spruce and fir.

Below 3,000 feet, the spruce-fir forest begins to merge with the hemlock– northern-hardwoods association, with white pine as a common associate. But since, unlike its neighbors, white pine is a pioneer species and not part of a true climax forest, ecologists consider it a "subclimax" tree of long duration, able to live in an area, if left alone, for hundreds of years. Such were the white pines of the virgin forests that towered before the first white inhabitants of America, and which provided masts for British sailing vessels. These titans were but the lingering pioneers from ancient blowdowns, or hurricanes similar to the one that hit Vermont in 1938, or fires set by Indians (early European explorers often remarked on the great many fires the Indians started to clear the land). If these survivors had not been cut down by the white settlers they would have eventually given way either to other coniferous or to deciduous trees, depending on the site. And today, where we see younger pines growing in pure stands, we can be sure they are filling former open land, resetting the process of succession.

Red pine is another native pine species, but not so common as the white and usually occupying poorer sites with sandy soils, where white pine does not do well. The best stands of red pine occur in dry upland areas in the Champlain Valley and, to a lesser degree, in the Connecticut River Valley. Only a few good natural stands grow in the interior of the state.

Red spruce and balsam fir are the climax species of the boreal forest in Vermont. They may grow together in near-pure stands, but often paper birch is present as a subordinate companion. This species of birch is a major pioneer in burned or cutover areas of the region, and its proportions may indicate the extent of a former fire or logging operation.

The boreal forest in Vermont, Canada, and states to the south has marked differences. As opposed to the dominance in Vermont of the red spruce, in Canada the white is the common spruce. Very much south of Vermont, Frasier fir supplants the balsam fir of the northern latitudes. Vermont's alpine boreal forest also differs from the low-level boreal forest in the Northeastern Highlands: heart-leaved paper birch, a subspecies of paper birch, is the important birch in the mountains, whereas at lower elevations it is not found at all.

Owing to its high elevation and inhospitable terrain, the alpine boreal forest of Vermont has been little touched by human beings even to this day. But the extensive coniferous forests in the northern part of the state form the center of a vital pulp and paper industry that has a long history in New England. Because of the limited technology of the 1880s, spruce was at first the only tree used in papermaking, and not even much of this species was taken, as the market was relatively small. But later balsam fir could also be used, and by 1912 even some hardwoods. With the advent of motorized vehicles in 1930 and the increasing demand for paper products, pulp production and transportation sharply increased, supplying Canadian and New England mills alike. This heavy use of the trees has continued up to the present, and a trip to the Northeast Kingdom can give the visitor an idea of the magnitude of the operations.

But people are not the only consumers of trees. In Vermont's northern regions periodic outbreaks of insect pests and diseases occur and often devastate thousands of acres of forestland. Many of the attacks seem to be a natural part of the ecosystem, however, since many animals—insects included—experience severe, sometimes violent, population cycles, from explosion of numbers to near-disappearance to explosion again. These cycles are most pronounced in the far north, where they are thought to be related, at least in part, to the lack of variety of plants and animals.

For instance, Vermont's coniferous forests have experienced a few infestations of spruce budworm, the caterpillar stage of which has a voracious appetite for needles of conifers. The latest outbreak began in 1974 and at this writing (1979) is still under way. More than 61,000 acres of trees were defoliated in 1978, and experts feel the peak has not yet been reached. The caterpillar's strict diet of needles can come from various trees, but the animal concentrates on balsam fir. So the boreal forest, almost exclusively spruce and fir, suffers greatly. But what usually follows such an infestation is a sharp decline of the insect population—due to lack of food, increased predation by birds or parasitism by other organisms, disease, or a combination of these controls. The budworm numbers then drop to harmless proportions, the forest is able to regrow over time, and the cycle is complete. For economic reasons, we usually cannot wait for the natural cycle to run its course, which would mean losing many revenue-producing trees. So we must take measures to short-circuit the cycle, most often with the use of target chemicals that kill the budworm before it has a chance to reach destructive levels.This use of pesticides must be made with great discretion, however, lest they harm or kill other insects and wildlife that are beneficial.

The deep shade under a dense evergreen canopy and the acidic soils derived from slow-rotting needles make the boreal forest a difficult place for most plants to grow. The understory

Connecticut River Log Drives. The Connecticut River was an important route in the nineteenth century for transporting pulpwood from northern Vermont and New Hampshire to mills in more southern New England. Crews would follow these drives down the river, traveling in long, narrow "bateaux," which could handle the fast waters and ledgy areas. The crews would have to free log jams that formed at bends in the river and at falls. Horses were taken on the drives, on rafts, and were used to pull jammed logs off the shore and into the river. As a last resort, dynamite was employed to free an especially difficult jam.

flora, what there is of it, is scarce and poorly diversified, and only a few small trees and shrubs enter the spaces between the canopy and the ground. Most frequent are mountain maple, hobblebush, and mountain ash (not an ash at all but a member of the rose family that has been used as an ornamental for its attractive orange-red berries). On the ground, the few flowering plants are often evergreens, such as goldthread (so called for the color of its root), shinleaf, partridgeberry, and, under pines especially, trailing arbutus, with its delicate violet-on-white flowers showing through the late snows of April. Other herbaceous plants (plants without woody tissue) are sometimes found here that are more widely distributed throughout the mixed forests in the state. Starflower, bunchberry (a relative of the dogwood tree), clintonia, the circumboreal (appearing in the boreal forest worldwide) twinflower, spinulose woodfern, and bristly club moss are some of these more cosmopolitan species.

A difficult environment for plants that require light, the boreal forest is well endowed with saprophytes, those plants that lack chlorophyll and thus need no sunlight to survive; instead, they live entirely off the decaying remains of plants and animals in the organic matter in the soil. Fungi are the most widely recognized saprophytes, but in many cases are unseen for most of the year. Only when they put forth their spore-

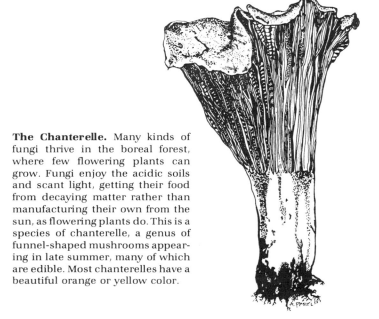

The Chanterelle. Many kinds of fungi thrive in the boreal forest, where few flowering plants can grow. Fungi enjoy the acidic soils and scant light, getting their food from decaying matter rather than manufacturing their own from the sun, as flowering plants do. This is a species of chanterelle, a genus of funnel-shaped mushrooms appearing in late summer, many of which are edible. Most chanterelles have a beautiful orange or yellow color.

bearing structures called mushrooms do we recognize their presence. Otherwise, they remain hidden as fibrous networks underground or under the bark of trees. Indian pipe is also a saprophyte, but unlike the fungi it is a flowering plant, with arched blossoms that straighten up when turned to seed and with scale-like leaves of a translucent, waxy white. Curiously, though, the Indian pipe lives in conjunction with a root fungus—each requires the other living being in order to survive.

The pink lady's-slipper, without doubt the most familiar wild orchid to people in the Northeast, grows relatively abundantly in the boreal forest. Like the Indian pipe, it and other members of the orchid family grow in intimate partnership with their own specific root fungi. It is thought that the fungus supports the orchid by securing nutrients from an acid soil, which the orchid is unable to do by itself; indeed, it is the fungus rather than the lady's-slipper that seems to require the acid environment of the forest. Despite its name, the pink lady's-slipper in a coniferous habitat grows in two colors, the common pink and the somewhat rare white one, the reasons for which are not well understood.

Mammals

As one passes on the earth from arctic, through temperate, to tropical regions, the number of species, whether plant or animal, grows, encouraged by the increasingly favorable conditions that last ever longer throughout the year.

The boreal forest in Vermont has a richer flora and fauna than the small tundra areas, but compared with the deciduous forest it is rather poor. On the other hand, the boreal forest, both alpine and lowland, is a refuge for some of the rarer and more intriguing wildlife of the state. This is owing in part to the special type of vegetation the forest possesses, but also in part to the large unpopulated and undeveloped stretches it encompasses, where the more secretive and elusive species can live without disturbance.

Two of the rarest mammals in Vermont are members of this group of boreal species, both of which were far more abundant everywhere before the white settlers entered the territory. Then they were trapped in considerable numbers all over the Northeast. The Canada lynx and the pine marten are the phantom emblems of this forest and are now virtually restricted to the boreal habitat. The lynx is a wildcat, resembling the bobcat of the hardwood forests but with more grizzled fur and wide, furry snowshoe-type feet, good for traveling over deep snow. The marten is a fair-sized weasel that weighs 2 to 4 pounds and, though not particularly fast, is very agile and a proficient tree climber. It not only looks like a large squirrel but can act like one, as well.

Both species are highly efficient predators. The lynx, however, seems to rely in great measure on the snowshoe hare as its main prey—a habit that seems to lock the fate of these two populations inextricably: when hare numbers are low, so are the lynx's, and when the hares build their population back in the absence of heavy predation, the lynxes, in response, also increase. The marten apparently is less subject to such cycles, since it, like most weasels, has a more catholic diet. The marten eats mice, voles, red squirrels, hares, snakes, amphibians, and various birds and their eggs, depending on availability and the season.

Both the lynx and the marten require large tracts of undeveloped coniferous forest for their hunting and living—conditions certainly met in the extensive softwood swamps and uplands of the Northeastern Highlands. But neither mammal has been definitely sighted in Vermont for many years; the last documented sighting of a pine marten, for example, was in the 1940s. Though both species still live in isolated regions in New Hampshire, Maine, and Canada, some biologists believe them to have been extirpated in Vermont, saying these predators were never very many in the best of times and were the losers in the long aftermath of the excessive land clearing of the mid-1800s. Other biologists feel that, barring overdevelopment and drastic alterations in the composition of Vermont's boreal-forest region, it will be only a matter of time before both of these fascinating species reappear. Whether gone or not, the Canada lynx and the pine marten are on the state's endangered-species list, and thus protected year round by law.

The word *predator* often strikes a resonating chord of apprehension, even fear, in some people. It can connote an aloofness, a wildness, a fierceness—even though such attributes are usually severely exaggerated to the point of becoming mythology. But nonpredatory wildlife in Vermont's remote boreal forest can also be awe-inspiring and fuel the imagination. One such is the state's largest mammal, and among the largest on the continent—the moose.

This ungainly-looking but magnificent animal was once a widespread resident of the vast evergreen wilderness across North America, but its numbers have shrunk considerably under the incursions of people into its native range. It existed in Vermont until land clearing in the 1800s pushed the mammal completely out of the state. But now the moose has edged back, to the point where twenty-five, thirty, or perhaps as many as fifty live here, mostly confined to the northeastern part of Vermont. There a person may be lucky enough to see a moose in its natural habitat, roaming the thickets around remote ponds or lakes, browsing on waterside plants, or wading out to uproot aquatic weeds. For Easterners, unused to such a sight, it is an unforgettable experience even to catch a glimpse of this creature.

An occasional moose may wander into the most unusual places and create quite a stir. Practically every year one is seen in a farmer's field grazing with the cows, or running down the middle of an interstate highway, or even poking through a downtown street! These individuals, far from what we consider their normal home, are often found to be suffering from what is called moose sickness. This disease is caused by a parasitic worm that bores into the brain tissue of the moose, resulting in the mammal's becoming progressively disoriented and uncoordinated, and in most cases eventually dying. The worm gets into the moose by way of a terrestrial snail that acts as a secondary host. The worm-bearing snail is consumed by accident by the moose along with the vegetation being eaten; the worm leaves

The Moose. Vermont has a growing population of moose, especially in the northeastern part of the state. Occasionally one will appear out of its normal range—the wild—and take up unusual residence, as this moose did on a farm near Morrisville. Such individuals often are infected with a parasitic brain worm, which will eventually cause their death.

the snail and then works its way into the moose's central nervous system and ultimately into the brain. In the brain the worm lays its eggs, which then develop into larvae and move down blood vessels into the digestive tract of the animal. Finally, the larvae pass outside in the moose's feces, are picked up by the snail, and develop into the worms, which repeat the cycle.

Unaccountably, although this parasitic worm very commonly occurs in white-tailed deer, it seems to have few or no ill effects on them. Many wildlife biologists believe that the brain worm may be one important factor in keeping the moose from extending its range farther south into deer country.

The lynx, marten, moose, and other larger mammals carry a romance and stature befitting the stereotyped picture of northwoods wilderness. But they are, of course, not the only mammals of these forests. Other smaller ones are an important part of the area, even if they take up less of our thoughts and dreams.

The red squirrel is the most often seen of these smaller mammals. It has a wide distribution and broad tolerance, being found wherever conifers grow, whether in urban parks or deep forests away from civilization. It even lives in more southern states, but there, where conifers do not grow, it shifts to deciduous trees, although only those of higher elevations. Less seen because of its nocturnal habits is the northern flying squirrel, not really a flier but a glider from tree to tree. This species nests and sleeps by day in tree holes left by woodpeckers or other natural cavities, and emerges at night to hunt for food. It is active all year and eats a greater variety of foods than other squirrels—the seeds from cones, which the red squirrel favors, but also insects, bird eggs, nuts, berries, and occasionally a small mammal. They will also pay surprise visits to home suet-feeders put out for woodpeckers!

Down out of the trees, other seldom seen mammals of the boreal forest are at work the entire year—in winter, under the snow. The widespread boreal red-backed vole, mentioned earlier, is common all over this region, including its mountainous portions, and, in the manner of all voles, feeds on a large variety of herbaceous material, such as leaves, buds, bark, and roots. Searching the needles and furrowing into the humus layers of soil for ground insects, worms, insect larvae, and even other small mammals is the tiny masked shrew—one of several insectivores (the insect-eating family of mammals) that are residents of both softwoods and hardwoods, wherever moisture is plentiful.

Taken as a group, the mammals of the boreal forest are a hardy lot, able to survive in a rigorous climate, in a region where the pickings are slim. The ecological relationships of animal-to-animal or animal-to-plant may seem simpler here than elsewhere, because here there are fewer species than in more southern parts of the country. But each individual animal, to

The Red Squirrel. A familiar inhabitant of coniferous woods throughout Vermont, this squirrel eats a variety of foods, including mushrooms, which it places in tree branches to dry. This species has two litters each year, one in the early spring, one in late summer. It is active all winter, though stays inside its nest during very cold spells.

make it through a day or a year in this demanding environment, is involved in an incredibly complex and tenuous endeavor.

Birds

Birds of the spruce-fir forests are an interesting and changing group: the few and notable year-round residents, the unpredictable and sporadic winter visitors from farther north, the ephemeral summer nesters, and the seasonal migrants.

Though winter is a lean time for the bird—and therefore the bird-watcher—it can be a most rewarding period, for unexpected and unfamiliar species then come into Vermont. Many of the birds that visit the state's feeders, fields, and mixed forests in winter are true boreal species, breeding only in Canada. They move into the United States to spend the winter here, to proceed farther south in New England or beyond, or to wander from place to place. Their appearances are quite unpredictable, since their movements are not a true migration, but more a quest for food.

Most of such winter visitors are finches, a family of small to medium-sized birds with strong bills that can crack open the shells of seeds and nuts. In summer their diet is broad, from berries and seeds to insect larvae, spiders, beetles, and other "animal" matter. But in winter their choices are narrowed, to seeds that still cling to branches, buds, or the occasional hibernating insects they discover.

In this family two species of grosbeak (appropriately meaning "big beak") are numerous and common in Vermont, although over the years they do not consistently appear in the state: the evening and pine grosbeaks. Most years the evening grosbeak does arrive, often traveling in large flocks, stripping the trees of their seeds and buds, leaving the snow beneath littered with cone scales, twigs, seed husks, and bits of bark. Usually in late winter, when they are on their way back north to Canada for breeding, they will stop at bird feeders for sunflower seeds, having earlier picked clean the offering of the trees. Though now widely recognized in New England, before 1890 it was an unknown species east of the Great Lakes. In the following decade it moved east rapidly. One researcher attributed this dispersal to the planting of box-elder as a shade tree in much of the East. When these trees matured to seed-bearing age, the evening grosbeak apparently leapfrogged to the East Coast, and once here was able to sustain itself on other foods. Still, one of the best places to observe evening grosbeaks is where box-elders grow—whether in towns or along river bottoms.

The pine grosbeak is more erratic than the evening grosbeak in its appearance, being abundant one year and totally absent the next. Furthermore, it may be present here in the worst of winters yet absent in the mildest. These unpredictable winter movements thus seem geared to food finding rather than severe weather. When the pine grosbeak is in Vermont it is conspicuous, especially the handsome male, with its burgundy-colored body and dark wings; in addition, this bird is somewhat the daredevil, picking up grit and salt on roads and waiting until the last second before flying out from under an onrushing car.

Wandering far down the United States on occasion, but not often seen in Vermont, are two species of crossbill, finches whose name describes their outstanding physical feature. Their sharp-pointed bills do not meet as most birds' do, but cross at the ends, an awkward-looking but effective arrangement for the food they eat: the bills work like shears to cut cones from branches and rip off or pry apart cone scales to reveal the seeds inside. The white-winged crossbill is the more common of two species occurring here, but the rarer red crossbill is the more striking for its plumage of deep red.

Crossbills are among the earliest birds to begin nesting in the north country. Their nests, complete with eggs and sometimes even young, have been found in the boreal forests of Canada as early as January and February, in the full fury of winter! Whether or not most of the young from these early nestings grow to maturity, however, is open to question. Though we have no positive record of either species nesting in Vermont, it is suspected that they may do so in the forest of the Northeastern Highlands, if indeed not other places in the state where good boreal habitat is available.

The crossbills, grosbeaks, and other smaller finches, our occasional companions through late winter, begin to move north in preparation for breeding as winter yields to spring. Among these, the pine siskins and redpolls fade from rural areas in March and April as they depart for points north. Dark-eyed juncos and white-throated sparrows materialize in Vermont at about this time, on their way back to the higher elevations and coniferous mixed stands from their migrations south. Although for the most part the boreal-forest finches keep on moving through Vermont, to breed and nest in the woods of Canada, a few do stay, including most commonly the juncos and white-throated sparrows, which are apt to be found nesting in many mixed or coniferous stands throughout the state. The evening grosbeak, too, is now known to nest here.

With the dawning of May the boreal forest stirs with the daily arrival of small birds migrating north, keeping pace with the hatches or emergences of multitudes of insects. Most of these insect-eating birds in Vermont are the restless, jewellike wood warblers, whose winters are spent as far away as the southern

United States, Central and South America, and the West Indies. As many as fourteen different species inhabit the coniferous forests in our state, some as breeders, others as transients on their way farther north—even as far as the Arctic tundra.

The nesting species fill in the slots and spaces in the forest, illustrating well the concept of "niches"—the utilization of the complete environment by the members in it. The northern parula, a warbler, feeds in the upper reaches of the tree crowns and builds a nest of one particular species of lichen that grows there (old-man's beard). In the same area, the magnolia warbler keeps more to the understory vegetation, while the Nashville warbler may be active high in the canopy, though placing its nest on the ground, under shrubs. Thus, although these birds occupy the same general area, there is no conflict: their activities are different and variously located, and since insect species change from place to place in the forest, their foods are also different. Living space is parceled out in discreet units that the warblers can use to best advantage.

But niches mean more than just spacing. They refer also to a faithful association of birds with certain tree species or forest

The Magnolia Warbler. This bird acquired its misleading name when observed in magnolia trees in the South, on its wintering grounds. It actually breeds in the coniferous forests of northern New England and Canada and is a fairly common warbler in Vermont, both as a breeder and as a visitor during migration.

types. The blackpoll warbler is a common nesting species in the higher elevations of the spruce-fir forest on Vermont mountains, whereas the black-throated green warbler and yellow-rumped warbler prefer hemlock of the mixed forests. The rarer pine warbler is sometimes heard trilling in the crowns of pine trees, especially where they grow in pure stands. Rare, too, is the Wilson's warbler, a species found in openings in wet areas, such as alder swales. Stopping over in migration in the tall, open spruce stands are the Cape May warbler and the bay-breasted warbler—they will continue up the continent and few, if any, ever stay to make Vermont their summer home.

Many other insect-eating birds are found throughout this region in spring and summer. Tiny ruby-crowned kinglets, smaller and even more nervous and darting than the warblers, pick at twigs and needles for insects, insect eggs and larvae, and spiders. So small are they that their hanging nests are woven together with spider webs. The larger, warblerlike solitary vireo moves more slowly after insects and is heard singing high in the treetops. Olive-sided and yellow-bellied flycatchers swoop out to catch meals on the wing, while the red-breasted nuthatch bobs up and around tree trunks looking for larvae or ants, then retires to its nest in a cavity of a tree.

A hike in the mountains may well reveal several species of thrush, a family whose more familiar members are the robin and bluebird of towns and farms. Unlike these two, however, the forest thrushes are dull in coloration, their browns and grays protecting them in the dusky woodlands. Thrushes seem to sort themselves out according to elevation below tree line, with some overlapping. Nearest the tree line lives the gray-cheeked thrush, its song often heard by mountaintop hikers. Lower down, the Swainson's thrush is the common one seen and heard. As one proceeds down even farther, into the mixed woods, the Swainson's fades and is replaced by Vermont's state bird, the hermit thrush. This kind of replacement continues with other thrush species even down into the hardwoods.

The summer passes quickly and the young have grown to flight. By September most of the birds are noticeably anxious, in preparation for another migration. By the end of October almost all will have gone from Vermont's rather solemn forests, having headed to milder southern regions, where winter food will be waiting.

Only a few birds choose to stay through the long, cold, snowy winter. Though these few may visit us only during some winters, they are unlike the wandering finches in that they remain in purely coniferous regions the entire year. In Vermont's northern boreal zone they may be considered permanent residents, since they have been found there throughout the breeding season, as well as at other times of the year. They have acquired the means to secure food in winter, when it is extremely hard to find (because of inactivity of insects, deep snow, and frozen surfaces). They are only a handful, and because of their relative rarity and isolated locations it is exciting to discover these birds.

Among these permanent residents is the boreal chickadee, almost identical to its ecological equivalent, the common black-capped chicadee familiar to most people, except for its cap color (brown versus black), slightly different song, and the habit of hunting for insects, insect larvae, spider eggs, and seeds closer to tree trunks than out in the branches. Seen less often and only in the larger bogs and swamps of extensive second-growth boreal regions is the black-backed three-toed woodpecker. This

The Gray Jay. The "whiskey jack" or "camprobber" to loggers of the north country, this is a bird of true boreal regions and a scavenger par excellence. The species is known to breed in Vermont in the Northeastern Highlands. Its beautiful low whistle can be heard in the deep coniferous forests there, where it may come close to steal your food or other items.

medium-sized woodpecker, strictly a North American species, is suspected of breeding in the northeastern part of Vermont, where it flies from spruce to spruce, flicking off the bark with its large bill to uncover its insect food below. Though elusive, it is not particularly shy, and may give the viewer many minutes of observation. Even rarer is the northern three-toed woodpecker, commonly called the ladder-backed for the pattern that distinguishes it from the black-backed. This species is infrequently seen, and only in winter, but has shown up in Vermont in such varied places as the boreal forests of the mountains, the Lake Champlain islands, and, strangely, in the vicinity of Burlington.

Confined in Vermont to the boreal forests north and east of Island Pond is a species of grouse (chickenlike, nonmigratory ground-dwelling birds) that is rare both here and in the United States as a whole: the spruce grouse. Similar in many respects to the ruffed grouse of other areas in Vermont, it is hard to find, but when discovered it proves to be a most unbashful bird. Like many animals that have had limited contact with people, it has developed little fear of them, a habit earning the bird the slang name "fool hen"—it has even been caught by hand, without weapons or traps. Although it prefers to remain on the ground, it will take to the trees to roost or avoid danger, and in winter, when ground food is scarce or snow-covered, it will feed heavily on spruce and fir buds (which impart a resinous or turpentiny taste to the bird's flesh, according to those who have eaten it.).

One of the more flamboyant members of this select northern group of year-round inhabitants is the gray jay, formerly known as the Canada jay. It shows an unnerving boldness, and woodsmen have dubbed it "camprobber" for its habit of stealing their food and other items from camps, sometimes right out of their hands! "In its choice of food the Canada jay is even more omnivorous than the blue jay. It attacks almost anything that seems edible, and in winter is said at times to feed on the lichens. ... There is no reasonable limit to its appetite. Any bird that will consume quantities of soap probably will take almost anything edible. Indians say that it will eat moccasins and fur caps, but its food habits have never been the subject of exhaustive investigation." (Forbush and May, 1925)

Birds of prey are busy in winter, trying to live off a catch that may come only infrequently. But unlike the species that have just been described, most are not confined to a boreal habitat. The goshawk has the reputation of being one of the fiercest, boldest, most ruthless of these hunters. It is indeed a powerful and aggressive predator, and is agile in the woodlands, but the reputation is overblown, probably owing to its large size (two feet tall), appearance (red eyes under frowning white "eyebrows"), hostility when its nest is approached in breeding season, and broad diet, which includes almost any living thing it can get its talons on, from small insects to large birds to mammals.

When passenger pigeons swarmed by the millions over forested areas of the northern United States, they supposedly were one of the favorite foods of the goshawk. As far as we can tell, the goshawk then roved well south into the broad-leaved forests, but with the extinction of the passenger pigeon in the early 1900s and the reduction of forestland all over New England, it steadily retreated to its boreal refuge, where it stayed until recent years. Within the past decade, however, goshawks have been returning to lower latitudes in increasing numbers. Nesting is not uncommon in Vermont now, even in the mixed woods, as several hikers have found out—much to their surprise and alarm—when dive-bombed by screaming defensive parent hawks.

Another group of predatory birds, the owls, are represented in the boreal forests. Though several species live there, the long-eared owl is the one most restricted to that habitat and is generally considered to be rare in Vermont. It is possible, however, that it is not so uncommon as we think, since it is a nocturnal bird, roosting quietly during the day, when it appears appressed to the trunks of trees, blending perfectly with its background.

In the course of almost every winter rare Arctic birds of prey show up in Vermont. These are believed to be driven south in search of food, which has become scarce in their native hunting grounds. Once, two, or sometimes several individuals of such foreign species stay the winter and set up territories in their adopted homes. Perhaps the most regular of these periodic invaders are snowy owls. They usually select flat, open areas that may resemble their tundra landscapes, and there they feed on mice the way they do on lemmings in the far north. Snowy owls have appeared recently on power lines and rooftops in Barre and on the breakwater of Burlington harbor. Another Arctic visitor is the very large rough-legged hawk, seen some years in substantial numbers, mostly as it hovers over the flatlands of the Champlain Valley. Among the once-in-a-lifetime sightings of Arctic birds in Vermont are the hawk owl that spent the winter of 1978−79 in a farmer's field in Westford, not far from Burlington, and the swift, pure-white gyrfalcon seen over Craftsbury the same winter.

Other Animals

The homogeneity of the boreal forest, its paucity of plant species, its sterile soils, and its harsh environmental conditions severely limit the numbers of other animals able to live there.

The soil acidity and the lack of humus, caused by slowly rotting needles, on top of the glacial sands and gravels keep soil organisms—worms, insects, other arthropods, and the small mammals that feed on them—to a minimum. The long, hard winters apparently restrict cold-blooded vertebrates, too—the amphibians and reptiles.

The most common amphibian in this region is probably the handsome black-masked, buff-bodied wood frog. Though it lives throughout Vermont, breeding in wet areas and moving to higher grounds later in the spring, it is found farther north than any other North American amphibian. It is known to breed not only in the boreal forest but even in the tundra, and has a habit that accommodates the extremely short frost-free season when it is active: it breeds very early in spring, often before the snow is gone, and after the female deposits her eggs in the water, she, unlike most other amphibians, abandons them, so that she can move on to other businesses of living. The eggs and young develop quickly, their time of maturation being compressed to keep in step with the short season.

Another boreal amphibian in the state, though with a less widespread distribution than in other regions, is the mink frog. So named because of the musky odor it emits when handled, the mink frog can be heard uttering its staccato mating call in a few areas of Vermont in spring. One can even hear it in certain high-elevation ponds and wetland spots in the mountains, as, for example, at Bear Pond and Lake of the Clouds in Mount Mansfield State Forest.

Reptiles are few and seldom seen in the boreal forest. The most frequently encountered is probably the semiaquatic painted turtle, either at the edge of a pond as it basks in the sun or in the woods as it makes its way in summer from the water to drier land for egg laying. Of snakes, the familiar garter snake, tolerant of many habitats, is the most common of a very few in boreal regions; it searches the forest floor for insects and small mammals to eat.

Anyone who visits the coniferous-forest regions in May or June knows that insects are abundant. Most notorious are the black flies, the small biting insects that begin hatching in early spring, in the rushing waters of brooks and streams. They rise out of the water in great numbers, the females (the males don't bite) quickly seeking blood meals from any source. They can be so many and so pesky that they drive animals into a frenzy and into the water for relief. Many fishing and camping trips, planned in winter when thoughts of insects are faraway and dim, have been ruined—or at least made near unbearable—by this small, black monster. The black fly will be discussed again later, in another context.

      *   *   *   *

    The boreal forest in Vermont has a character and identity that must be felt as much as seen or described. With this background distillation of what these regions are like biologically, a visitor can then add his or her own impressions and experiences in the quest for why these woods have such special appeal to so many people.

7

The Northern Hardwoods

When the Europeans first took possession of North America, it was
one continued forest, the greatest on earth. . . . Much of the largest
part of Vermont is yet in the state in which nature placed it.
Uncultivated by the hand of man, it presents to our view a vast tract
of woods abounding with trees, plants, and flowers, almost infinite
in number, and of the most various species and kind.
—Samuel Williams (1794)

Legend has it that the early American hardwood forest was
so large, dense, and uninterrupted that a squirrel, if it wanted to,
could travel from the East Coast to the Mississippi River without
touching the ground. An exaggeration, no doubt, but nevertheless it must have been a grand and imposing scene, even a
forbidding one, that stood before those first white settlers.

But the wilderness meant something other than grandeur to
the pioneers of those years, and their approach to it and way of
life have left only fragments of the former virgin forest. In our
state these areas are but small bridges from presettlement Vermont to today.

But though the virgin woodlands no longer dominate our
landscape, and despite the changes in the forest that have been
wrought, Vermont's woods have retained much of their original
character. The hemlock—northern-hardwood trees that were
cleared by our ancestors have returned, and although they exist
in a different form from their predecessors, they are still a major
component of the state, both spacially and in terms of economics.

This is the forest of fall color, picture postcards, and maple
syrup. It is a forest of great commercial uses and potential. It has
been the area in Vermont most densely settled, and it harbors a
wide variety of plants and animals.

The hemlock—northern-hardwood association is part of a
large and fascinating forest system—the Eastern Deciduous
Forest, encompassing most of eastern North America except for
the central and southern maritime regions. Though most people
who live in it take its seasonal transformations for granted, on the
world's scale it is a unique forest. Only China has a geographic
region with a comparable climate and environment that results
in a similar flora, but even there many of the species are different

and the flavor of the land is not quite the same. In few other places on earth do the trees put on delicate green leaves in spring (with wild flowers blooming on the ground), then continue through summer, and finally drop their leaves in a blaze of color in autumn. In few other places do the trees stand leafless through winter, storing their manufactured food in the protection of their roots.

In general, the hemlock – northern-hardwood association occupies most land in Vermont below 2,400 feet, except for that which is boreal forest or such special habitats as marshes and ponds – or space preempted by human beings for roads, buildings, and farms. All together this association accounts for 68 percent of the state's 4.5 million forested acres. Since forests of all kinds make up 75 percent of the state's land, this means that hardwoods grow in more than half of all of Vermont.

The classic climax hemlock – northern-hardwood forest is a mixture of species and varies with the topography. Sugar maple, American beech, and yellow birch are the dominants on well-drained, rich soils, with lesser quantities of white ash, black cherry, basswood, red maple, red oak, hemlock, and others. In higher elevations, the pioneer trees paper birch and quaking aspen might persist for a long time into the climax stage. In more poorly drained areas and bottomlands, red maple, butternut, balsam poplar, black ash, eastern cottonwood, and silver maple are found in greater proportions, as was American elm before its near-obliteration by the Dutch elm disease.

White pine grows throughout the region and often in pure stands, usually indicating a former opening in the canopy or a clearing of the land, to where it could gather enough sun and rise to maturity; several of the pure stands of pine bear witness to where the 1938 hurricane blew down whole tracts of forest. White pine also does well in abandoned fields, especially where other seed-bearing pine trees are not far away and are thus available to provide the source for a new generation. Red pine fulfills a similar role on poorer, sandier soils, although this species is less common now than it used to be.

Northward and higher in elevation, conifers become increasingly abundant. Southward and lower, red oak become more noticeable (they are virtually absent north of a line drawn from Burlington to Montpelier). Within this general distribution, the forest changes in composition and character with terrain, local climate, exposure, and other factors. Indeed, little of the forest is what might be called "pure" hemlock-northern hardwoods. Most is a mishmash, befitting its position as an ecotone: an area of transition from one landscape to another.

The changing climate over the past 3 million years brought

the glaciers, which brought the tundra and boreal forests to Vermont. The tundra is believed to be a disjunct community, one separated from its parent region to the north (in this case), remaining here because the mountaintop climate is like that of its ancestral home. But other disjuncts also remain in Vermont, having come from other directions and staying for other reasons.

In the protective cradles of the Champlain and Connecticut River valleys live tree species more typical of the South than the North. Black gum, a common tree in Southern swamps, tulip poplar, sycamore, chestnut oak, black oak, sprouts of the near-extinct American chestnut, pitch pine, and red cedar crop up as individuals or as modest-sized colonies. These are remnants of a southern forest that undoubtedly spread well up into Vermont during what is called the climatic optimum, or hypsithermal interval, a period, as mentioned in chapter one, about 4,000 to 6,000 years ago, when the climate was at its mildest. When the climate cooled 1,000 to 1,500 years later, it drove this forest back South, but in a few protected Northern pockets trees could still survive and the species have persisted to this day. Trees are the most noticeable relics of the climatic optimum, but shrubs such as redbud, flowering dogwood, sassafras, mountain laurel, and

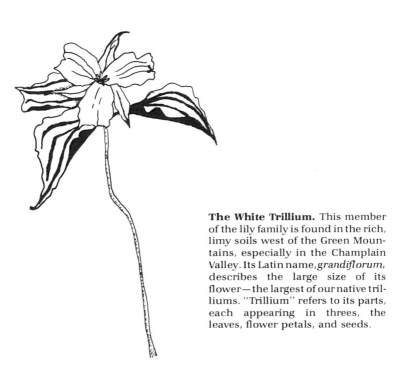

The White Trillium. This member of the lily family is found in the rich, limy soils west of the Green Mountains, especially in the Champlain Valley. Its Latin name, *grandiflorum*, describes the large size of its flower—the largest of our native trilliums. "Trillium" refers to its parts, each appearing in threes, the leaves, flower petals, and seeds.

great laurel are also products of it. Even bog species such as pitcher plants, sundews, and wild orchids, growing side by side the tundra species, owe their presence in Vermont to this warm interglacial period.

In addition, tree and plant communities best developed in yet other geographical regions of the continent are represented in Vermont. The northern Lake Champlain Valley and adjacent lowlands give us species more typical of the northern Midwest and West, such rarities as jack pine and bur oak. In the lower Champlain Valley and the Taconics are communities closely tied to the New York—southern-Midwest region: the oak-hickory association of white, black, and red oaks, three species of hickory, and such occasionals as black walnut and scarlet oak.

So the picture of Vermont's plants is not simple, the state's being situated as it is, between several distinct forest types, the Northern and Southern, the Eastern and Western. When the large variety of landscapes, soils, bedrocks, and habitats is added as another component of the makeup of Vermont, we see the reason for Frank Seymour's statement, in *The Flora of Vermont*, that the flora here is *five* times as diverse as the rest of New England's.

Plants

Before the new leaves of the forest have unfurled completely, even before the snow has gone in many places, the wild flowers begin to blossom as the sun warms the sodden ground. The spring wild flowers of the Eastern United States are a special—in fact unique—flora. As in the case of the trees, China has a similar spring flora, since it has similar geographical and climate regions, yet even there the species do differ considerably from those of North America. The native herbaceous plants of Vermont are mostly perennials, taking many years to grow to flowering age, and each fall dying back to a rootstalk. They bloom very quickly during that brief time between the end of winter and the full leafing out of the trees, when the canopy closes out the sun.

Very early in spring in the rich hardwood forest rises bloodroot, with its delicate, almost ethereal white flower. Like other members of the poppy family, bloodroot has an opaque, poisonous sap, but, as noted by its name, the sap is red rather than the usual white. Trilliums seem to be everywhere. The most common, red trillium, grows throughout the region. The larger and less common white trillium is restricted to the limy soils near Lake Champlain and its islands; in fact, the best colonies of white trillium, nowhere common in New England, occur here—some places look as if they are covered with snow when it blossoms. Painted trillium grows in the intermediate elevations where conifers become more plentiful and the environments more boreal in character.

Smaller flowers open daily under the increasing warmth of the spring sun. Common are the violets, in all their shades, the perfect spires of foamflower, the stars of starflower, the variable-colored round-lobed hepatica, and the nodding, yellow dog-tooth violet, or trout lily (so called for the markings on its leaves, which resemble a brook trout's). Above the tracery of blue-green leaves dangle windflowers and Dutchman's-breeches. And on rare occasions the woodland traveler comes across the purple-and-white flowers of the showy orchis, one of the state's few woodland orchids.

Flowers that come later in the spring are usually not so conspicuous. Jack-in-the-pulpit hides its cluster of fleshy flowers at the base of a leafy cup. The purple-brown flower of wild ginger often goes unnoticed, since it is at or below the leaf litter on the ground, at the base of the plant's two heart-shaped leaves. Wild sarsaparilla, a widespread plant in Vermont that looks like a small, misshapen white-ash seedling, has a green spiked ball of nondescript flowers beneath a parasol of leaves.

Through the summer, colors continue to subside and even fewer flowers are to be seen in the deeper shade cast by the trees. A group of tiny woodland orchids, collectively called rattlesnake plantains, that bloom from midsummer to fall are often over-

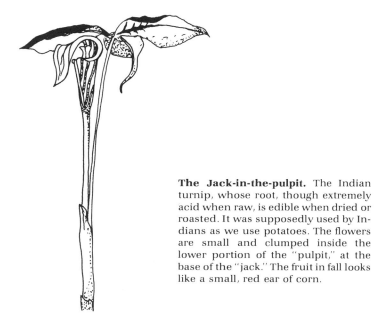

The Jack-in-the-pulpit. The Indian turnip, whose root, though extremely acid when raw, is edible when dried or roasted. It was supposedly used by Indians as we use potatoes. The flowers are small and clumped inside the lower portion of the "pulpit," at the base of the "jack." The fruit in fall looks like a small, red ear of corn.

looked because they are so small. Their leaves are usually only 1 to 2 inches long and pressed against the ground; their patterned greens blend perfectly with the surroundings. Like almost all other orchids in Vermont, the rattlesnake plantains are considered rare and endangered.

Certain wild flowers signal autumn's approach. Bottle, or closed, gentian is such a flower, growing along many trails at the forest's edges. (This plant is so named because its flowers generally do not open, but remain shut like a bud, looking like a bottle. When the flowers open briefly for pollination by bees, the insects that linger too long inside get trapped.) The first frost may have taken place or not be far away, even in the guardianship of the woodlands, when two asters appear—whorled aster and white wood aster, both of which have white flowers. These two are members of a large worldwide "modern" family, most of which are field species, such as dandelions, sunflowers, daisies, thistles, and goldenrods.

The wild flowers add an attractive dimension to the forests, but other kinds of plants also make an important aesthetic contribution to Vermont's woodland scenery. Most notable are the ferns and their allies the club mosses and horsetails. Our state has more than 50 species of ferns and many more hybrids, perhaps half of which occur in the hardwood forest, its edges, and closely related but specialized habitats. The ferns, club mosses, and horsetails we see here today are relatives of the tree-sized species that existed more than 200 million years ago in the huge, sprawling inland swamps of Pangaea. It was the incredible amounts of peat (partially decomposed organic matter) produced by the decomposition of these plants—their trunks, leaves, and even spores—that went into the making of the enormous coal deposits mined today in the United States and elsewhere.

There seems to be a fern for every situation. Many are tolerant of a wide variety of environmental conditions, and thus are widespread. Others, however, are more restricted to the rich, moist woodlands of broad-leaved trees. Still others prefer the younger open woods, where the light floods in. Even the wet bottomlands and riverbanks have their own species, such as crested shield fern, marsh fern, and ostrich fern, the last being the "fiddlehead" fern of spring foragers.

In limestone areas with cliffs, ravines, forest pockets, and other unusual landforms one may discover some of New England's rarer fern species. Many of these are probably disjuncts from both the north and south. The Vermont Valley, adjacent slopes of the Taconics and Green Mountains, and the eastern side of the Champlain Lowlands form a gallery of interesting, unusual ferns. The Brandon region at its center is sometimes called the "fern capital of the East" because of this diversity. Such exotic species as narrow-leaved spleenwort and male fern grow in the cold, moist ravines, while wall rue and slender cliffbrake hide in the ledges of cliffs and outcroppings.

Mammals

The mammals in Vermont's hardwood forests, especially the larger animals, have figured importantly in the state's economy through the years, both in the early days of white habitation, when trappers supplied fur to markets far beyond Vermont's borders, and now, when hunting and other recreations dealing directly or indirectly with wild animals are so popular.

In many ways, mammals have been the barometers of what has happened to the land. Numerous species were driven out by the initial cutting of the virgin forests; some left and never returned, but others—often with human help—have come back with vigor to the new forests of the twentieth century.

Before the white settler ever set foot in Vermont, far-ranging wilderness mammals lived over the region. The caribou, today found mostly in Canada and Alaska, was undoubtedly here, probably living in coniferous-forest swamps. So, too, was the elk, or wapiti, now an inhabitant of only our Western mountainous states, but which formerly was the most widely distributed of North American hoofed animals. It is certain the elk was in Vermont, because its antlers have been found in bogs in the western part of the state. The scourge of the northland wilds, the wolverine, a large weasel of legendary ferocity, once lived at the northern limit of the state. And the bison, too, may have roamed into southern Vermont, where the burning of the forest by Indians produced an open range that would have been suitable for grazing. Although we have no evidence of the bisons' presence in Vermont, it is highly likely they lived here, as their bones have been found in Massachusetts, near Cape Cod.

These species disappeared early, being true wilderness sojourners and totally incompatible with the changes brought by the white settlers. They probably were gone prior to 1750. Others remained into times of denser settlement but eventually they gave way to land clearing and civilization. The timber wolf was one of the more famous of these animals.

Long the stereotyped villain of tooth-and-claw ferocity, the wolf was hated and persecuted by early sheep and cattle farmers, who saw it as the archenemy of their herds. An early Vermont historian, Samuel Williams, wrote in 1794:

One of the most common and noxious of all animals is the WOLF.... His eyes generally appear sparkling; and there is a wildness, and a fierceness, in his looks.... This animal is extremely fierce, sanguinary, and carnivorous. When a number of them associate, it is not for peace, but for war and destruction. The animal, at which they most of all aim, is the sheep.... They attack the deer, foxes, rabbits, and are enemies to all other animals; and their attacks are generally attended with the most horrid howlings.... There is nothing valuable in these animals but their skins....

The wolf was bountied in 1779 and from that time until about 1820 it was a great sport to organize wolf hunts that served the purpose of ridding the countryside of what was seen as a severe danger. Concurrently, the breakup of the vast tracts of wilderness forest drastically reduced the territory the wolf required for its hunting. Together these factors served a death warrant to the timber wolf, and by 1900 it was gone from this region.

The history of the catamount in Vermont ("cat of the mountain," otherwise known as the mountain lion, puma, panther, or painter) is not unlike that of the timber wolf. This large feline—

The Last Mountain Lion. This was the last catamount shot in Vermont. It is posed with its hunter, Alexander Crowell, who killed it in 1881 near the town of Barnard, in central Vermont. It was also the largest catamount on state record, weighing 182½ pounds and measuring 7 feet from nose to tip of tail. It now stands as a mounted specimen, beside the gun that shot it, in the Vermont Historical Society Museum in Montpelier.

the largest ever recorded in Vermont weighed 182 pounds—was feared for its strength and allegedly wanton predation. It even had the reputation of hunting human beings. Evidently the stories were not completely fanciful, as authentic accounts relate how men and horses were chased. Even so, there is no record of deaths due to the mountain lion. Like the wolf, the catamount was bountied in the very early years of settlement, in 1779. Although questionable bounties were still being paid as late as 1894, it is believed that the last cat in Vermont was the one killed thirteen years earlier in the town of Barnard. This individual was mounted and is now on display at the Vermont Historical Society Museum in Montpelier.

Until recently and despite persistent rumors to the contrary, most authorities have believed the catamount to have been exterminated in Vermont since the killing of the animal in Barnard in 1881. In the last few years, however, several reputable people have made close and clear sightings of what they claim to be mountain lions and, even without evidence of specimens or photographs, some of these reports are hard to discredit. A dead catamount was recovered in January 1968 from the bottom of a steep cliff at Saranac Lake, New York, a short fifty miles west of Vermont. This individual apparently slipped off the icy cliff and died of a broken neck. Although even these sightings and the New York specimen do not convince some people of the presence in our state of the native mountain lion—they argue that the animals seen may be individuals of the Western breed of mountain lion that have been released here or escaped from captivity—it is nevertheless a distinct possibility that the catamount has returned to Vermont after its long absence. Certainly the proper habitat to meet its needs has been restored in many areas, and perhaps soon we will have the evidence we now lack. But for the time being, it must remain but an exciting possibility.

These are the most vivid examples of animals that were too sensitive to endure the coming of the white settlers and the changes they brought. They fuel our imagination about the nature of that former Vermont. Most appear to have gone for good, their homes too much altered or their ways back too remote and full of obstacles for them to return. Despite this demise for many animals, however, there were others that, on the way to extinction, reversed their decline and have come back strongly. Often we have helped them return.

The white-tailed deer—a symbol of Vermont, in a way—is our largest, most popular game animal. The embodiment of a rural, tempered wildness, it is a mammal of versatility and great adaptability. We all know it, but we almost lost it.

In the virgin forests of America the white-tailed deer apparently was present in substantial numbers, providing much food and clothing for the Indians. But the arrival of white settlers and loggers soon changed that: deer were hunted the year round, supplying commercial meat markets; their forest habitat dwindled; no laws protected them. Their population dropped precipitously within a relatively short period of time.

Even before Vermont was a state, people were aware of the plight of the deer. The first laws to protect them here were establishd in 1741 by the New Hampshire Grants (the land of Vermont was at that time divided down the Green Mountains, belonging to the "New Hampshire Grants" to the east of them, and New York State to the west). As an independent territory, Vermont in 1779 set its first statute prohibiting the hunting of deer, from January 10 to June 10. This was the first closed season

The White-tailed Deer. A big buck in the fall. The species in Vermont was nearly extinct in the mid-1800s, owing to the clearing of its wooded habitat, but it is now the most abundant large mammal in the state. Its population here probably exceeds 160,000. The deer's prime territory is the hills of the southern half of the state.

and it coincided with the institution of bounties on the deer's natural predators, the wolf and the catamount.

But despite this protection the deer had great trouble recovering from its earlier decline, and by 1800 it was nearly extinct in the East. In response, game laws became stiffer, the closed seasons longer, and ultimately it became illegal to hunt deer in Vermont.

But slowly the scene changed. To bolster the almost non-existent population, deer were brought to Vermont from out of state and released. All the while, the deer-preying wolves and catamounts continued to decline to insignificant proportions, and over time the forests made a comeback from the height of land clearing in the 1860s and '70s. With protective laws even tighter, freedom from predation, and shelter and food from the new forests, the whitetail's fortunes changed dramatically. By 1930 deer were once again secure in Vermont—as it turned out, too secure for their own good.

The white-tailed deer is supremely equipped to live in modern Vermont. It thrives on the interspersion of fields and forests, young timber and old, hardwoods and softwoods. It browses on the vigorous low growth of the young forest, and fattens in the fall on the nuts of beech, oak, and hickory. It grazes on the sweet grasses of fields and the grains of standing crops. It retires to the haven of the softwoods for winters, where it finds cover and food. In short, the way we have shaped the land suits the deer's needs very well.

Hunting today is rigidly controlled and predation other than by human beings is slight. But our well-intentioned protectiveness, perhaps inherited from earlier years when deer were so few, has allowed them to overpopulate their range. As a result, each year thousands face starvation, especially during the lean time of winter, when twigs and buds within a small radius of the deer yards (wintering grounds) are the only available foods. Many of the animals that don't starve are malnourished and weakened to the point that they are susceptible to disease and stress, from which they eventually die.

In 1878 17 deer had to be *imported* to Vermont from New York, to attempt to bring them back from the brink of extinction. In 1978 biologists estimated the deer population in the state to be 160,000. Vermont today has one of the highest densities—if not the highest density—of deer in the United States. However, this population is not necessarily composed of the healthiest or biggest individuals.

Until 1979, Vermont was one of the few states in which only bucks could be hunted. But since one buck can mate with many does, and since people are virtually the only predator of deer, hunting that claims less than 10 percent of the animals is not enough to bring the deer's numbers in line with what the land can stand. Their population continues to increase, while their territory, already too small for their numbers, remains the same. Eventually, something must give.

Wildlife biologists have felt for many years that Vermont's deer herd is on the brink of disaster—too many deer making demands on too few food resources. Estimates of winter deaths range from one to two times the total number killed in the hunting season, or from ten to twenty thousand!

The season of 1979—80 will be the first in a long while in which does can be hunted, on a limited and highly monitored basis. It is sure to create arguments: some will say that mothers and young should still be protected. But biologists believe that only by such thinning out of the deer that actually account for the population increases—the does—can the numbers begin to drop to a point at which few will be faced with food shortages. Correcting the current imbalance will take time and be fraught with controversy, as it has been in other states. But if conducted properly and phased in gradually, this program could restore health and vigor to Vermont's deer, qualities lacking now for many years.

Although the white-tailed deer were a great and unexpected boon to the early white inhabitants of Vermont, as a source of both food and clothing, beavers drew the most intense interest, because their pelts were in high demand in Europe for fashionable fur hats. White traders from the fur companies accordingly hired the Indian natives to supply them with beaver and other skins. The result was that within a short time after this trade was begun, many mammals in the East had been trapped to near-extermination. This relentless, single-minded plundering of the beaver, accompanied by the clearing of its prime habitat across the country, caused the animal to fall close to extinction in a broad region from the Atlantic seaboard to the Mississippi River. Zadock Thompson in 1849 remarked that this once common mammal in Vermont was probably gone from the state even before the middle part of that century.

Again, our immediate remedial action to cure this "sickness" was to institute protective laws. Beavers were first afforded year-round protection in Vermont in 1900. This measure brought little success, however, so that attempts were then made to restock the depleted population. In 1921 several animals were live-trapped out of state and brought to southern Vermont, and in 1932 some beavers imported from Maine were released in Vermont's northeast. All the while, the forests were rising anew, offering quantities of vigorously growing aspen, a favorite commodity of the beaver for its food and building materials.

Thanks to these efforts, today this largest North American native rodent is firmly reestablished in Vermont, as well as other New England states, and it is now highly successful on its own. Many people have seen the work of the beaver—felled trees, dams, lodges—if not the wary animal itself. It is now of sufficient numbers to allow trapping during a regulated season in winter, and in some areas it has actually become a serious pest, causing floods and gnawing into young timber stands.

Though beavers were the most plentiful and sought-after furbearers before white settlement, another mammal was the most valuable, per pelt, of any in the forest. The elusive and mystical fisher, often called "fisher-cat," sold for as much as $350 for a fine pelt, an enormous sum in the seventeenth century, not to say today.

Despite its name, the fisher, neither primarily fishes for its food, nor is it a kind of cat. It is really a large weasel, with males weighing up to 12 pounds (the females much less), similar in shape to the marten, but sleeker, blacker, and bigger.

The fisher was never abundant in Vermont, because it requires a large home range: it is estimated that one animal's territory is 3 to 4 square miles, but within this area it may actually crisscross a total of 100 miles in its hunting. And since it was such a prize to trappers, and one of the easier mammals to trap, even the relatively few in Vermont were soon depleted, their extermination greatly accelerated by the clearing of the forest. Like the beaver, the fisher was to all intents extinct in our state by the mid-1800s.

Being a night hunter and an efficient predator, the fisher has been endowed with an aura of ferocity and evil comparable to that of the wolverine. It has been credited with carrying off dogs, cattle, and even children! The stories become ever more fanciful. But one of its real prey, an unlikely one at that, has played a decisive role in both its depletion and restoration: the porcupine. The fisher is one of the porcupine's few natural predators, being agile and quick enough to knock the porcupine out of a tree and attack its unprotected belly without getting quilled and apparently it can withstand some quills without detrimental effects.

As the young forest matured in the last quarter of the nineteenth century and the first quarter of this one, porcupines became a serious problem to the wood-based economy of Vermont, as they ate their way through the bark of many valuable timber trees. Porcupines grew rapidly in number, encouraged by the ideal habitat of the revived forest, the abundance of food, and an absence of enemies.

The Fisher. This large weasel hunts at night in a wide territory, for rodents and other small game, and it is especially noted for its skill in preying on porcupines—a welcome activity as far as foresters are concerned, who are at war with the sapling-eating porcupine. Once nearly extinct in Vermont, the fisher has reappeared in sizable numbers. Note the paired tracks left by the animal, typical of all weasels when they are running.

To combat this problem the Vermont Department of Forests and Parks, in cooperation with the Vermont Fish and Game Department and the U.S. Fish and Wildlife Service, began a program in 1959 to restore fishers to the state, a recolonization the animals apparently were unable to do on their own. Theoretically, fishers could, in a natural way, control porcupines more effectively and cheaply than could human beings, with their artificial means of control. Between 1959 and 1967 124 fishers were live-trapped in Maine, brought to Vermont, and released in porcupine-problem areas. These imports were to supplement any native stock that might still remain and provide the nucleus for a renewed population.

The program has worked well: it appears that fishers have returned to their rightful place in Vermont. They have taken hold quickly, expanded their range perhaps even farther south than the original one, and have proved a significant control on the porcupines. They have built such a strong population here that they may now be trapped, as has been done under a highly monitored season since 1974. From trapping results wildlife biologists will gain insights into the population dynamics of this exciting "black ghost" of the forest.

The white-tailed deer, beaver, and fisher are some old acquaintances that have gone through hard times, at first hurt by our hand but later helped by us. There is at least one animal, however, that is almost brand new to the state, having made it here quite on its own, even in spite of us: the coyote.

No coyote had been seen in Vermont before 1948, but from the time of that first appearance until now it has found its way into nearly every section of the state—indeed, throughout the East. Many people have heard its ringing nighttime howls during the winter mating season or seen it loping along a field or through the forest.

The race here is the eastern coyote, distinct from its smaller counterpart, the western coyote. The eastern is believed to have acquired a larger size through generations of crossbreeding with the timber wolf of northern Michigan and Ontario. One author has named it "new wolf" for its characteristics intermediate between the wolf and the coyote. It is a pure breed and not a dog-coyote cross (the "coydog"; such crosses do take place but offspring after the first generation are a mixed litter, the individuals bearing the attributes of one or the other parent, or even earlier forebears: this means that coydogs do not breed true, and thus are not a distinct species).

The coyote's amazingly rapid immigration to Vermont, probably via Canada, is due to several factors: its ability in many ways to take the place of the wolf, a high reproductive rate (the average litter is 6), the absence of natural predators, a renowned cunning, and an omnivorous, scavenging, opportunistic feeding habit. It is also a most hardy soul, having survived bullet holes, feet severed in traps, and, in one case, a missing lower jaw.

This wild canine has been criticized as a despoiler of deer populations, but the claim is unjust, for evidence shows that

The Coyote. One of the state's newer species pads through the winter forest. This scavenger-predator has been immigrating steadily eastward in the United States, arriving in Vermont in 1948. Its numbers in the state are now estimated in the thousands.

predation on deer is the exception rather than the rule. A coyote occasionally may bring down a weak, injured, or sick deer, but does not have the means to cope with a strong, healthy one. More likely, it will eat the carcass of a deer previously killed by free-running domestic dogs or dead from other causes.

The coyote has been an important addition to our fauna—for most people a welcome one—providing a legitimate service as a scavenger, cleaning up remains within the natural community. It is one large mammal that can live alongside people and still remain wild, two traits our burgeoning civilization is increasingly requiring of wildlife.

But the mixed forests of Vermont continue to harbor a share of true wildlife, which can stir within us the romantic feelings only distance from humanity can bring. Perhaps none does this so well as the black bear.

Few people have seen this large animal (weighing up to 500 pounds), whose numbers in Vermont are estimated at between 1,000, and 1,200. It is reclusive, wary of human beings, most often seen by hunters in the fall, when it is preoccupied with gorging on nuts, berries, fruit, seeds, honey, and insect larvae in preparation for its dormancy in winter. The black bear does not truly hibernate, like a woodchuck and some bats, whose metabolic processes grind to a near-halt and body temperature falls to within a few degrees of freezing. Rather, it semihibernates for long periods, occasionally stirring during winter's warmer spells. Its temperature remains close to normal and the female even brings forth her tiny young (weighing only a few ounces) every other year during this rest. Bears emerge from dormancy looking healthy, plump, and as if they had been active all winter, but soon become emaciated and ravenous, searching feverishly for food.

The black bear has experienced many ups and downs in its residency in Vermont. It was bountied as late as the 1940s, as a supposed threat to people, sheep, and crops. Its numbers are low enough now so that hunting results must be closely scrutinized, and biologists and wildlife managers must recommend timely management actions for its continued well-being. The greatest threat to the bear, as,for so many wild animals, is the destruction of the habitat it needs to survive—the development of large currently unsettled forests will certainly have adverse effects on this grand and imposing creature.

The bobcat, too, has gone full circle in its relationship with man, having been bountied until 1971 and now being protected by a restricted hunting season, which was initiated in 1976 and tightened in 1978. Contrary to its reputation, this predator feeds very little on deer, but rather, mostly on rodents, small game, and, extensively, carrion. It is a mammal that intrigues us, but about which we know very little. Scant data are available about its life or population in Vermont, but perhaps a thousand live in the state, undoubtedly many fewer than in presettlement times, yet more than at the probable low point of fifty years ago.

All these mammals have experienced one thing in common, change. Disappearing, reappearing, fluctuating, immigrating. And regardless of human influences and intentions, change will

The Black Bear. Although this is the smallest species of bear in North America, individuals can reach weights of 500 pounds; Vermont's record is 413 pounds. The breeding season here is as early as June and July, but development of the fetuses is slow. The young, weighing only a few ounces, are born in winter to semihibernating sows, and then they remain with their mother for about 16 months. Brother and sister cubs stay together for another year, after which the family ties are broken and the bears become quite solitary.

always be the way of nature. Such patterns are not restricted to these glorified members of the Vermont forest wildlands, either. Many of the "lower" mammals have also exhibited them.

The gray fox, for example, has worked its way into Vermont from Southern states and now lives in every forested region here. (Zadock Thompson in 1849 gave only brief mention of it, as it had not then extended its range far into Vermont.) This tree-climbing brother of the red fox is still a relatively unknown species, because its fur has not been pursued as has the red fox's, and it stays deeper in the forest, rarely coming out in the open.

Among the lagomorphs (the order encompassing rabbits and hares) in Vermont, once the sole representative was the snowshoe hare, which changes coat color from summer to winter. But in the mid-1800s the New England cottontail—almost indistinguishable from the common eastern cottontail—appeared in southern Vermont and began to move up into brushy areas, clearings, and mountainous locations. Now it lives everywhere in the state except the boreal region of the Northeastern Highlands. Shortly after the appearance of the New England cottontail, the eastern cottontail also arrived, but remained primarily in the Champlain and Connecticut River valleys and other bottomlands, where it still lives; the period of this rabbit's greatest influx was 1900 to 1916, corresponding to the stage in the forest succession that was favorable to its existence—the shrubby, small-treed stage, which offered protective cover with access to open areas for feeding.

As could be expected in such a forested state, squirrels have done well in Vermont, although they, too, have experienced change. Red squirrels have always been abundant in the coniferous and mixed woods, as have the less noticed, nocturnal northern flying squirrels. The population of eastern gray squirrels, of deciduous areas, has fluctuated more, though they have never been scarce. (In the 1700s the black squirrel, now known to be identical to the gray squirrel except for its coat color, lived here in considerable numbers; in fact, it is estimated that they were as common as grays. However, for unknown reasons, their numbers dwindled in the following century and they are now completely gone from the forests, leaving us familiar with only the gray phase.) The gray squirrel undertakes periodic mass migrations, apparently triggered by poor nut years, which follow fast on the heels of years of abundance, which have allowed their numbers to build. The last major migration took place in 1936, when hordes moved across Vermont from east to west, through the trees, over land, swimming the rivers and ponds.

Even the smallest of Vermont's mammals show pronounced highs and lows in population from one year to the next. White-footed mice (of the woodlands) and deer mice (of fence rows, shrubs, and forest edges) are undoubtedly dependent upon the seed crop and its availability throughout the winter, the severity of winter, and other variables. Predation helps to control their numbers, but increased predation is usually a response to increased numbers of the prey and only later becomes instrumental as a damper on population size.

Vermont forests house one marsupial—a primitive mammal that suckles its young in a pouch called the marsupium—the opossum. A native of South America, it is one of the champion long-distance movers as far as mammals are concerned. It has progressed north through Central America and up the length of the United States, and first appeared in Vermont in 1920. Since then it has marched almost to the northern border, one showing up in Maidstone State Forest in 1977. With its naked tail, muzzle, and ears, it is seemingly ill prepared for the harsh winters here, but climate has not been a deterrent to its dispersal—it has gone from tropics to sub-Arctic zones despite a few frozen-off tail ends and tips of ears!

In many ways, the hardwood forests are more difficult places for mammals to pass the winter than is the boreal forest. Without the protection of the leaves on the trees, the winds penetrate more bitterly and the snow accumulates in greater packs. Night can be brutal, as any heat gained during the day is quickly reradiated to the open sky. But the greatest threat to survival is the scarcity of food in these areas during the cold months.

To cope with the problems of the winter forest, animals have arrived at several solutions. A few hibernate in the true sense of the word. Others, such as black bears, chipmunks, squirrels, striped skunks, and raccoons, go into semihibernation, from which they can emerge during a January thaw or other warm spell to recharge themselves on food stored or found in nearby sources. One mammal, the white-tailed deer, moves out of the hardwoods and into the softwoods, where it finds food and shelter. It also grows a new coat of hollow, insulating hair for the winter. And some keep up the search for food all winter within the hardwoods: the white-footed mouse and the insectivores, a group of insect-eating mammals that includes the mole and the shrew.

These small winter-active animals, with their extremely high metabolisms, demand a near-continual supply of food; they can starve within hours of eating. In winter they live beneath the snow. The odd-looking star-nosed mole works underground in the moist soil of riverbottoms and especially near lakes, deeper in the winter than in the summer as it moves down below the frost line in search of prey. It uses its fleshy tentacled nose to sense the movements of earthworms or grubs, then digs furiously with its spadelike front paws to reach them. A smaller relative, the short-tailed shrew, scours higher up either in the humus and leaf litter of the soil or in the low vegetation itself. This is the most widely distributed insectivore in Vermont, occurring across many types of habitats, at many elevations. Though small, it is a fearless hunter day or night and will attack mice and other prey larger than itself, as well as earthworms, insects, land snails, and other terrestrial organisms. Presence of this and other shrews is obvious in winter from the maze of tunnels that course through the snow.

Thus we have seen that season by season, as well as century by century, the Vermont forest changes, and the animal inhabitants must follow its lead, either in the normal cycles of their lives or in response to what happens to their land. The mammals, whether the exciting wildlife of forest lore or the lowly creatures more in evidence, have been central to these intricate plays: the same stage, different scenes and actors.

Birds

After the piercing winds and cold-white silences of winter, the Vermont forests soften under the spring song of birds. But these sounds of rebirth actually begin much earlier, for those who tune an ear. The great horned owl signals the start of its courtship during warm spells in late January or early February. This largest of our common resident owls is the first bird of the season to mate and raise young in the hardwoods or mixed forests, and since the eggs are usually laid about March 1, the parents must incubate them continuously to protect them from freezing temperatures and heavy snow. Its feathers certainly help in energy conservation: the bird is well insulated from talon to beak, and even the toes and nostrils are covered. Like its relative the goshawk, the great horned owl has the reputation of being fierce, the fiercest of all owls.

Breeding somewhat later, and slightly smaller and more a resident of moist woodlands and richer bottomlands than the great horned owl, is the barred owl. This species has no "ear" tufts, is steely gray- and brown-streaked, and has one of the most recognizable calls: a hollow, barking phrase that has been described as "who-cooks-for-you, who-cooks-for-you-all." The screech owl and the saw-whet owl are the smallest year-round owls in Vermont. Both are cavity-nesters and often use the abandoned holes excavated by woodpeckers. The screech owl is a miniature version of the great horned owl, but has two color phases, red and gray, the reasons for which are not understood. The saw-whet owl is an elfish little thing, half a foot high, that preys on small rodents and insects of the night. It is bold and tame, often perching within arm's reach, at eye level, cocking its head as it looks at you.

The Saw-whet Owl. A 6-inch-tall owl that has become increasingly abundant in Vermont. It lives in the mixed woods in summer but prefers the protection of conifers in the winter. Active mostly at night, it hunts insects and small rodents. Its name comes from one of its "songs"—a thin sound like a saw being filed.

March in Vermont is hardly considered full-blown spring if measured by human feelings, with snow still deep in many places and more snowstorms yet to come, but it ushers in the first bird migrants, those that arrive to scrape a living off the previous year's remains in the trees or on the ground, or peck at the emerging signs of new life. Crows return from a winter in the milder lowlands nearby or south, out of state. Phoebes, earliest of all the flycatchers to appear, snag the few insects that have hatched or awakened from hibernation. Later in the month come flickers and yellow-bellied sapsuckers, two common species of woodpecker, in preparation for nesting; the males set up territories, marking the bounds by hammering on hollow trees, sap pails that hang on maple trees, or even tin roofs.

In March, too, comes the plump, peculiar-looking woodcock, a shorebird that for feeding and nesting prefers the upland habitat of forests and forest edges. The woodcock is restricted to the woodlands east of the Great Plains, and Vermont has one of the highest populations anywhere within this region. It has big eyes for night vision, a long, pliable bill for probing for earthworms, and short wings for rapid flight through the trees—attributes that have given this important game bird the colorful local names timber doodle and bog snipe.

The male begins a strange but fascinating courtship ritual in early spring, a ceremony unlike any in the bird world. In the evening or early morning, sometimes even in night's darkness, he spirals into the air from his resting spot in a clearing. With a twittering of wings he rises, often to 300 feet or more. Then he drops, chirping, straight down to the spot he left, where he sits motionless, uttering an occasional buzzing "peent." After a while he repeats the performance. This elaborate activity is thought to be an effective way for the male to attract a mate and advertise its territory, as less ostentatious displays might not be noticed at night.

In May, new migrants arrive in the hardwoods daily, most pacing their progress north with the emergence of the myriad hopping, flying, crawling insects that crowd the summers in Vermont. The drab flycatchers return—the large great crested flycatcher to the tree crowns and the medium-sized wood pewee and the little least flycatcher to branches lower down. They sit almost motionless on their chosen perches until insects fly by, then swoop out to capture them and return to perch again.

Warblers and vireos migrate at night in large flocks, and if grounded by a spring storm they may descend upon the hardwood forest in great variety and number. The two families are similar in size, habit, and appearance. Vireos, however, are slightly larger, slower, and heavier of bill than warblers. Further, male and female vireos look alike, whereas warbler males are the more strikingly marked and brightly colored of the sexes. The red-eyed vireo is considered the most common of all birds in the summer forests of New England; hardly a woodlot seems to be without one. Its repetitious song goes on when other birds are silent, through the day, through the season. Correspondingly, the redstart, a beautiful bird decked out in black and orange in the male, black and yellow in the female, is likely the most common warbler in Vermont woodlands, favoring the second growth so prevalent here. Both species feed in the upper canopy for the most part, yet drop down to understory saplings for nest building. Each constructs the nest typical of its family—the redstart's is wedged in the vertical prongs of a forked tree branch, the red-eyed vireo's is suspended from horizontal forks of a sapling branch.

Songs reveal the birds. The ovenbird's "teacher-Teacher-TEACHER" is an unmistakable soft-to-loud phrase that swells up from the ground or near it, close to where this species builds its domed-over nest (this shape resembles an old-fashioned brick oven, hence the bird's name). The black-throated blue warbler buzzes up the scale, "trees, trees, trees," from the obscurity of the understory, while the black-and-white warbler courses the trunks of trees much like a nuthatch, issuing a thin, high buzz as it goes.

The thrushes, too, stake out vocal claims on their piece of this seasonal forest home. There is no mistaking their presence: the lucid flutes play from the shaded greens low in the forest and, in the evening especially, these songs impart a peace to the cathedrallike setting. In fact, the family of thrushes is considered to have some of the most beautiful songsters in the world, including the famous "lover's bird" of Europe, the nightingale. Like that species, the North American thrushes often sing at night, often in flight during migration. The three thrushes of Vermont's deciduous forests are the wood thrush, the hermit thrush, and the veery. All are a mellow brown above and white below, but differ in that the wood thrush has a heavily spotted breast and rusty-red head, the hermit a rusty-red tail, and the veery a faintly spotted breast. They are perhaps easiest to identify by song. Though their songs have a similar, beautifully flutelike quality, they are easy to tell apart.

The thrushes of the forest are well camouflaged in their subtle shade of brown, and they keep safely away in the understory and on or near the ground, where they feed and rest. But higher up, more brightly colored species (the males at least) weave in and out of the protective obscurity of the leaves. The male scarlet tanager, for example, the "black-winged red bird" of earlier days, blazons the canopy, and may be heard calling loudly—he is less often seen than heard—from a branch in a tree crown. (The silent and drab gray-green female is rarely seen, as she tends to business of the nest lower down within the branches.) The tanager is fond of oaks, or rather the insects parasitizing oak leaves and acorns.

Sharing the broad-leaved forest with the songbirds, and occasionally dining on them, are the winged predators—the owls mentioned earlier and, especially, the hawks. The accipiters (members of the genus *Accipiter*) are the most forest-oriented hawks, being able to maneuver easily and fly rapidly through tight spaces and the maze of branches. These hawks are equipped with narrow bodies, long tails that act like airplane flaps, and short, rounded wings for fast beats and quick changes of direction. Once the most common accipiter was the Cooper's hawk (the notorious "chicken hawk"), but it has declined sharply in the last ten to fifteen years, and is now being considered for endangered status in Vermont. Its northern range seems to be filled more and more by the smaller sharp-shinned hawk and, to a lesser degree, the larger goshawk, both fellow accipiters.

Most of the buteos (the genus of large-bodied, large-winged, fan-tailed, soaring hawks) enter the forest only for nesting, since they are ill equipped for hunting in confined spaces. They are

Hawk Silhouettes. Identification of the main groups of hawk is made easier by comparing differences in their silhouettes and flying habits. Size is not exactly proportional here. (1) Buteos: large bodies, broad wings, fan-shaped tails; they soar and circle high. (2) Accipiters: smaller bodies, short, rounded wings, long tails; quick and darting fliers with a wingbeat sequence of flap-flap-flap-soar. (3) Falcons: long, pointed wings, long tail; the fastest fliers, with a rowing style of wingbeat. (4) Turkey vultures and Harriers (Marsh hawks): possess similar silhouettes, with long wings and tails, but vultures have larger bodies and smaller heads. Both glide and soar, but vultures hold their wings in a more distinct V and tilt from side to side.

neither so swift nor so agile as the accipiters, and thus they capture few birds as prey, concentrating instead on slower mammals and other land animals. The most common buteo statewide is the red-tailed hawk, usually seen circling high above a meadow or standing watch from a sentinel tree, looking for small rodents, rabbits, snakes, insects, or perhaps an unwary bird. The more streamlined red-shouldered hawk is most often met in its preferred habitat, the wet woods, rich bottomlands, and swampy areas. There it is regarded as the daytime counterpart of the barred owl—one writer mentions an instance of these two predators' taking up communal residence, using the same nest, both raising young, but working separate shifts! The smallest of our nesting buteos is also the most complete woodsman: the broad-winged hawk is never far from the forest, staying concealed within its branches or flying close over the tops of trees. It is a rather quiet bird in the breeding season, only occasionally calling "pewee" in flight.

With all their appealing variety, color, song, and activity, the songbirds and raptors (hawks and owls) depart from the forest before we're ready to see them go. Fall migrations begin even before the summer has ended, with many flycatchers leaving in late August and the majority of warblers in September. With nesting done and the young grown to flight, a drying stillness settles over the forest. A new season is defined by the going of the birds.

For these birds the migration in fall is less hurried and the period is less concentrated than in the spring. The birds seem to drift south, quietly, without the urgency of the migration that calls them to nest, done now with the defense of territory and the demands of rearing their young. To us, they pass less noticeably, not bunched in great flocks, as in spring, and the males of many songbird species have changed their brilliant breeding plumages for less conspicuous fall feathers that they will wear through winter.

Earliest of the hawks to depart is the broad-winged hawk. This species forms large, spectacular flocks (some composed of thousands of birds) that begin to move out in early August, with a peak in mid-September. These flocks use rising thermal air currents to give them lift over the mountains: the birds enter low in the valleys, spiral up the updrafts, then peel off at the top and shoot down and south again. These are the famed "kettles" of broadwings that many people observe from mountain peaks here in Vermont and elsewhere in the East. Along these peaks, too, one may see other hawks passing in their time, the red-tailed and red-shouldered in late October and early November, the sharp-shinned in early October, and the goshawks in early

November. (Appreciable numbers of the red-tailed do stay in Vermont, however, for they are able to hunt the open lands throughout the winter.)

Although most of Vermont's birds leave in the fall, a few other than the red-tailed hawks do remain behind. The birds that habitually stay through winter are not necessarily the same individuals year to year, but rather the same species as a whole. These birds have the wherewithal to survive given a source of food, as food, not climate, is the critical factor. This is as true for the seemingly fragile small birds as it is for the large—all can make it through the most frigid times if enough food is available.

Besides the solitary red-tailed hawks, other species of birds form nomadic feeding and roosting flocks for spending the winter in Vermont. Blue jays gang up in small numbers, aggressively searching for seeds, vegetable matter, or the remains of dead animals. Smaller birds, such as the black-capped chickadee and the goldfinch, congregate in larger flocks, scouring the areas for seeds still clinging to trees and shrubs or for hibernating insects and spider eggs tucked in bark crevices.

Sometimes these winter flocks attract individuals of more solitary species. White-breasted nuthatches, for example, are frequent winter companions of chickadees, although they keep to themselves within that loosely formed group. Indeed, the white-breasted nuthatch is one of the few species that shows territorial behavior in winter, as it guards feeding sites from others of its own kind. Moreover, it is unusual in that it maintains the male-female pair bond formed in the breeding season, whereas most small birds break the bond for winter and make a new one the following spring.

Whether or not woodpeckers stay for the winter depends on the diet of each species. The flicker, which feeds on ants, and the yellow-bellied sapsucker, which drinks tree sap, depart for obvious reaons. Some woodpeckers, however, are able in winter to chisel insects—hibernating adults or larvae—from bark or wood, using their long, barbed tongues to reach into the deeper tree recesses. The common hairy and downy woodpeckers remain with us, and are frequent visitors of suet-feeders in towns, as well as the trees of the forest. Pileated woodpeckers also stay, as our largest, nearly crow-sized woodpecker species. Once met it is not easily overlooked, with its great flaming crest, long bill, and resounding "ka-ka-ka-ka" call. Its work is obvious, too—it literally excavates dead trees in search of its favorite meal, the carpenter ant, making gaping holes a foot or so wide and several feet long; sometimes it almost reduces a tree to a pile of chips. It also carves out large cavities for its nest, and though it may nest in the same tree year after year, it never uses the same cavity twice. Perhaps this serves as a prevention against contaminating its young with lice or other parasites that have possibly infested a hole.

The pileated woodpecker is currently experiencing a population resurgence, having fared badly during the years of clear-cutting and the subsequent young forest regrowth, as it requires large mature or old trees for feeding and nesting. Now that such trees are once again part of Vermont's scenery, the species has responded well and appears to be flourishing, much to the delight of winter bird-watchers.

One of the best-known birds of the winter woods is the ruffed grouse, or partridge, as it is known in the Northeast. Like the spruce grouse discussed earlier, it is a nonmigratory, chickenlike bird with a big body and short, powerful wings suitable only for brief, fast flights. Owing to its relatively small home range, it eats many different types of food. One researcher found that it will feed on 120 kinds of items, including various insects, seeds, fruits, nuts, catkins, buds, twigs, leaves, needles, bark, and mushrooms.

In winter the ruffed grouse turns to buds as a staple of its diet, and aspen buds are sought most of all. This preference has been noted by wildlife managers, and in one state game-management area where grouse are being encouraged, sections of the forest are periodically clear-cut to allow quaking aspen to thrive (male trees of the species are favored, as their buds are larger and more nutritious than those of the female). To avoid enemies, endure cold spells, or simply spend the night, the ruffed grouse often plunges full-flight into a snowbank and buries itself. Many a cross-country skier or snowshoer has been startled by this bird blasting out from underfoot, in a shower of flakes and a thunder of wings. Unfortunately, the grouse is sometimes entombed in this snow den by icy crusts that develop on the surface and prevent its exit.

The ruffed grouse has for a long time been widely distributed over Vermont, wherever mixed open woods exist. Conversely, its larger relative the wild turkey has had a checkered career in Vermont, and has only recently been moving north from the state's southwest corner.

In the time before white settlement the wild turkey lived in this section of Vermont, where ample nut-producing trees supplied its major source of food. The turkey was also plentiful south and west of the state, especially in the mountainous regions of New York, Pennsylvania, and Massachusetts, where beech, oaks, hickories, and American chestnuts provided bounty for this big bird. As these forests fell, however—the chestnut to virtual annihilation by the chestnut blight, a deadly fungal infec-

tion brought from overseas, and the others to the heavy cutting of
the 1800s—the turkey became rarer and rarer. It is believed to
have become extinct in Connecticut by 1813, in Vermont by 1842,
and in Massachusetts by 1851; luckily, it always remained in the
remote mountains of central Pennsylvania and New York.

With the redevelopment of the forests a good turkey habitat

The Ruffed Grouse (Partridge). A male puffing up and displaying his tail
feathers during spring courtship and territorial defense. Part of the display
involves beating his wings rapidly, or drumming, at a clearing or on a special
log: the drumming starts slowly then increases, sounding like the distant throb
of a motor starting. In the north, grouse populations fluctuate from high to low
to high again every 9 to 10 years.

returned to Vermont: where the chestnuts once grew, the oaks became even more dominant, offering their acorns as food. But the turkey is a nonmigratory bird and is restrained by geographical barriers such as lakes, rivers, and mountain ranges, so that it was unable to recolonize its former range in Vermont. Accordingly, in 1969 the Vermont Fish and Game Department live-trapped 31 turkeys in Pennsylvania, brought them to Vermont, and released them in prime range in the southwest. This was the beginning of what is now an unqualified success story. Turkeys have exploded into new areas, bolstered by an active in-state trap-and-transfer program. In a few short years they have reproduced so well and have swelled to such numbers that controlled spring hunting was instituted in 1973 and spring and fall seasons

The Wild Turkey. A native of North America that in many parts of its range, including Vermont, was driven to extinction before 1900 by the disappearance of the forests it needed for food and cover. It has now been successfully reintroduced to the state and is expanding its range rapidly, with human help. The male gobbling in the spring can be heard today in many parts of Vermont, wherever hardwoods and foods on the ground are present year round.

were opened in 1977. By that year turkeys had showed up as far north as Johnson, Stowe, and Chelsea, an indication that they have exceeded their original range by a good deal. Now, it is Vermont turkeys, that, besides being transferred north in the state and across the Green Mountains, are being exported to the wilds of New Jersey, Maine, and even West Germany for similar stocking programs.

Other Animals

Although they do not bask in the limelight in which birds and mammals seem to shine, other animals of the forest are plentiful, important, in fact integral to this community. They not only help give a complete expression to the diversified character of the hardwood forest, but they are also essential ties between the lower and higher forms of life. Significant among these animals are the amphibians and reptiles.

Many amphibians are members of the hardwood forests, and even though they spend some part of their lives in water, most are landlubbers as adults. So, implicit in their existence are seasonal movements, usually from water to land in the summer, after they hatch and pass through the early tadpole stages, then from land to water for the late-fall and winter hibernation.

Seen by most summer hikers are the red-spotted newts — in their more familiar land form called red efts — which hatch from eggs laid on plants rooted in a shallow pool or pond. They spend the first summer as gilled larvae totally in water. After three or four months, they crawl to land, having resorbed their gills and developed lungs for air breathing. They then become the beautiful orange creatures we see making their slow way over leaves and around rotting logs. After a few years on land, the efts go through another series of changes: they return to water, change base color to olive green, and grow a tail with a fin. Once in water, they stay there to mate, and the circle of their lives is drawn.

Since the adult has lungs and no gills, one may wonder how can it "breathe" underwater. Like frogs, these salamanders can respire in water through their skin and the lining of the mouth. Even on land, when hibernating, the red efts get some of their oxygen in this manner, as do another group of salamanders in our forests, the so-called lungless salamanders. These indeed have no lungs, and so would be expected to live in water. But this is not the case; most are land-bound as adults. Nevertheless, they must keep moist to allow gaseous exchange through their skin, which is why, when handling them, one must make sure they stay wet. Scientists believe the lungless salamanders evolved in mountain streams, later shifting to a woodland habitat — lungs in animals living in fast-moving water would be a distinct disadvantage, of course, so over time and the natural processes of evolution they lost their lungs. The change to life on land was permitted in part by the moisture in the rich forests, which allows respiration to continue through other organs in contact with the air and soil. Thus, lungs in these salamanders simply were never needed. Most of the lungless salamanders in Vermont show this old affinity with streams or pools, spending their larval stages there and later remaining near them always. The red-backed, dusky, and less common two-lined salamanders are the state's three lungless species.

Woodland frogs and toads are everywhere here, also. The American toad, with its warty skin, plump body, and short hind legs, is the common species, with the Fowler's toad occasionally showing up in the extreme southern portion of the state. The American toad is familiar by appearance and its mating song, a continuous trill that can be heard throughout the spring and summer. The tiny spring peeper and somewhat larger gray treefrog—both treefrogs with sticky pads on their toes allowing them to hold on to twigs and branches—hatch in wetlands or ditches very early in spring, move to higher and drier ground later in summer, then move back to water in the fall in preparation for hibernation. When they awake in the spring we hear them clearly, especially the peeper, whose voice is surprisingly strong for such a little fellow, announcing its time of waking up and mating.

One of the most attractive frogs is the wood frog, mentioned earlier as a member of the boreal forest. Like the other frogs, it begins life in the waters of a swamp, pond, or pool, and moves as a young adult to land. This amphibian, with its remarkable tolerance for cold climates—found even well north of the Arctic Circle—is one of the earliest risers in spring, often quacking at the close of maple sugaring in late March or early April.

Vermont has relatively few reptiles and even fewer that might be called woodland. This apparently is owing to its hard winters of relatively long duration. Some people look on this as a blessing, since to them reptiles mean snakes and snakes mean danger. In actuality, there are some eleven species of snakes in Vermont, but only one is poisonous to human beings. That one, the timber rattlesnake, has a small population and a very limited range, is seldom encountered even there, and is most timid. It does not, therefore, pose much of a threat. But even early in Vermont's statehood, the timber rattler carried a bad name and was bountied for a dollar apiece, and later snake hunters reduced its small numbers even further.

The timber rattlesnake lives in the southwestern portion of the state, where in the rugged terrain of cliffs and steep rock outcroppings it dens up for hibernation through the colder months. In summer it moves out among the rocks or down to the more open areas to hunt, primarily for rodents. Though there is always the chance of meeting the rattler in the summer in these areas, the risk of snakebite is very small: the snake flees from people and strikes only if fearing for its life. Indeed, there have been no documented fatalities from snakebite in Vermont.

Of Vermont's other snake species, some, the garter snake, for example, are widespread throughout the state, including the boreal regions. Almost everyone recognizes the garter, with its black and yellow stripes running the length of its body (making the animal look like an elastic garter). Others, such as the black rat snake of the southern part of Vermont, are more localized and sensitive to environmental change. The black rat snake is non-poisonous, but can leave the impression that it is dangerous because it may act aggressively and bite if bothered. It is a constrictor, suffocating its prey by squeezing before eating it. It also climbs trees with ease, and often eats bird eggs or fledglings. To identify this snake, one should note that it is all black except for the mottled underside, and is shaped in cross section like, to quote one author, "a loaf of bread." Small, secretive, and harmless species of snakes are found under stones or logs in the hardwoods and neighboring fields. Woodpiles are a favorite nesting place for two, the northern ring-necked, with a yellow belly and ring around its neck, and the red-bellied, with a red belly

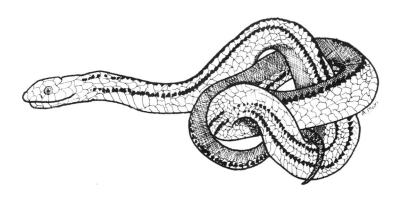

The Red-bellied Snake. One of several small, harmless-to-humans snakes in Vermont. This species with the beautiful crimson belly remains mostly in the woods, under fallen logs, and in woodpiles near houses. In winter it hibernates in underground dens, often residing with dozens of other snakes—ring-necked snakes, garter snakes, and the like. As with most snakes, the red-bellied lays eggs from which the young emerge in spring.

and three large yellow spots on the back of its head. Both feed on worms, slugs, insects, and some amphibians.

Terrestrial turtles are few indeed. The wood turtle spends some of its time in the water but is usually seen far away from it. This turtle's shell looks something like a small snapping turtle's—gray and composed of rows of conical plates that give it a sculptured appearance. Moving slowly over the land in summer, it eats a variety of foods, including berries, leaves, beetles, and slugs. But as winter approaches it heads toward a pond or lake, and by the time ice begins to form it has taken position on the bottom or buried itself in the mud, there to spend the cold months, well insulated by the water and ice above. During this period of dormancy, physiological processes in the turtle come to a near standstill, though at times it may move about on the bottom. Although totally submerged in water it is still able to breathe through highly vascularized anal sacs, much in the way that frogs and salamanders breathe through their skin.

In the repertoire of Vermont wildlife, the reptiles and amphibians are the least understood—their distribution, numbers, and activities throughout the year. Current research is under way to disclose more about these residents of our state, and it should add much to our knowledge of the north country.

III   Waters and Wetlands

A loon I thought it was
But it was
My love's
Splashing oar.

—Chippewa Indian love song

8

Brooks and Streams

In traveling over the lands of Vermont, one cannot go very far without meeting water. The state gathers a lot of it as rain or snow in its passage through the year, channels it to rivers, and collects it in ponds and lakes. Vermont is dotted with almost 600 bodies of water, covering almost a quarter of a million acres. It is crisscrossed with waterways, more than 4,800 miles of streams and rivers.

The countless rushing streams that wind their narrow ways down sides of mountains, cutting thin channels, are quite young. They are the products of the Ice Age, when glacial rock debris laid new grounds and dammed old drainage patches, and the melting water in all its volume and force began to carve new channels. These boulder-strewn brooks are in a hurry: geologists speak of them as being "immature" not so much because of their age as because of their physical characteristics, yet for the most part, by geological standards they are very young.

Many of our waterfalls are streams that are energetically cutting through rock—these streams are "sawing" their way back into higher elevations. They are shallow, clear, turbulent waters. Beginning cold from the direct runoff of melting snow or newly exposed ground water, they stay cold, for they are shaded by overhanging trees. In addition, the tumbling waters are well aerated, so the streams are saturated with oxygen. In this rush of water any soils and other eroded material are carried quickly downstream, leaving only the heavier rocks and gravel on the bottom, a composition we see in almost every mountain stream-bed.

Plants

The violence of the streams creates rigorous living conditions for any organisms found there. The few plants growing in this environment are small and form mats closely adhering to the rocks, or else they are free-floating. Green algae grow as slippery, tightly knit blankets on rocks, close to the stream surface, in such a way that the rushing water will not strip them away. Several species of diatom—microscopic plants with intricately patterned glasslike shells—and other unicellular algae float in considerable numbers in the waters, even though many are borne away on the currents.

Insects

A surprising number of insects, mostly as larvae, inhabit Vermont's streams; each species exhibits remarkable adaptation to the swift waters. Some, such as the nymphs of certain mayflies, have slender bodies that glide in the currents. Stone-fly nymphs

A Stream. Fishing for brook trout in central Vermont. The erosional work of water, rocks, and sand can be seen in the smoothly rounded bedrock and "potholes" (upper left of photograph). Potholes are formed when a resistant rock becomes trapped in a crevice in the softer bedrock and the rushing waters' swirling of the rock causes it to scour out a hole.

are flattened and have filamentous gills located on their legs, these two traits allowing them to appress themselves to the undersides of rocks and thus minimize the effects of the current, while at the same time permitting them to get oxygen from the passing water. Where quieter pools eddy behind logs or rocks, water striders skim over the surface in search of small organisms to eat.

The infamous biting black flies are born in mountain streams. As larvae they look like black moss on the underwater rocks, holding on by means of small grappling hooks at the bases of their bodies. They have an ingenious way of gathering food while rooted to the spot: they make a net of salivary material and float it out into the stream, where it traps organisms and draws them back for eating.

Larvae of caddis-fly species find other solutions to the problems of living in the stream environment. Some build protective cases of sand or small pebbles around themselves by cementing the particles to one another and to the bottoms of rocks. The cases are open at the head and face upstream. Food drifting by is captured in a net made of the same cementing material and the larvae pull it into the case to consume it. Almost any Vermont stream, at any elevation, will reveal these small cases fixed to the bottom of rocks. Other caddis-fly larvae are free-floating but have hooks and claws on their legs for grabbing on to rocks and holding themselves in place.

Fish

The larvae of the stream, as well as the airborne adults, are vital food sources for the stream fish, the most prominent of which is undoubtedly the brook trout (or "squaretail"). This fish is a New England native that, with human assistance, has spread to almost all suitable waters of the northern United States. It is one of the smaller members of the salmon family, averaging a pound or less, although the state record to date is 5 pounds 12 ounces. Even at 1 pound it seems large for many of the mountain streams, but it is well made for life in the swift waters, with a smooth, torpedo-shaped body. The species favors clear, cold, neutral-to-slightly-acidic fast-moving waters, and in October it moves upstream to spawn in the shallow gravel beds of headwater streams. There the rushing waters circulate oxygen through the nests (redds), and keep the eggs healthy. The brook trout can, however, also survive in ponds if conditions are right. For example, if beavers dam a mountain stream containing trout, the fish may continue to live in the impounded area if the water remains cool enough and free of silt. In addition to good water quality, brook trout require areas where they can take refuge from predators, as well as lie as in wait for catching their own prey: undercut stream banks, submerged logs, large rocks and boulders, and the like, places well known to trout fishermen.

Rainbow trout share many streams and cold brooks with brook trout, but they also range into rivers and lakes if these waters are clear and well oxygenated. The rainbow is indigenous to the West Coast but has been transplanted all over the world, and in Vermont it seems to do best in streams that are more alkaline than acidic, as are its ancestral waters. In contrast to the brook trout, rainbows spawn in early spring, most heading upstream from the larger rivers into smaller tributaries with gravel beds and fast-moving waters. Interestingly, some forms of rain-

A Beaver Pond. Backwoods beaver ponds often remain good trout-fishing areas for many years if the impounded water stays cool enough in summer and does not become loaded with silt.

bow trout migrate to spawn and others do not. The migrating forms are physically different, with a flinty, plain coloration, from which they get the prename steelhead. A remarkable display of their movements takes place each spring at Orleans, a town in the northeastern part of Vermont. There, steelhead rainbows that have spent the year in Lake Memphremagog swim en masse up the Willoughby River and struggle up and over a long series of falls at the outskirts of town. Fishermen and spectators alike line the banks, watching fish a few feet away as they rest in shallow pools between the rapids on this arduous trip that is their annual ritual.

The Rainbow Trout. The steelhead rainbows migrating. These are among thousands of the species in Vermont that try to leap the falls near the town of Orleans, on their spring spawning run up the Willoughby River from Lake Memphremagog. This remarkable display can be seen from only a few feet away, drawing crowds of fishermen and spectators each year.

Birds

Only a few birds come to the mountain streams to feed. The belted kingfisher waits patiently on an overhanging tree branch, then bombs into the water after a small fish. If the attempt is successful, it will first stun the fish, by beating it on a branch, before either eating it or taking it back to its young. The spotted sandpiper is a common sandpiper of exposed banks of streams and rivers, the only one of its family that nests regularly there. During breeding season it is easy to recognize, by its spotted breast, teetering walk, and unusual flight, in which the wings are flapped tensely below the horizontal, creating the effect of a tightly strung bow twanging close to the water.

During its migrations the little northern waterthrush—not a thrush at all, but a warbler with the color and markings of a thrush—is occasionally seen at streamside, walking over and among the rocks. It will not stay long here, however, as it begins its journey to South America before mid-September. The kingfisher often lingers as long as the water remains open. But finally, with the departure of these species, the streams will be without birds, and the sound of rushing water will be muffled by new-fallen leaves and then the snows and ice of winter.

Mammals

The stream is home to but a handful of mammals. Mink often live in dens adjacent to streams and readily enter the water for fish. Hikers sometimes see the northern water shrew—big for a shrew, being larger than a mouse—swimming in search of small fish or aquatic insects. This species is perfectly designed for its life in streams, rivers, ponds, and bogs of northern regions: its large hind feet serve as paddles, and its thick, water-repellent fur sheds water and insulates against the cold.

Tracks of deer, weasels, raccoons, skunks, and jumping mice indicate these animals' regular visits, for food or drink, During summer nights, also, come several species of bats, flying over in search of hovering insects. The tiny, yellowish eastern pipistrel, one of the country's smallest bats at less than a quarter of an ounce, is one of these nocturnal hunters.

*   *   *   *

So, the picturesque streams—vigorous and apparently hostile as they dash and plummet down the shaded slopes—are in reality full of special lives, molded to their special conditions.

9

Rivers

As the streams cut their way down the mountains they join and evolve into rivers—the wider, deeper, less turbulent waters of the lower elevations. Rivers collect the sand and soil brought down, and so are more turbid than the mountain waters. These bottom deposits accumulate and build a substrate upon which some special plants can root. The rivers have thus become habitats different from the streams above them.

Often it is hard to distinguish a river from a stream. Like any location of ecological transition, there are always zones of merging where the wildlife represents both contributors.

Rivers are generally much older than streams. Many have been cutting and eroding for not just thousands but millions of years. Most in Vermont are termed "mature," lying in the broad valleys they have helped to sculpt. Mature rivers have wide flood plains and a sinuous passage through the land.

Under natural conditions, rivers are subject to periodic flooding—especially in a place as wet as Vermont and particularly in the spring, when tons of melting ice and snow rush down the mountains. Late fall is also a prime time for flooding, when the ground begins to freeze and rainwater can no longer seep down, but rather travels over the surface to collect directly in rivers in quantities greater than the banks can hold.

Vermont's history contains records of a few severe floods, the most devastating of which occurred in November 1927. That flood, brought on by an Atlantic-coast storm that moved inland, caused 88 deaths and millions of dollars' damage statewide. The hardest-hit region was the Winooski Valley from the Barre-Montpelier area to Burlington, where whole villages were swept away and 55 people lost their lives. To prevent a future calamity the newly created, soon famous Civilian Conservation Corps (CCC) began construction of three flood-control dams across tributaries of the Winooski River, one just north of Montpelier, one at East Barre, and one at Waterbury. Completed in the 1930s, they are still in use today. Several other flood-control dams were later built in other sectors of Vermont.

But most floods are not so bad or destructive as the one of 1927. Many riverside plants and trees are adapted to cope with seasonal flooding, and indeed many depend on it. Flood waters, if not too torrential, deposit a great deal of silt and fresh organic matter in lowland areas, thereby enriching the soils. In fact, flood plains, especially the broad ones of Vermont's major rivers, are sites of some of the most productive farmland in the state. In addition, as we shall see later, many fish and other wildlife rely on flooding for completion of their life cycles.

Most of the valleys we see today were cut by the rivers flowing within them. Some, however, were originally cut by ancient rivers and streams that flowed through the same general areas but which have long since disappeared and been replaced by the present rivers. The Connecticut River Valley was made in this way, where several smaller rivers were "captured" into one river and followed a glacially modified channel.

The oldest valleys have been continuously cut since the beginning of the Appalachian system by "subsequent" rivers: rivers that are parallel to mountain ranges. Most of Vermont's subsequent rivers therefore flow north-south. Some valleys, however, run predominantly east-west, having been cut by "superimposed" rivers running at right angles to the ranges— the Lamoille and Winooski rivers and part of the Batten Kill are good examples of superimposed rivers, flowing east to west right through the Green Mountains. Their valleys predate the rise of the mountains, following older rivers: as the new mountains rose up, these existing rivers sawed through them. This explains why they originate east of the Green Mountains, where normally they would be in another drainage (going east into the Connecticut River), and flow west to Lake Champlain.

A few rivers, or portions of them, are classified as being in "old age." These meander through flat terrain, have numerous oxbows, and are laden with silt. The final repositories for materials brought down from above, they are almost at the end of their time of eroding. Dead Creek in Addison County, sections of Otter Creek, and the Winooski River as it approaches Lake Champlain are fine examples of rivers in old age.

River wildlife is rich. Most rivers have aquatic vegetation emerging from their edges, where the current is weak and bottom sediments have had a chance to build; old-age rivers have the most margin plants, because of their thick mud deposits. Aquatic insects, especially those that can propel themselves, appear in great numbers, as both larvae and adults. Freshwater clams, crayfish, and other bottom dwellers live in the fertile muds, and the sluggish currents help them secure their food. Such vegetation, insects, and other organisms in turn attract larger creatures in search of food, most particularly fish, which, in their turn, bring human beings.

Archaeologists have good evidence of substantial Indian settlements along many of Vermont's rivers, especially the larger ones as they approach Lake Champlain. The excellent fishing there provided year-round food, and, at least in the Champlain Valley, the climate was more tolerable than deeper inland. In addition, the rivers could carry the Indians into new territory, and the openness of the water gave them views of approaching enemies.

Fish

The brown trout, like the rainbow a nonnative trout species, lives in Vermont rivers of widely varying characteristics. Brought over from Europe in the last century it has become an important addition to the state's cold-water fisheries, particularly as it is more tolerant than are other trout of the increasingly silted, warm, and partially polluted rivers that are the results of agriculture and industrialization. As elsewhere south and west, the brown trout of Vermont has also become a major game species, reaching large sizes (the state's record is 11 pounds 12 ounces) and possessing a cunning nature that entices the sport fisherman.

As one proceeds downstream from the mountains, the waters become deeper and more placid, the bottoms muckier with muds and silts; widening out from the shelter of trees, the rivers warm somewhat in the summer sun. In many places, in fact, the rivers come close to being ponds, where marginal vegetation increases, aquatic insects cruise the quiet pools in search of prey, and bottom inhabitants such as clams and crayfish become more numerous. The trout of the colder waters give way to smallmouth bass in many such rivers. Bass are better able to live in warmer waters, and with their laterally compressed bodies slide more easily through the weeds. Where the rivers flair out as tributaries of marshes, ponds, or lakes, northern pike may enter.

The pike is a long, large (commonly attaining 20 pounds or more in Vermont) warm-water fish closely related to the smaller, common chain pickerel. It is most noticeable in the spring, after the ice of the lakes has melted, as it enters the weedy, shallow riversides or adjacent flooded fields to spawn, thrashing the waters in a feverish activity. Its fighting nature makes it a fine sport fish, but it is also an important "tool" of the fisheries biologists, who use it to restore healthy proportions of game-fish populations to ponds and lakes that have "gotten out of whack" owing to the domination of "trash" or "pan" species—yellow perch, crappie, pumpkinseed, pickerel, and others. These undesirable species prey heavily on the eggs and fry of the game fish, particularly trout and bass, resulting in an overpopulation of the trash fish and declining numbers of the game. Moreover, the increased number of pan fish results in a decrease in the available food, and the game fish become stunted. The pike is a tough, highly effective predator—known at times to pull swimming ducks underwater—and when introduced into such bodies of water quickly reduces the pan fish to an acceptable level, thus helping the game fish rebuild their numbers.

The deeper water of some of the state's northern rivers— those connected to such large lakes as Champlain and Memphremagog—contain muskellunge, the famous trophy fish of the North Central states and Canada. In its prime range the muskellunge grows to great proportions, reaching 70 to 75 pounds, but Vermont is on the edge of its range and here it grows only to the size of the northern pike—for which it is often mistaken— reaching a record size in the Missisquoi River near the Canadian border of 23 pounds 8 ounces (1975).

The Atlantic salmon and American shad were two species that once came to Vermont rivers by the hundreds of thousands to spawn, running in from the sea to places far inland. Before 1800, salmon appeared each spring and summer in hundreds of rivers in New England, including the St. Lawrence, the Connecticut, their tributaries, and those of Lake Ontario and Lake Champlain. (The salmon of Lake Ontario's tributaries, however, apparently lived in the lake and did not migrate to the sea, as did the salmon of the other waters). In Vermont, the Connecticut River runs were among the most anticipated and celebrated rites of spring, testimony to the fecund cycles of Nature as she brought to reality this annual promise. But, once so plentiful, these two species both disappeared in the early 1800s, when dams, pollution from the by-products of the new white culture, and excessive commercial fishing by nets placed across the mouths of the rivers blocked their access to ancestral spawning grounds. It seems to be another of the tragedies of modern times, but this story has an epilogue, and maybe soon even a happy ending.

Salmon and shad are anadromous fish—they spend their adult lives in the ocean but move into rivers to spawn. The young fish hatched in the rivers remain in the place of birth for one or two years, until of age to travel downstream to the sea. At that stage they are called "smolts." They then stay in the ocean for a few years before achieving breeding age, at which point in spring they come back to spawn at the place of their birth. Unlike the Pacific salmon, the Atlantic species does not die upon spawning but makes its way back to salt water, and may breed for several years following.

Before white settlement of New England, the Connecticut River was the major way into the state for enormous numbers of salmon and shad. They entered from Long Island Sound and proceeded north through Connecticut and Massachusetts into Vermont and New Hampshire. The salmon continued upstream almost to the Canadian border, passing into smaller streams along the way, but the shad went only as far as Bellows Falls, prevented from further migration by the falls, and spawned only in the main channels of the Connecticut.

Salmon, in addition, evidently came up the St. Lawrence River, entered the Richelieu River, then moved down into Lake Champlain, though they stayed in the northern part of the lake, no farther south than Otter Creek. From Lake Champlain, the fish progressed up suitable rivers—including the Winooski—and streams to spawn. However, Lake Champlain was presumably a secondary point of entry as it was the Connecticut River that carried the reputation for the famous runs.

With the development of the white people's culture in New England, this annual passage of fish was disrupted. Improper commercial fishing took its toll. Siltation of the clear water that the salmon needed was the result of heavy deforestation and agricultural uses of the land. Small dams built on streams to provide energy for local communities blocked off the return routes for many salmon. Later, several major dams across the Connecticut River cut them off completely: the first was built at Turners Falls, Massachusetts, in 1798, and four others followed, none equipped with ladders to allow the fish to bypass the structures. Thus, as early as 1814 salmon and shad were gone from the Connecticut River. In the Lake Champlain region, the increasing siltation and pollution of the lake and the St. Lawrence River, along with the dams built across the spawning streams, had effectively eliminated salmon from here as well. So the fish no longer came to Vermont. In fact, they were practically extinct in New England—only to Maine did they continue to come, and then principally to one river, the Penobscot.

Concern for the welfare—the very existence—of both species led to attempts at their restoration as early as the mid-nineteenth century, futile though the attempts proved to be. Finally, in 1966 a program involving cooperation among Vermont, New Hampshire, Connecticut, Massachusetts, and the federal government was established to bring the salmon and shad back, once and for all. Under provisions of the agreement, all dams across the Connecticut River would have fish ladders, water quality would be improved to acceptable levels for the fish, and hatchery-reared young (fry) would be imprinted to streams and rivers throughout the original range, so that they would return as spawning adults.

Encouraging signs appeared within the decade following the program's inception. The first adult salmon showed up in the

Connecticut River in 1974, albeit dead when found. By 1977 seven adults had swum their way to the Holyoke Dam, in Massachusetts, some 85 miles from the ocean. Then in 1978 a run of 99 salmon arrived at the Holyoke Dam and at the Rainbow Dam on Connecticut's Farmington River, the best run in 150 years. These were caught for spawning, although only two survived, owing to a deadly fungus infection that spread rapidly through the stock.

Of the shad, in 1977 nearly 203,000—a record since observations were begun in 1954—were counted and lifted over the Holyoke Dam. These were part of the nearly 400,000 shad that now travel up the Connecticut.

The restoration program continues, with eventual success still a way off and only tentative. But with hope arising from past achievements and steady progress toward the project's completion (including a new hatchery in Bethel, Vermont), the Atlantic salmon and American shad may once again come as messengers from the sea, time-honored riches from our treasured heritage.

Mammals

Down to the rivers come many mammals, to fish or hunt for waterside animals, to drink and wash, even to play. The ever-present raccoon, one of the country's most "successful" animals—despite an unbroken history of being hunted and the victim of other environmental pressures—pays its nightly visits to the river for amphibians, insects, and small fish that it is able to grab. White-tailed deer quietly edge in to drink, while mink run the banks or swim the open waters with equal ease. Beavers waddle inland from their riverbank dens to cut the trees that are destined to be their food.

The river otter, largest member of the weasel family in Vermont (weighing up to 25 pounds), was once much more prevalent than it is now. Otter Creek—a major river on the western side of the state, which was important to the Indians for its fish and the transportation route it provided—was named by early settlers for the great numbers of otters living along its length. Despite their reduced population, owing to being trapped for their fur, otters are still with us, sparingly, along many of Vermont's rivers and lakes. They are seldom seen, however.

Otters dig dens in the sand of riverbanks or under logs not far from the water's edge, each den equipped with several underwater entrances. These mammals have a deserved reputation for playfulness, as apparently purely for fun, they wrestle a good deal on land and in the water and "sled" down well-worn snow and mud slides near their homes. They are among the swiftest and most agile of mammalian swimmers, able to catch a trout in open water. Naturally, their main prey is fish, but they also hunt a variety of other animals — mice, muskrats, frogs, crayfish, and even the occasional duck.

The otter is supremely adapted for work in the water, even in winter. Its thick, well-oiled coat (oil from the large anal glands possessed by all members of the weasel family) both insulates the animal and repels water, the properties that made the fur so popular in earlier years. Webbed feet and a powerful muscular tail are used for propulsion and steering, and the otter can stay underwater for up to two minutes while fully active.

Birds

The rivers attract many birds, too, both those that fish for food and others. The great blue heron stands among the aquatic plants in quieter pools, ready to stab at a passing fish. A kingfisher will loop down the channel, rattling its call. A spotted sandpiper scurries around the sandbars in search of small organisms, and bank swallows sweep a few yards above the water surface, snaring insects. In the shrubs at the river's edge a male

The River Otter. The largest species of the weasel family in Vermont. The otter breeds in winter and early spring, and the young are born nine months later. Otter families travel repeated circuits in their search for aquatic foods, moving from place to place as the supply is used up. In winter the otter does not hibernate, but it may not be seen, because during cold weather it lives underground and under the ice. The naturalist Ernest Thompson Seton in 1929 estimated that the population of otters in the United States was half of what it had been before white settlement. This drop in numbers was probably due to heavy trapping and increasing development along rivers and lakes.

yellow warbler often sings "sweet-sweet-sweeter-than-sweet" as his territorial proclamation.

One might even be lucky enough to spot an osprey, especially during its peak migration periods in April and September, slowly flapping overhead or stationed in a tree with a good vantage point of the river. When on the move for food, this large fish-eating hawk hovers over its prey, then descends, wings folded back, hitting the water with an explosive clap and grabbing the fish in talons that are fitted with fine serrations for holding the slippery catch. Thereupon it bears the fish away to feed on it piecemeal in a tree, tearing it apart with its sharp, hooked beak.

In earlier times we would have had a good chance of seeing another fish-eating hawk working the rivers and lakes, but today our chances are slim indeed: the bald eagle, which if ever sighted now is seen in the fall or winter. There are no recent records of this raptor's breeding in Vermont, and those individuals seen

The Great Blue Heron. Herons nest in colonies (rookeries), never very far from water. The largest Vermont rookeries occur in the Champlain Valley swamps. This photograph shows typical stick nest, with an immature bird on guard. Herons are in the same family as bitterns, and have many characteristics in common—including flying with crooked necks. (See the text for further discussion of herons and bitterns.)

here are the Southern race of bald eagle, breeding in January or February in the southern half of the United States and wandering as youths or nonbreeders to the North. Whereas the osprey eats only live fish that it has caught, the bald eagle is not so fussy. In addition to what it can catch on its own—fish or otherwise—it will eat dead fish and other carrion, and will even steal from other predators, especially its near-rival, the osprey.

The peregrine falcon (a hawk with the older name of duck hawk, acquired from its habit of hunting waterfowl) formerly bred in Vermont, nesting in many cliffs high over rivers and lakes. This falcon is one of the fastest, most exciting of birds, diving on its prey at speeds close to 200 miles per hour, hitting the victim in full flight, and then circling back to claim the fallen prey. At one time more than 40 nesting sites, called eyries, were documented in Vermont, in every sector of the state. Unfortunately, these eyries were also well known to falconers and egg collectors, who would rob them for eggs, new birds, or simply as proof of their daring rock-scaling adventures.

But now the peregrine has gone from New England; worse, it is thought that the Northeastern subspecies is extinct. The last known eyrie in Vermont is believed to have been on the rocky cliffs bounding Lake Willoughby. Not one peregrine falcon has nested in the state since the early 1950s; the infrequent examples seen today are migrants to and from breeding locations in northern Canada. We have lost a thrilling, graceful member of our wildlife. Falconry and egg collection can be blamed for only some of that loss. There is a far more pervasive, insidious culprit responsible for this extermination.

The peregrine, bald eagle, and osprey have become the most publicized innocent bystanders of the lethal effects of the hard pesticides used for many years in this country. The infamous DDT apparently was the main cause of their decline when it was being broadcast with abandon to cure a variety of pest problems. This chemical persists in the environment long after its use, accumulating in organisms progressively up the food chain. Though amounts in small animals may be minute, the predators at the end of the food chain, such as these three hawks, collected massive doses of DDT from the food they ate, often to levels a *million* times that of the environment. The adverse effects on the birds were many. Not only did it kill them outright, but it also impaired their reproductive physiology, deformed their embyros, and, most devastating of all, disrupted their calcium metabolism so that the weakened shells of their eggs were crushed by the incubating parents. Thus, whole generations, not just individuals, were wiped out in a short span of time.

The prohibition of DDT in 1972 was a major step toward

halting the alarming drop in population of these birds and many others. Since then the osprey has shown positive increases, including even a report of one bird's nesting in Vermont in the past few years. The bald eagle has not been so resilient and still is in trouble over all its range. It remains on both state and federal endangered-species lists.

The peregrine is the focus of a rehabilitation program in the East that Vermont is participating in. Though the native sub-species of peregrine in the Northeast is believed to be extinct, the young of other, very similar subspecies have been brought here, acclimated to scientifically chosen nest sites, trained to fend for themselves in the wild, and left on their own, in the hopes that they will return to the nest sites in the future, when it is their time to breed. This program is part of a national effort being made by several states and the federal government, with the help of Cornell University. Vermont's entrance into it was in 1977 with the release of three nestlings at a location in the Green Mountains; more such releases in other areas are scheduled for 1981. As of

The Osprey. Called the fish hawk, this bird has a large curved beak used for tearing fish apart—it eats only fish, which it catches in its talons. Owing to its diminishing numbers all over the United States, the osprey has been on federal endangered-species lists for several years. It was probably the victim of DDT, the pesticide that causes eggshell thinning as well as other detrimental effects in birds. Since the banning of DDT, the osprey in Vermont has been seen more frequently, on migrations, but there is no sign yet of its return to nest as before the days of DDT.

the winter of 1979 there has been no sign of the return of the young banded peregrines released in the Green Mountains, but biologists are hopeful that next year at least one will show up, by then an adult, having made it through the toughest years toward maturity and breeding age.

These martyred hawks have served as gauges of our environmental health. We have tried to eradicate the evil by banning DDT, but as yet we do not know if our response has been adequate or in time. After doing so much harm to the wildlife we must consider ourselves lucky to have been sufficiently sensitive to read the signs and thus had the chance at least to attempt to correct the wrong.

     *   *   *   *

The history of humankind in Vermont has been tied closely to the rivers. The rivers have provided animals and plants for food, good sites for settlement, and means of access into lands farther inland. Indians concentrated their activities near them and to this day much of Vermont's population is located on rivers. Times, however, have changed greatly in some respects, and our lives are no longer bound so intimately to the flowing waters. But for many people the rivers are no less important today than they ever were—if only for the spiritual gifts they proffer.

10

Marshes

Leveling out, a river of Vermont glides into a pond or lake, and we notice changes. The river has become sluggish. The water is shallow and shows the rich, muddy bottom. The plants reach out into the channel and begin to dominate the scene. One has entered the special world of the marsh.

Marshes are the first type of wetland we have encountered in this study; the two other types in Vermont are bogs and swamps. All wetlands are alike in that they are water-saturated—although they are not necessarily underwater—the year round. Their differences are most obvious in the vegetation. Marshes have herbaceous, grassy-type plants; swamps have trees and/or shrubs; and bogs develop a floating mat of sedges, heaths, and sphagnum moss. Additionally, marshes and swamps have some water flowing through them, whereas bogs are near-stagnant, with water slowly passing through only under certain conditions and at certain times of the year.

In most cases marshes are a specialized zone of a lake or slow-moving river. This zone, called the littoral or shore zone, is well on its way to becoming land. The marsh is one of the biologically richest ecosystems in the world, and therefore one of the most fascinating. It has flora and fauna of wide diversity, and produces, purely in pounds of vegetation, much more than forests or grasslands. It is a breeding place for many birds and a spawning ground and nursery for crustaceans, mollusks, worms, insects, amphibians, reptiles, and fish. It is a hunting ground for mammals of several species and a vast feeding and resting area for migrating birds, both waterfowl and others. In short, for many of Vermont's residents it is home, and for the large numbers of birds we share with other states and even countries, it is an irreplaceable oasis.

Although marshes may be the littoral zone of lakes, not all lakes have them. The physical structure of a lake basin, its location, and the kind of bottom sediments (or lack of them) may prevent the formation of a marsh. Lakes or lake sections that have steep sides cannot support plants of the shallows. Similarly, lakes with rocky bottoms, lacking the necessary clays and silts for soil, do not have the organic base upon which a marsh must sit in order for plants to grow. And where plants can't grow, a marsh can't exist.

Many areas along the eastern shore of Lake Champlain and its tributaries have excellent marshes. There the littoral zone is wide and declines slowly, is filled with clays brought down from the uplands to the east, and is practically without currents, which would remove the soil buildup. Other areas of Lake

Marsh Plants. Some common emergent and floating-leaved marsh plants. In the foreground: flat leaves and a flower of spatterdock, or yellow pond lily. Right: leaves of a common cattail. Background (middle): the pointed leaves of duck potato, or common arrowhead.

Champlain on the Vermont side and most of the New York side are unsuitable for marshes. Steep walls and deep bays along the thrust fault line in Burlington Bay and Shelburne Bay, for example, prohibit this kind of development.

Marshes are sensitive environments, constantly changing under the seasonal fluctuations in water level, always in the middle of the battle between land and water. They are dynamic communities, whose inhabitants and visitors depend on these very tensions for their propagation. For instance, most marsh plants are very choosy about conditions. Some, such as the smartweeds, require sites that are alternately wet and dry. Others, such as wild rice, grow on deep, rich soils that are covered with 1 to 3 feet of slowly circulating, nonfluctuating water. Some species of fish (the northern pike and bullhead) spawn in newly flooded fields nearby, while many ducks time their egg laying to the high-water period in spring, instinctively counting on the level to drop gradually, so as not to threaten the nests of their newborn.

But, vital as marshes are to wildlife, people have not always recognized their value or treated them with the respect they deserve. Since they occupy flat, low-lying areas and are usually in scenic surroundings, they have been filled for building developments. Those who view them as wastelands dump in them the refuse and by-products of human consumption. They have been drained for mosquito control or conversion to farmland. Because marshes are a great purifying filter for the waters entering them, they have become sewers ever since the tremendous pollution of rivers upstream of them. Even altered drainages in areas outside their bounds affect marshes adversely: stabilized water levels kill the marsh, because they discourage the propagation of many marsh plants and thus accelerate the shift to dry land.

Vermont is fortunate in possessing some of the finest marshes in New England, thanks to the fact that it has so far escaped the massive developments undergone farther south. Nevertheless, even here much has been lost, and the future is as questionable in Vermont as it is elsewhere. Public conscience must preserve what we have left.

One of the major controversies in New England within modern memory is the impending construction of a large flood-control dam across the Richelieu River in Canada, which would affect the water levels of Lake Champlain and thus its associated wetlands. The proposed dam would have a movable up-and-down plate within it and would work in concert with a widened and deepened river basin. Together these features would allow a greater volume of water to flow out of Lake Champlain during flood times, especially in the spring, thereby preventing inundation of the farms and houses built on the Richelieu floodplain. Although operators of the dam would attempt as much as possible to mimic the natural cycles of the water level of the lake, the peaks that cause flooding would be eliminated. And flooding is essential to the vitality and ultimate existence of the wetlands. Extensive research done over the past three years on the potential effects on plants and wildlife in the Lake Champlain wetlands indicates that as much as 28 percent of the total wetland acreage would dry out, and the spawning, nesting, nursery, and feeding areas of countless species of fish, birds, mammals, and other animals would be destroyed.

At this writing, Canadian and United States negotiators are still discussing whether or not the dam is to be built. There are huge pressures both pro and con. For those who consider the wetlands priceless and irreplaceable, the decision on the Richelieu Dam will be a momentous precedent—it is looked upon with great trepidation.

Plants

In the thick, fertile underwater soil the marsh plants take root. Further enriching the mud, the plants that die add nutrients to what is brought downstream. The water circulates slowly, replenishing the oxygen and distributing dissolved minerals. The foundation of the marsh is laid.

The plants grow aligned in fairly distinct zones, determined by water depth, exposure, and other factors. Farthest out, in the deepest water, is the zone of submersed plants. There such species as milfoil, elodea (the "algae" of aquariums), and pondweeds spend all their lives at or near the bottom, never even breaking the surface. They generally have finely divided leaves and lack the firm outer layer of tissue (cuticle) found on land plants. Since the water buoys them up, the plants also do not need reinforcing tissue. Instead, they have air cells throughout their stems and leaves that provide flotation and act as oxygen reservoirs. These specializations allow the plants to absorb nutrients and oxygen directly from the water, which is necessary because their root systems are little developed, if at all, and the soils in which they grow are oxygen-poor, owing to the concentrated decomposition of dead plants. This ability is one important reason the submersed plants flourish in waters that have become polluted by sewage and the runoff of artificial crop fertilizers. They thrive, to the point of excess, on these abnormally high amounts of what to them are nutrients, and can in fact choke out shallow bays and ponds, as has happened in many places in Vermont and elsewhere.

The next zone toward land from the middle of the marsh is that of the floating-leaved plants. In this area the marsh bottom and surface have been brought closer together by the buildup of organic matter from submersed plants and the accumulation of sediments. The tough, wax-coated horizontal leaves of the water lilies float and ride the waves at the surface, while their long, leathery stems bridge the gap to soil, where they are more firmly rooted than the submersed plants.

The next zone, that of the emergent plants, is usually the most extensive. Plants here have thick, flexible air-filled stems and bladelike leaves, which rise out of water and bend and sway with the winds. Roots are well developed and supporting, and the large underground tubers persist for years, unless muskrats or ducks uproot them for food. Within this zone there are further subdivisions: in deeper portions wild rice, pickerelweed, and arrowheads may grow; in shallower areas are burreed and cattails. In places more like soggy fields than water-covered marshes, many species of sedges and rushes are conspicuous.

The expanses of marsh vegetation harbor innumerable insects, fish, birds, and other organisms. The tubers of burreed and arrowhead are a favorite food of muskrats and ducks, and the nutlets of the former abundantly nourish migrating waterfowl in the fall. The tall, golden "meadows" of wild rice, too, yield their crop of seeds to thousands of ducks, geese, and songbirds fatten-

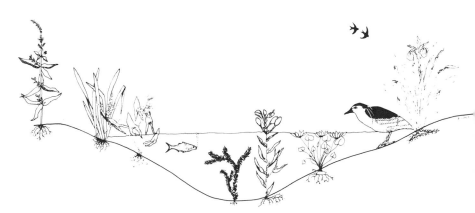

Marsh Profile. The inhabitants of a marsh. Nearest the edge are the emergent plants (iris, loosestrife, burreed, arrowhead), which have most of their leaves and stems above the water. Farther out, but not in the deepest areas, the floating-leaved plants grow—water lilies and some pondweeds—with long, flexible stems and flat, floating leaves. Deepest are the submersed plants (here milfoil), totally below water, from which they get their nutrients, rather than from the soil. Birds and wildlife are active in all zones of the marsh.

ing in autumn. But more than food, the plants are also a maze within which the nests, young, and adults of many species of birds are protected throughout the year.

Birds

The black duck, mallard, and blue-winged teal are the only common ducks that nest in great numbers within the marsh vegetation in Vermont. These are in the group variously known as "puddle," "dabbling," "pond," or "marsh" ducks. They ride high in the water, tip (not dive) into the water for food, and can fly directly into the air from either a standing or a floating position—this ability is a definite advantage in the tight, narrow

Mallards. Now the most common ducks in western Vermont, mallards also closely rival the black ducks east of the Green Mountains. They may hybridize with the blacks, as well as with domestic ducks. Here ducks and drakes feed together in shallow water. The females are the quackers; males (here distinguishable by their dark heads) have a quiet nasal "peenting."

spaces of a marsh. The mallard has been a highly successful species that originally came from the prairie states but moved steadily east, its immigration assisted by people who raised it as a domestic bird and then released it into the wild. Mallards and black ducks are closely related and have similar habitat and food requirements; occasionally, mallard—black-duck hybrids occur. Since the mallards' arrival in Vermont, many authorities believe that they have been competing with, and supplanting, the blacks. But though mallards now outnumber blacks west of the Green Mountains, east of the range, and statewide over winter, the black ducks still are the more abundant.

Another common dabbler is the wood duck, the variegated male of which is without question one of the most beautiful birds in North America. Though frequent in marshes, it has a wider distribution in swamps and wooded pond areas, where it nests in the cavities of trees and feeds upon nuts, tree seeds, and the smaller grains and vegetation at waterside. We shall take another look at this species later.

The other group of ducks are the diving ("bay") ducks, which ride lower in the water, dive underwater for their food (vegetable and animal), and must skitter over open water before they can become airborne. Consequently, they mostly work the deepest water, near or beyond the zone of submersed plants. The one diving duck that regularly nests in Vermont marshes is the ring-necked duck, but it is generally found only in the boglike sedge and heath marshes of South Bay of Lake Memphremagog (Coventry Marsh, see Appendix I), where it finds suitable nesting material. The other diving ducks nest in Canada or in other habitats where mature woodlands are within flying distance of water. These species will be discussed in more detail in chapter thirteen, "Ponds and Lakes."

All Vermont ducks breed early in the spring, and soon after mating lie low throughout the incubation, brooding, and raising of their young. The females stay on or close to the nest, while the drakes, once done with mating, move off to be by themselves. Both sexes molt all their flight feathers soon after breeding, which renders them incapable of flying. Being so vulnerable, they remain in seclusion until new flight feathers grow in, and during this time they are silent and very hard to find. Both sexes molt all their body feathers as well, but the drakes then change "clothes," donning a drab plumage like their mates'. In the fall, the drakes molt back into breeding feathers and will keep them through the winter until the next "eclipse" molt the following spring. This unique molting pattern appears to be related to the particular reproductive physiology of the family: ducks form pair bonds on their wintering grounds—which is why the drakes require their breeding finery in winter—and move north together in early spring. This allows them to set up nesting very quickly, without the time-consuming courtship and breeding rituals that most other birds perform. Moreover, ducks can "afford" to molt only in summer, since even though flightless they can still obtain food then, and a molt at other times of the year would leave them either exposed in the cold months or unable to migrate.

The dawn of a spring day is the time to hear and see others of the extraordinary birds of the marsh as they cackle, babble, chuckle, croak, whinny, laugh, or sing their strange mating and territorial messages. The Virginia rail trots over and around the roots, stems, and leaves of the aquatic vegetation, its way through this mini-forest made easier by a laterally compressed body and wide, splayed feet. This is the most common rail in Vermont, nesting in drier patches within the marsh, usually on mats made of cattails. The closely related, darker common gallinule is more visible than the Virginia rail as its swims out from cover, bobbing its head as it paddles around by means of partially lobed feet. Its weird henlike cackle is a sure clue to its presence. The little "hell-diver," the pied-billed grebe, looking much like a small duck, with its long neck, small bill, and stubby tail, has the ability to adjust its position in water by expelling air from or taking it into air sacs within its body. When in danger it lowers itself like a submarine, with only its eyes and nostrils above water, but when swimming freely it rides high, with a good view. This grebe is a regular nester in Vermont, and in summer is sometimes seen swimming around with its tiny young on its back, in the manner of all grebes. It moves quickly around the marginal vegetation, in and out of the marsh, then sinks below the surface after a fish, or circles closer to land for insects and crayfish.

Standing on firmer ground or in the shallower stretches of the marsh, an American bittern may be seen, a secretive but relatively common bird of this habitat. The bittern is much like a heron in appearance and in its habits of dainty wading and snatching fish with its long bill. But unlike herons, it nests in pairs or loosely formed colonies within the marsh, rather than in well-knit but often large colonies in trees. It has a variety of colorful nicknames, such as "stake-driver," "thunder-pumper," "stump-knocker," "butterbump," and "bog bull," most of which are attempts to describe its strange call. Listen to the marsh. You can often hear this liquid, pulsating throb, which seems made more by machine than bird.

Terns are usually thought of as fliers of ocean coasts or large lakes, circling and plopping into the water after fish they have spotted. But the black tern seen over larger Vermont marshes is an exception. It looks much like an oversized swallow as it twists after insects it captures in flight. Furthermore, it builds its nests on floating rafts of vegetation within the protection of the marsh, rather than in large colonies in open, rocky prominences, as do other terns. Small colonies of black terns return to Vermont each year to nest in a few marshes along Lakes Champlain and Memphremagog; one of their best breeding populations is in the Little Otter Creek Marsh west of Ferrisburg.

Smaller, nonaquatic birds reside in the upper levels of emergent marsh plants. The ubiquitous red-winged blackbird slings its cup-shaped nest between stalks of cattails and the little long-billed marsh wren and swamp sparrow often keep each other company, mixing their bubbling, chattering songs. The rarer short-billed marsh wren is found farther up in drier areas, nesting in sedges and other wet-meadow plants adjacent to the marsh proper.

The American Bittern. When alerted to danger this bird will stand straight up, among the marsh grasses, bill pointing to the sky, and stay motionless except for a slight swaying to mimic the movement of the vegetation. This vertical stance, combined with protective coloration, causes the bird's stripes to blend with the marsh plants, making the bittern practically invisible.

As one might suspect, hawks and owls are not common sights around marshes, since theirs is not the world of dense, low vegetation or pervasive water. In earlier times the peregrine falcon might have come rocketing over to snatch a duck or other bird in flight, and perhaps it will again someday. But now the harrier ("marsh hawk") is the hawk most frequently seen, as it tilts, tips to change direction, hovers low, then drops straight down to catch a snake, frog, rodent, or bird within the vegetation. The short-eared owl seems more hawk than owl, and indeed in many ways it resembles the harrier. It hunts a great deal by day, especially in the evening and early morning, flies with the gliding, twisting, hovering motion of the hawk, and is one of the very few owls that scrape together a nest in the openness of field or marsh edge—most other owls retire to tree holes left by woodpeckers, which they modify. And like the harrier it hunts in a variety of nonforest habitats: fields, marshes, croplands. With all these traits in common it is not surprising that these two birds may be found together, though usually only in the spring or fall, as the short-eared owl rarely spends the summer here, moving north for breeding.

For migrating birds, the waterways of Lake Champlain and its marginal marshlands (most of which are on the Vermont side of the lake) make up a major branch of the Atlantic Flyway, one of the routes between breeding grounds in the Canadian prairies and tundra and wintering grounds in the South or along the Atlantic coast. The Connecticut River is another branch of that flyway, but with smaller concentrations and varieties of birds. In these areas there is a magic about October and November, in the restless southbound waterfowl passing over, dropping down to feed and rest, congregating by the score for the evening to rise again by morning. The puddle ducks filter into pools and shallow-water areas: blacks, mallards, blue-winged teal, wigeons, pintails, shovelers, wood ducks, gadwalls, and the later-arriving green-winged teal. At the fringes of the submersed-plant zone and out into the clear open water flock the divers, including common goldeneyes, buffleheads, ring-necked ducks, and the greater and lesser scaups.

The bittersweet stirring of autumn drifts down in the honking of Canada geese and in the flash of the white-and-black wingbeat of snow geese. Flying high, they are almost part of the sky, until they wheel in for evening feeding. Before 1954 the Canadas had been only migrants through Vermont to their breeding grounds far north around Hudson Bay, James Bay, and the Northwest Territories. But in that year 44 wild geese were pinioned and released at Dead Creek Waterfowl Area in Addison, and a small flock has bred there ever since, and even attracted free-flying wild individuals. Now 200 to 300 goslings are hatched here each year, and upwards of 4,000 geese stop down in fall migration.

For people who love the outdoors the autumn marsh has a special feel, an ineffable nostalgia that comes of the smell of dying leaves, the golden-brown trim of cattails, and the sharp blue sky. Through an early fog the sounds bring us closer to winter, remind us of the sadness of losing summer. Unseen wings beat on the water, the wind glances over the jacket. The marsh has meaning like no other place on earth.

Mammals

For hunters, bird-watchers, and other observers of nature, the birds of the marsh are the most relished discoveries, receiving the greatest attention. But one can scarcely be unaware of the other lives that are part of this rich reservoir.

One of the most evident of these other beings is the muskrat, known mostly from its cattail lodges. This rodent actually builds two types of lodges, a smaller one for feeding only, and a larger, thicker, well-insulated one for year-round living and the raising of young. In winter the 'rats swim beneath the ice to cut and gather plants for food, and return to the lodges via one of several subsurface entrances. Muskrats that live by rivers or ponds usually do not build lodges but rather dig their homes into soil banks, much as beavers do.

The muskrat was one of those fortunate mammals in the early years of our country's settlement whose fur was scorned when that of so many others was in huge demand for coats and other fashionable items. It apparently has always been abundant in Vermont and elsewhere in the East, and even today, when muskrat fur has become more prized, its population remains high and steady, owing to proper management and closely regulated trapping.

The mink, also a formerly undesired species but now a valuable furbearer, often dens up in unused muskrat lodges or digs burrows at the land-water interface, from which it can move out quickly to capture fish, frogs, insects, snails, birds, and small mammals, including the muskrat. Minks are the year-round archenemies of muskrats, often plundering the muskrat population in an area. This usually occurs in low-water years, when the muskrats' lodges are left high and dry or their bank dens are separated from water, so that the animals are forced to travel overland. Being exposed and ungainly on land, they fall extremely susceptible to predation by minks, which are as comfortable and quick on land as in the water.

There are countless more stories of the marsh, and many go untold: the multitude of insects that swim through the underwater spaces or fly out from hatching to other areas, small crustaceans that are invisible to us as they cartwheel in the water or settle in the bottom ooze, fish that zigzag in search of smaller prey, tadpoles that become toads, frogs, or salamanders. But the stories are there if we listen closely enough, or read them thoroughly. They tell us of one of the most splendid mysteries in the natural world.

11

Bogs

Many people regard bogs as places to be avoided, as soggy wastelands unsuitable for agriculture, forestry, recreation, or other worthwhile activity. But as a special kind of wetland, bogs are significant and intriguing ecosystems, unlike any other. On the world scale, they occupy enormous portions of Canada, Russia, and Scandinavia, where they are used for many commercial purposes, including mining for fuel substances and peat moss. Though most in Vermont are tiny by comparison with the bogs of those countries, the state boasts some of the best, most unspoiled bogs in the United States.

A Kettle Bog. A small bog in southern Vermont exhibits the classic kettle-bog appearance. The open water is surrounded by a quaking mat of heath shrubs and sedges; the white tufts are the flowers of a cotton grass, in the sedge family. The thicker mat is covered with sphagnum mosses, and the trees here are predominantly tamarack—a species of conifer that loses its needles in the fall.

The occurrence of bogs in Vermont depends on several key environmental factors, abundance of water being one of the most critical. North in Canada, the boglike landscapes spread for thousands of unending miles as "muskeg." There water is almost always available, since evaporation is reduced by the short ice-free season and in many areas the permanently frozen ground (permafrost) just below the surface acts as a barrier to the downward-percolating water. But in Vermont, where summers can be somewhat dry and permafrost does not exist, bogs have developed only in depressions where drainage is slowed or stopped and water collects in the low areas. With impeded water flow and little or no oxygen supplied from the outside, decaying plant and animal remains rapidly consume what oxygen is available in the basins. Eventually, the waters become deficient in oxygen and stagnate. At that point, dead matter cannot be well decomposed, as the agents of decay (primarily bacteria and fungi) cannot live without oxygen. Thus, whatever dies here is "pickled" in this acidic, watery environment. In this way, the organic matter accumulates as peat builds into mats in which plants and animals are often preserved intact. In fact, in some European bogs human bodies (probably those of executed prisoners) have been almost perfectly preserved for thousands of years.

The process of peat formation has been taking place for millions of years. Indeed, peat is the precursor of coal—given enough time, material, and compaction, peat is transformed into soft (bituminous) coal, and then to hard coal (anthracite). The vast coal beds in this country and elsewhere around the world were made in just that way, in enormous boglike swamps that existed long before the Ice Age, more than 200 million years ago. When we burn coal today (or peat, as is still done in several countries) we are merely completing the decomposition begun so long ago, but in a greatly accelerated way.

Technically, a bog is only one type of peatland. The formation of different types of peatlands is due to different combinations of basin topography, seasonal water level and flow, minerals present, climate, and the vegetation itself. In peatlands with deep basins and almost totally blocked drainages sphagnum mosses and heath shrubs predominate. These are the true bogs, whose peat builds to a point where the surface of the mat, the only area of growth, rises above the water table, and the living mosses and other plants on the mat become isolated from the water and nutrients below; rain and snow are then the only suppliers of these essential ingredients.

In peatlands that have some water flowing through them, sedges and grasses are the dominant plants, with sphagnum mosses being scarce or lacking entirely. These are called fens, and their vegetation remains in contact with the ground water throughout the year. Whereas bog water is often highly acidic, fens may be mildly so or even basic, owing to the flushing away of acids, replenishment of minerals, and introduction of some oxygen by the moving water. Under certain circumstances both bogs and fens support trees; bogs generally have black spruce, fens tamarack and, if calcium is present in the substrate, white cedar.

Many older bogs in Vermont began as kettles—ponds or small lakes created at the end of the Ice Age when huge blocks of ice became separated from the retreating glacier and were lodged in steep-sided depressions in the land. These blocks were then buried in glacial till and the depressions were sealed. As the ice slowly melted, the depressions eventually transformed into ponds. Conditions were right for boglike plants to invade, and the process of bog formation began.

In these kettles, peats accumulate on the bottom of the basin, while the buildup and expansion of the mat and its peat over the water create "false land" at the surface. Mats may be very thick (some are more than 40 feet deep) yet may still be floating in the water. But the mats are not like floating pieces of wood; rather, they resemble saturated sponges, forever sinking with the added weight of live and dead plants, yet remaining in suspension. In certain rare circumstances, a mat can become thick enough to support a person—anyone who has walked on a "quaking bog" must agree that it is appropriately named, as its sways and bobs with every step!

Development of peatlands is unimaginably slow. Though they may be initiated in the relatively short span of 100 to 200 years, many present-day bogs were formed early after the waning of the last glacier, about 10,000 years ago. Less well developed bogs are much younger, of course, some in Vermont being only two to three thousand years old. All biological activity in the bog is drastically slowed down, owing to the environment's cold temperatures, acidity, and lack of oxygen: for example, an 80-year-old tamarack in a bog might be only 3 inches thick, with annual growth rings so narrow they can hardly be seen, whereas a tamarack of the same age on land nearby might be 12 inches in diameter.

Plants

The bog plants growing in the mat are among the most exotic and beautiful of North American flora. Many are found only in bogs, partners to the rigorous features of these places. And, no bog exactly resembling another in physical, chemical, and biological characteristics, the bog's vegetation may include many species or few; a plant may blanket the mat in one bog and be absent in the next.

Plants of the bog have to contend with a gamut of adverse conditions: a sterile "soil," as organic matter is little decomposed; acidic water within the mat; scant oxygen for respiration and growth; direct exposure to the elements, especially in treeless bogs; unsteady footing for roots; and, always, the wetness. In many ways, these conditions are similar to those in the tundra on the mountaintops, and though individual species may differ in these two places, the manner in which their plants handle the problems is much the same. Indeed, two families—sedges and heaths—are among the most prevalent plants in both areas.

Ironically, though water is pervasive in bogs and is essential to their formation and development, it is largely unavailable to bog plants, mostly because of the acidity of the peat waters. The plants have acquired several adaptations that allow them to conserve what water they manage to collect. Sedges have thick, solid stems and narrow-bladed leaves, both of which reduce potential evaporating surfaces. Sphagnum mosses have two types of cells, live ones at the mat surface that manufacture food and absorb water from the rain and air, and dead subsurface ones that act as water-storage vessels. Common heaths— leatherleaf, Labrador tea, bog laurel, bog rosemary, blueberries, cranberries, and others—have tough, woody stems and firm, leathery leaves, both attributes helping to restrict the amount of water passing through the plants to the outside.

The problem of obtaining nutrients, especially nitrogen and phosphorus, in such a sterile environment is solved ingeniously by three bizarre plants that actually trap and consume insects and other small organisms. Botanists believe that these carnivorous plants extract essential nitrogen directly from their victims instead of from the soil, as do plants in other environments. Strangely, the carnivorous plants are of Southern origin, not from the North, as are most of the bog members. Evidently, they grew in comparable wetland areas in the South and were pushed North during the climatic optimum, found a satisfactory home in our bogs, and stayed even after the climate cooled.

The pitcher plant is the largest and most conspicuous of the carnivorous species. Its big, hollow vase-shaped leaves are equipped with little downward-pointing spines on the lips surrounding the opening. Insects attracted to the odor inside the leaf crawl through the opening, follow a "path" of red veins downward, slide down the smooth interior walls of the leaf, and fall into the liquid at the bottom; their escape is prevented by the smooth leaf surface and the spines. The liquid in the leaf contains digestive enzymes that immediately begin to dissolve the

insect, and one can often find at the bottom of the leaf the
chitinous remains of insects, the indigestible leftovers.

The Pitcher Plant. The leaves of pitcher plants growing from the sphagnum-moss mat of a bog. This carnivorous plant's structure and special
mechanisms for capturing insects are described in the text.

Sundews are tiny carnivorous plants, almost hidden in the sphagnum, and though there are several species, each captures insects in the same manner. Sticky spines radiate out like a star-burst from the flat, quarter-inch leaves. When an insect alights on the leaf, it is instantly stuck as if on flypaper. The leaf responds to the presence of the insect by folding around it, and remains that way until the insect is digested, whereupon the leaf slowly opens to set the trap for the next meal.

Within the mat or floating in pools in the bog are species of carnivorous aquatic plants, bladderworts. Found also in other habitats, such as marshes and shallow ponds, they are closely related to the butterwort, the carnivorous species in the high alpine area of Smugglers Notch. The bladderwort has tiny (1/16-inch-long) sacs on its finely cut leaves, and each sac has an opening with a minute "trapdoor." When a microscopic aquatic organism swims by the sac and touches a hair sticking out by the opening, a stimulus triggers the inflation of the sac. This inflation creates a current that sucks the organism into the chamber. The victim cannot swim out the opening, because it is blocked by the trapdoor. As the organism is "eaten" the sac deflates, the trapdoor relaxes, and the plant is ready to repeat the process. The most common species in Vermont bogs is the horned bladderwort, although it lives unseen by most bog visitors until it puts up a beautiful yellow flower in midsummer.

Of all bog plants perhaps the greatest visual treasures are the wild orchids. Though unexpectedly small, their blossoms are exquisite in design and color, and even in bogs most orchids are uncommon. These qualities have made them rewarding finds for botanists, naturalists, and photographers, but also, unfortunately, for those few people who collect the plants for selfish personal possession. Many bogs have suffered through loss of their orchids by such unscrupulous collectors. Not only does the collector deprive us of something in its natural setting, but by taking the plant that person is disrupting the botanical environment. Scientists now know that most orchids grow in close, inextricable association with underground fungi: there is one specific fungus for one specific orchid. Without this symbiotic relationship neither survives. Thus, removing one partner destroys both this relationship and, therefore, the two plants.

Orchid flowers are of all colors, from the purest white of white bog orchis, to the sulphur of the yellow lady's-slipper, to the variable pinks, lavenders, and blues of calopogon, rose pogonia, and arethusa. They may be single flowers, such as the several species of lady's-slipper, or multiples on a stem, such as the lady's-tresses. The plants are as small as the inch-high twayblades and as tall as the two-foot showy lady's-slipper. In all, close to 30 species of orchids grow in Vermont bogs or in swampy woods nearby. Though they are a relatively minor component of these landscapes, they certainly have gathered attention.

Wildlife

The strange lure of bogs does not rest with plants and wild flowers alone. A good variety of insects in the bog attract some food-seeking vertebrates, such as the four-toed salamander, which works its slow way over and through the moist sphagnum mosses. In bogs with open water, painted turtles are not uncommon, being seen with their heads poking above the water surface or swimming along the edge of the mat. The small bog turtle one would expect to be found in Vermont bogs, as it is in neighboring New York State, but so far it has not been sighted here. This turtle is rare even in its main Western and Southern range, where it seems to be almost exclusive to bogs and boglike habitats.

Mammalian inhabitants are mostly small rodents that feed on the vegetation and stay within its protection. Of particular interest is the southern bog lemming (lemmings are vole-like natives of the North, especially boreal and tundra regions.) This tiny lemming uses runways and tunnels in the bog mat for traveling from place to place, and for nesting and raising its young.

Birds

The bird life of the bog is not exceptionally rich, but a few fairly rare species may appear, some even nesting. Breeding here has been ascertained, though infrequently, for the Lincoln's sparrow, a northern species that builds its nest well hidden in the sphagnum mat. The red-capped palm warbler, another rare but possibly Vermont-nesting bird, uses two habitats: bogs in breeding season, open grasslands and fields in migration. One might see a yellow-bellied flycatcher higher up in the trees of a bog, waiting for a flying insect to come near, or hear the mighty call of the tiny ruby-crowned kinglet from the thick maze of spruce branches. One might also see a small flock of rusty blackbirds flying over to the swamp trees outside the bog.

*   *   *   *

Bogs intrigue and attract a variety of people. Whatever their purpose, most visitors pause upon entering, feeling the strange, special qualities inherent to these places, the aura of unearthliness that human beings of all times past have surely sensed.

12

Swamps

The word *swamp* conjures up impenetrable jungles of vines, Spanish moss, underbrush, and fallen trees with snakes dripping off branches and the waters dark with sinister, unseen dangers. This may be the picture of tropical swamps, but Vermont swamps are nothing of the sort. Rather, they are a wetland and a type of forest all their own. Southern swamps are generally deep-water and can be explored well only by boat. Northern swamps as we have here, however, are shallow-water, more suited to foot-slogging than boating.

Swamps are considered wetlands because they are water-saturated at all times of the year. They differ from marshes in that they contain woody vegetation—shrubs, trees, or both. In many cases, swamps are the final stages of the filling in of a pond. Although technically swamps are the penultimate product of changes in the landscape proceeding from open water to marsh to shrubs and trees and finally to dry land, because of water saturation the final stage may never be reached—or at least it may be extremely slow in evolving—so for all intents and purposes the swamp is in fact the end product of this evolution.

Plants

Swamps exist in either boreal- or deciduous-forest regions. Some of the best-developed and most extensive swamp systems in Vermont occur in the spruce-fir regions of the Northeastern Highlands, where they are composed largely of tamarack, black spruce, balsam fir, and perhaps some white cedar, all trees typical of certain types of bogs. Deciduous areas with flood-plains, riverbanks, deltas at the mouths of rivers, and edges of marshes support swamp white oak, silver maple, cottonwood, red maple, black ash, and elm, their proportions in the forest depending on locale. Pure hemlock swamps are also frequent, especially in cool, shaded ravines. Some of the finest deciduous swamps are in the Champlain Valley, tied closely to the large marsh and river systems there.

The trees living in a swamp must be able to get oxygen to their roots and support themselves in a tenuous footing in soggy soils. In deep-water swamps, the trees may therefore develop "knees" (pneumatophores), which buttress the trunk and raise

153

part of the root system completely out of the water. But the trees in Vermont's swamps, which are shallow-water, rarely have such structures; rather, they have shallow, spreading root systems, which create a broad base and put the roots in closer contact with the air, although not completely out of the water.

Bushes and shrubs are strangely lacking in the treed de-

A Swamp. A silver-maple—swamp-white-oak forest near Lake Champlain. The plants and animals here are adapted to the seasonal flooding. Note the high-water mark on the trunks of the trees.

ciduous swamps of Vermont, but understory vegetation is usually lush. It grows atop the hummocks of fallen trees, where it can get a foothold, as well as relief from saturation. Sphagnum mosses, true mosses, and ferns—tall cinnamon and royal ferns—are particularly luxuriant. Jewelweeds, nettles, the early-blooming, golden marsh marigold and turtlehead are common rooted flowering plants. Tiny duckweeds, whose flowers are almost microscopic, float like a dense algal mat in the many pools, dangling their free roots into the water.

In shrub swamps, the vegetation may be thick and difficult to get through. Viburnums are well represented, with witherod, nannyberry, and arrow-wood all to be found. Speckled alder, winterberry, whose berries stay bright orange red through the snow season, and many species of willow may also be present. The fragrant sweet gale (one of the bayberry family), leatherleaf, and mountain holly are common to many shrub or boglike coniferous swamps in central and northern parts of Vermont.

One truly Southern swamp tree grows in a few isolated pockets in the state, a reminder to us of the existence of the climatic optimum of more than 4,000 years ago. Individual trees of black gum, or tupelo, occur in part of the Champlain Lowlands or as small, aged relict stands in the most southeastern corner of Vermont, in the Connecticut River Valley. The black gum grows to be one of the oldest trees in New England: one researcher determined it to reach more than 400 years in age in a virgin stand in Maine. The trunks and branches of these ancient trees are often contorted and the bark is deeply furrowed—one can almost feel the weight of their years bearing down on them.

Mammals

Wildlife in a Vermont swamp has not the distinction of a Dismal or an Okefenokee. For the most part, animals in our state's swamps either are typical of a wet wood or are passing through the area while foraging or hunting. When the swamp is located next to a lake, however, many water-based birds and mammals may take refuge or come to nest in the swamp. This is a perfect habitat for minks (sometimes called water weasels) and raccoons. Both make their meals of fish, frogs, or other aquatic animals, as well as land prey. Raccoons, in addition, take advantage of the fruitful offering of trees and shrubs.

Swamps house many mammal species that live in other habitats as well. The woodland jumping mouse, with its long tail and kangaroolike feet, is not uncommon in many wet-woods situations and may be quickly identified by its very long jumps—almost leaps—over fallen trees and plants. The smallest mammal in the world, weighing 1/9 ounce, the pygmy shrew is busy hunting its food day and night, summer or winter, in swamps and other forest areas here and across northern North America: this little insectivore must keep up a feverish search for prey in order to fuel a body that consumes more than its weight per day! Red squirrels, snowshoe hares, otters, fishers, bobcats, black bears, and white-tailed deer are present in varying numbers in the larger, more remote, and especially coniferous swamps, either residing there or traversing the area in their forays for food.

Birds

The barred owl and red-shouldered hawk nest in many

The Raccoon. A mammal of great versatility, the raccoon is at home in swamps as well as towns. In swamps it will usually den up in tree cavities and eat a variety of foods, including bird eggs, various plants, insects, amphibians, and fish.

swamps, along with a multitude of songbirds. Where conifers are abundant, the yellow-bellied, olive-sided, and alder flycatchers are three of that family to be seen or heard. Also, without much trouble, one may view sizable flocks of rusty blackbirds and hear the vociferous winter wren and northern waterthrush. The last is a warbler that is more "swampish" than most others in its family, walking around the fallen logs and hummocks, building its nest on the ground, and issuing a strident song that rings through the swamp.

Perhaps the most notable birds of the larger swamps near Lake Champlain are the herons. There they congregate for nesting. The large great blue heron we often see stab-fishing in river shallows, marshes, or the edges of ponds, but the smaller green heron, more oriented to the swamp or marsh, stays away from the eyes of the average visitor.

Heron nesting colonies (called rookeries) are often large. Those of the great blue may contain hundreds of birds, the green heron's rookeries being smaller and not so tightly knit. The nests themselves appear to be a loosely thrown-together mass of sticks and twigs and, in the case of the great blue, often are placed high in the canopy. Despite the protection afforded by height, the young great blue herons are made nervous by intrusions, especially by human beings, and will regurgitate a recently devoured meal of fish if approached too suddenly. It is strange to hear the plopping of dead fish as they rain down from the high nests to the ground!

Swamps are also choice nesting sites for some of the state's cavity-nesting ducks, when they are within striking distance of suitable bodies of water. The wood duck is, by far, the most abundant, but not so long ago it was almost a thing of the past in Vermont and elsewhere in New England. Extensive logging of the mature trees needed for nesting, drainage of wetlands for crops and urbanization, heavy predation on its eggs and young by the ever-present raccoon, and the relative ease with which hunters could shoot it all helped to bring wood-duck populations to a precarious low by the turn of the twentieth century. It was threatened to such a degree that in 1918 both Canada and the United States declared a moratorium on its hunting. Thanks to this protection by law, the maturation of America's forests, and the willingness of adult wood ducks to adopt man-made nesting boxes (which were placed out in the marshes and on the edges of ponds, away from raccoons and other predators), this beautiful bird was able to build back its numbers. In Vermont the wood duck is now at its best in regions containing nut-bearing trees—the oaks, hickories, and beeches—since nuts make up a major portion of its diet.

Although several duck species nest in tree cavities, there is always a touch of incongruity about such water-oriented birds standing or sitting in trees. But one soon realizes their rightful place there, as expressed by the wildlife biologist Reuben Trippensee (1953):

> The nest of wood ducks is made in cavities in trees made by pileated woodpeckers or gray squirrels, or just cavities where decay has removed the heartwood. Such sites may be near the water or at considerable distance from it. . . . The entrance hole can be unbelievably small and still be large enough for the female to enter. She flies directly into the opening and by some unknown mechanism stops with little injury to herself. . . . After the eggs are hatched, the female coaxes the young from the nest by calling to them and leading them to the nearest water. The young birds are able to swim as soon as they are dry and look like yellow bumblebees on the water.

A widely distributed diving duck of ocean bays and large inland lakes, the common goldeneye (known to hunters as the "whistler," for the sound its wings make as it flies) also builds its nest in tree cavities in swamps, but heads to the open water for

Wood-Duck Box. Wood ducks readily use such man-made boxes for nesting, substituting them for the tree cavities that are their normal homes. The boxes have helped the wood-duck population build back from serious lows earlier in the century, when large trees suitable for their nesting were severely depleted by intense logging. Now the species is one of the most common ducks in the Eastern wetlands. The conical predator shield below the box keeps out raccoons and other predators of nests. Notice the spider web constructed in the birds' absence, a quick way to see if the box is inhabited or not. In addition to wood ducks, other cavity-nesting animals use these boxes, among them common mergansers, owls, and flying squirrels.

clams, crustaceans, and submersed aquatic vegetation. The breeding population center of this medium-sized duck is in Canada, with Vermont as its southern limit.

The other cavity-nesting ducks of the swamp are the mergansers ("sawbills"), which use their narrow, tooth-edged bills for catching fish. Two species of these divers frequently nest in Vermont: the common merganser and the smaller hooded merganser. Their habitats and food preferences keep them from competing with each other, even though they may nest in the same area. The common merganser pursues small or medium-sized fish such as perch and pickerel in the waters of lakes and large rivers, whereas the hooded feeds mostly on small fish, tadpoles, insects, and even some vegetation in the pools, sloughs, and slower rivers, never far from the forest.

On several occasions, two or even three cavity-nesting ducks have used the same site at the same time: eggs of wood ducks, hooded mergansers, and goldeneyes have all been found together in one nest box at several wildlife refuges in Vermont. But these nests, called "dump nests," are usually formed very early in the breeding season and are unsuccessful, as they are abandoned.

Reptiles and Amphibians

The swamp is a fertile breeding area for reptiles and amphibians. Frogs are the most noticeable, especially in the early spring, when they arise from hibernation and fill the days and nights with their territorial and mating songs. Spring peepers and gray treefrogs are especially active then, as is the larger, terrestrial pickerel frog, identified by a call that is described as "a finger on a balloon." Salamanders, though silent, are also working their way toward water for egg laying. This is the favorite habitat of the two-lined salamander and two species of "mole" salamanders—those that spend most of their lives under logs, in the ground, or variously buried, but emerge for spring breeding or in summer rainy periods.

One mole salamander, the Jefferson, is rather plain and slender. The other, the spotted, has big yellow spots on a black background and is one of our larger and more handsome species. It often takes up winter residence in house basements, after having moved over considerable distances from the waters of its hatching, and is found crawling over the floor when the basement has been partially flooded by rain or melting snow. After winter this strong migrant will travel steadily until it reaches water by mating time. Recent studies indicate that Vermont's mole salamanders have declined drastically in the past few years, and the suspected reason is the "acid rains" that result from industrial air pollution in the East and Midwest, which are brought here by the prevailing winds and "dumped" in the rain and snow.

The northern water snake lives in the swamp, as well as other watery areas — it is equally likely to swim in marshes, rivers, and ponds, or slide over the land nearby, for this reptile is semiaquatic, able to hunt on land as much as in the water. Though it has a distinct skin pattern of irregular dark-and light-brown bands and patches, in water this snake seems to be completely dark, and has led many people to believe that the poisonous cottonmouth (water moccasin) has somehow found its way into Vermont. In reality, the cottonmouth comes no closer to us than southern Virginia, but this unfortunate mis-identification has caused the water snake much persecution. Though it is defensive to the point of biting if handled, the water snake is nonpoisonous. It feeds mostly on small "trash" fish, amphibians, and other aquatic animals, in addition to several land species, and it may actually do a service to the fisheries by helping to weed out the less desirable pan fish, leaving more space for the game species.

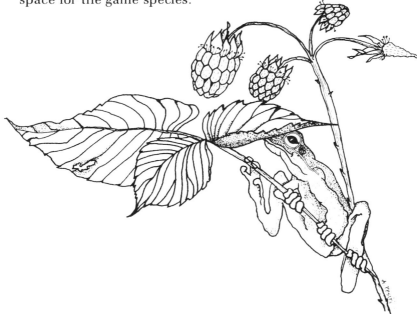

The Gray Treefrog. The largest of Vermont's two species of treefrogs, but only 1½ to 2 inches in length. Its long legs and digits, and sticky pads on the toes, allow it to climb plants, particularly shrubs and small trees. When giving its sustained trill at spring mating time, the male inflates his chin sac like a tiny balloon.

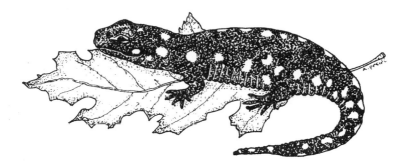

The Spotted Salamander. One of the largest salamanders in Vermont, measuring 6 to 7 inches from nose to tip of tail. A so-called mole salamander, this species spends much of its life buried in the mud or under logs; in winter it often migrates to hibernating areas, such as house basements. With its large yellow spots on a black background, a handsome animal.

13

Ponds and Lakes

We sail out into open water. We have come to the end of the flow, to where the current stops and the water is gathered into reservoirs of many sizes and shapes. They are the virtual end of the line, in many cases, for most of the water from the uplands around them.

These reservoirs are usually classified as ponds or lakes, but the distinction is not always clear. Ponds are on the whole

Vermont Lake. The contemplative time of sunset fishing, at Great Averill Pond in extreme northeastern Vermont.

smaller and shallower than lakes, and have more extensive bottom vegetation. Since ponds are shallow, their waters are heated uniformly in summer or cooled uniformly in fall, whereas lakes are deep enough to develop thermal layers. In summer, a warm layer lies above a cool one; in winter, cool above warm (in reality, the lower layer remains more constant in relation to the changeable upper layer). As we shall see later, this stratification, or lack of it, determines to a great degree the types of fish that inhabit each body.

Some lakes occupy sites that have been around for millennia, dating back to geological processes associated with crustal movements and plate tectonics more than 500 million years ago. Lake Champlain, as we mentioned before, sits in a deep, long trench, thought to be created when a massive block of bedrock dropped down more than 700 feet between the Adirondacks and the Green Mountains; Lake Dunmore, near Brandon, is a low place in a series of metamorphic-rock folds on the western side of the Green Mountains. Of course, these ancient sites subsequently were much modified by the glaciers, and most of the lakes we see today owe at least part of their character in one way or another to the ice sheets.

The glaciers made lakes in one of two different ways: by gouging out ("overdeepening") preexisting basins, valleys, or pockets, or by depositing material they had eroded and transported, blocking old drainages and building new basins.

Most of the gouged basins contain deep, clear, cold, and highly stratified water. Lake Willoughby is a classic example: the rock between the masses of Mounts Pisgah on the east and Hor on the west was ground out and eroded by an ancient river that ran between the two peaks, which had probably begun by following a long crack (fault) in the rocks. The rivers and glaciers enlarged and deepened this trough until it became one of the deepest lakes in New England, dropping to more than 300 feet in some places. Glacial till from the outwash plugged the north and south ends, creating the long, scenic lake we now see. Also in the northern part of Vermont, Crystal Lake, Great Averill Pond, Maidstone Lake, and Lake Seymour exhibit features of gouged basins. So, in more southern parts of the state, do portions of Lakes St. Catherine and Bomoseen.

Though lakes lying in gouged basins usually have cliffs and other tourist-drawing postcard-pretty scenery, they are in a minority in Vermont. Those made by the deposition of glacial till and damming are far and away the most common here. These are ordinarily rather shallow, have a sandy-gravelly floor overlaid with muds and silts, feature much vegetation at the edges, and do not become thermally stratified. Lake Carmi, Lake Elmore, Emerald Lake, and parts of Lake Champlain well illustrate these attributes.

Kettles, mentioned earlier, are a special class of depositional ponds, beginning as depressions in the land where an isolated block of glacial ice was trapped and melted, and where no proper inlet or outlet existed. Kettles are usually fairly symmetrical in shape, often nearly round and small. Many of them have become bogs, as perhaps will many more of them. Spectacle Pond at Brighton State Park near Island Pond is a large kettle, only 8 to 10 feet at the deepest, with a thick bottom of muck. Silver Lake in Barnard is another fine example of a large kettle pond.

Size, however, is not always a good criterion for determining whether a basin was gouged or was formed in a depositional moraine. Many of the small high-elevation ponds in the Green Mountains, such as Bear Pond, Lake of the Clouds, and Sterling

A Vermont Pond.
Some of the activity of a small pond, depicted in cross-section.

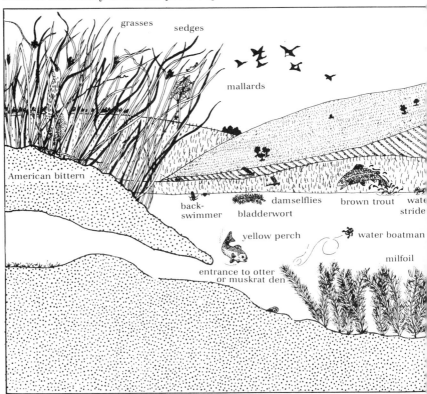

Pond (all in the Mount Mansfield State Forest), are shallow and nearly filled with organic matter, but they are gouged basins. On the other hand, some or portions of some of our larger lakes are depositional, such as Island Pond and Lake Bomoseen.

Like any of the habitats we have talked about, ponds and lakes are not static: they are constantly evolving. They pass through stages of vegetation development as surely and predictably as grasslands or forests, only in the case of these bodies of water they are in the process of being filled in, with sediments brought by rivers and matter from dying organisms, to become dry land at some future time. Centimeter by centimeter, year by year, century by century the lake bottom builds. Finally, the lake is shallow enough for the sun to call forth plants, and then as plants die, the soil accumulates even faster. The lake thus transforms into a marsh (or perhaps a bog), next into a swamp, finally into the familiar forest. The lake by then has died and land has

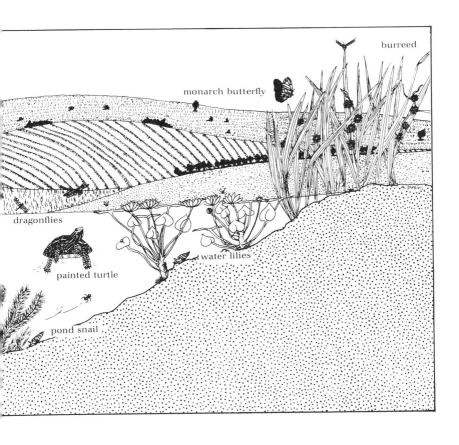

been born. It seems to be a one-way journey to extinction, but future lakes may come from the mighty movements of continents, the warping of mountains to make valleys, and, perhaps in the distant future, more glaciers.

Many outside influences can change the course of development of a pond or lake. The rate of sedimentation, water quality, basin depth, and the speed of water flowing through them are all important factors. Great quantities of fertilizers coming from agricultural runoff and phosphates from detergents have resulted in abnormally fast and luxuriant plant growth in many lakes (eutrophication), causing clogging of the shallower bays with water weeds and premature aging of the lakes. This is a great problem, especially in portions of Lake Champlain, where water chestnut and milfoil are making many harbors and swimming beaches unusable.

The modern phenomenon of acid rains—the turning of our rainwater into mild (and sometimes not so mild) acids by the reaction of industrial air pollutants, particularly sulfur, with atmospheric moisture—has altered the basic water chemistry of many lakes and adversely affected the wildlife populations within them. The problems are most severe in the Adirondacks, where lakes have become "acid baths" and entire fish populations have been wiped out. Vermont, being somewhat protected from the prevailing winds by the Adirondacks to the west and the White Mountains to the east, so far seems to be suffering less, though there is mounting evidence that our bodies of water— and mountain vegetation—are indeed being affected.

Lake Zones

Most lakes are divided into zones, as based on physical dimensions and biological characteristics. Each zone has a distinct identity and figures importantly in the dynamics of lake life. Nearest the shore is the littoral zone, where shallowness and light penetration allow plants to root and grow making it the most biologically productive area. A marsh is really a highly developed littoral zone of a wide, slow-moving river that is, for all intents and purposes, a long lake (the outstanding marshlands on the eastern side of Lake Champlain are, in effect, part of that lake's littoral zone that has been cut off from direct contact with the lake). Though often called the shore zone, the littoral zone is not just shoreline; some shallow ponds have nothing but littoral zone, since vegetation grows out to the deepest middle parts, covering the entire surface of the water.

The littoral zone, whether a marsh or a portion of a pond or lake, teems with insects and other invertebrates. The large nymphs of dragonflies, highly predatory, propel themselves through the tangle of vegetation in pursuit of other aquatic insects and even small fish. Backswimmers, whirligig beetles, and predaceous diving beetles, all free-swimming as adults, carry an air supply down with them on their dives underwater for prey. On the water surface skim water striders and small spiders, while on the underside of the film flatworms and tiny snails are able to glide and move about in their scavenging. Hanging down from the surface film are mosquito larvae, their minute breathing tubes poking through to the air. These various invertebrates represent an important component of the productivity of the lake, as they are a major source of food for many larger insects, amphibians, reptiles, fish, and birds that cruise in and over the area in search of meals.

The open water beyond the littoral zone—but including the bottom and only to a depth where light still reaches—is referred to as the limnetic zone. This is the realm of plankton, the floating, microscopic organisms, both plants and animals, the former of which are able to use the sun to manufacture their food. This is an important hunting ground for some larger predatory fish: such warm-water species as largemouth bass, northern pike, and walleye spend much time here, although they also move into the outer limits of the littoral zone in search of other game.

The benthic zone is the bottom beyond the littoral and beneath the limnetic zones. It contains numerous creatures in the sedimentary muds, many more than the littoral mud, for it is better aerated than the highly organic, poorly oxygenated bottom closer to shore. Clams, crustaceans, worms of many kinds, and other invertebrates live off decayed matter lying there or the dead plankton that "snowfalls" from the waters above. These bottom animals, in turn, become food for diving ducks and bottom-scouring fish. The brown bullhead ("horned pout," alluding to the poisonous spines on its pectoral and dorsal fins) is a native catfish in many of Vermont's warm-water ponds and lakes, where at night it uses its "whiskers" in these muds to feel out its slow-moving prey.

Finally, the deeper, colder lakes have a fourth zone, the profundal. This is the region of open water below the limnetic zone into which insufficient light penetrates for plants to grow. Because no plant plankton can live there, the few bottom-dwellers below this zone obtain food solely from what drifts down from the limnetic zone. Since this zone is far from the air insulated by the waters above it, it remains cool in summer and thus may harbor some cold-water species of fish. There is not enough food here, however, so the fish travel elsewhere to hunt.These fish may roam the various lake levels and zones during the temperate times of the year, but during the hot days of summer and the ice-covered months of winter they retreat to the profundal zone.

Fish

More than 60 species of fish inhabit Vermont ponds and lakes, from the tiny minnows to one of the largest freshwater fish in the world, the lake sturgeon. Most of these species are of the so-called warm-water variety, those that prefer ponds and shallow lakes, where the waters are uniformly heated in summer and abundant vegetation grows at shoreside.

Of these warm-water fish, the yellow perch is, by far, the most common. It is often ignored by sport fishermen but it actually constitutes, in total pounds taken, the most important food fish in Vermont. It can be caught almost any time, anyplace, and is most popular in winter, when it can be taken through the ice and its flavor seems best. Chain pickerel, northern pike, largemouth bass, sunfish, bullhead, suckers, and several others are also common warm-water fish in these waters. Some people regard these as "trash" fish, worthless for sport and harmful to game species, but others value them. For example, northern pike have long been considered by many to be vicious predators; these people will take every opportunity to eliminate them, including shooting them in flooded fields, marshes, and shallows as they spawn in the early spring. Other people, however, look at the northern pike as a fine sport fish, with a spirited fighting nature and a good trophy size; many come miles just in search of the pike.

In the lakes where the lower layer of water remains cool or cold the year round, the cold-water species are to be found: trouts of several kinds, smelt, and, in special places, salmon. These fish, strongly associated with the north country, spend most of their time in the depths, although in some cases they may move into shallower water or even into rivers to feed or spawn.

Rainbow trout are often found in the cold waters, as are the lake trout. The latter, largest of our trout species, prefers the very deep lakes where there is a high dissolved-oxygen content. It is a nonmigratory native species, feeding and spawning in the deepest parts of the open water (unaccountably, however, in some lakes outside Vermont it spawns in shallow areas). A fine sport fish summer or winter, the lake trout may weigh 25 pounds or more and maintains stable populations in such cool northern lakes as Willoughby, Maidstone, and Seymour, and Great and Little Averill ponds. It was known to inhabit Lake Champlain in fair numbers before 1880 but, for as yet unexplained reasons, has virtually disappeared from there. The several hypotheses for the fish's decline include the influx of the parasitic sea lamprey that decimated the Great Lakes' population of lake trout, ruining a huge commercial fishery there; the possible severe predation on young lake trout by the smelt, a species that shares the trout's region of a lake; and a general worsening of conditions in Lake Champlain. Whatever the cause, almost no lake trout have been caught in Lake Champlain in a hundred years, even though the proper habitat seems available and despite a modest program begun in 1958 to reestablish the species through hatchery-raised stock. The situation could change, however, once the reason for the trout's decline is discovered and with the proposed increases in hatchery releases of fish, along with the improvement of Lake Champlain's water.

One species of salmon lives in a few lakes in Vermont and apparently has done so since glacial times. The landlocked salmon, otherwise known as the Sebago salmon (after one of its ancestral homes, Sebago Lake, Maine), is believed to have evolved from a stock of the Atlantic salmon that was denied reentry to the sea by an intervening barrier created by the receding glacier.

The landlocked salmon retains much of its kinship with the Atlantic salmon, both in appearance and in its schooled migration from lakes upstream to spawning grounds in rivers. It is as if the species shifted its instinctive attraction to salt water to the fresh water of lakes. In Vermont its native range was traditionally restricted, a few inhabiting Lake Champlain, but mainly most of the species living in Lake Memphremagog and its major tributary, the Clyde River. There it was relatively abundant until the 1930s, but soon after that it began to fade under the developing industrialization and dams and the unstable water levels they caused. By 1950 the species was rare and by 1965 it was almost gone.

To reverse an impending permanent loss, the Vermont Fish and Game Department initiated a landlocked-salmon-restoration project in the 1960s. Young fish from a remnant population of the Lake Memphremagog strain had some years earlier been taken to Maine to be raised as brood fish. Fry from these captives were brought back to Vermont, raised in hatcheries here, and released in tributaries of various lakes that were deemed suitable for their survival and growth. The program is still under way and appears successful to date. In addition, a proposed hatchery on the shores of Lake Champlain may well provide the seeds for future populations of landlocked salmon in that big lake, as well as elsewhere.

Lake Champlain's 440 square miles contain rich and varied fisheries, which in times past supported a thriving industry, and which have always been a great attraction for sportsmen.

It has both warm- and cold-water species, depending on the
geographic region and the depth of water. Perch are abundant in
practically every shallow area. Smallmouth bass, typical of
clearer and cooler waters, are the most common of the black

Stocking Salmon. A Vermont Fish and Game Department warden and
fisheries biologist release hatchery-raised landlocked salmon in a northeastern Vermont lake. The department has been active in strengthening the state's
landlocked-salmon population by bolstering the ancestral colony in Lake
Memphremagog and establishing new ones in suitably cold-water lakes in the
Northeast Kingdom. A similar program is planned for Lake Champlain.

bass, though largemouth bass also live here in sizable numbers. American eels spend their adult lives in the lake (as well as in most rivers of the state outside the Northeastern Highlands), then migrate out to the Atlantic Ocean for spawning—just the opposite cycle from the Atlantic salmon. The small, silvery-gray smelt is one of the cold-water species most often caught in winter; it is relished for its fine flavor.

The 1800s and early 1900s were when the lucrative commercial fishing industry existed on Lake Champlain. Walleye (pike perch) and whitefish (a relative of the trout) were the mainstays of the fishery and were principally caught in nets when they massed on their spawning runs—the walleye in spring, the whitefish in the fall. The catches were large: from 1893 to 1904, for example, yearly averages of almost 40,000 pounds of walleye and 38,000 pounds of whitefish were taken, supplying both the Canadian and the American markets.

The netting of these fish on their spawning runs and grounds created bitter controversy in those years, a controversy that has continued in various forms up to today. Walleye has always been the focus of this debate, since, as one of the finest-tasting fish, its spring migration would draw hundreds of fishermen. Walleyes schooled by the hundreds of thousands in Missisquoi Bay, coming from both the United States and Canadian waters of Champlain. They would then spawn in the bay or in the channel of the Missisquoi River, where they were netted. Public pressure resulted in 1911—12 in laws preventing the netting of walleyes in Vermont, but the Canadians continued this practice, not only for their own markets, but for the American ones as well—an added insult to the Vermont fishermen. Finally, however, in the 1960s Canada also outlawed the indiscriminate netting of spawning fish.

The walleye, being a favorite game fish, has always been in the public eye, more so than the whitefish. That species, though a substantial part of the old commercial enterprise, and though still abundant in Lake Champlain is hardly talked about anymore. It is a resource that is almost untouched today, for reasons hard to determine.

Some fish in Lake Champlain and its major tributaries are found nowhere else in Vermont. Several are "living fossils," belonging to ancient lines of fish now extinct, and their presence here can be traced back to the effects of the Ice Age.

One such ancient species is the lake sturgeon, among the largest freshwater fish in the world. Individuals weighing more than 300 pounds have been caught, though in Vermont the biggest have been just over 125. The physical attributes of this bony (ganoid) fish testify to its antiquity: a skeleton of cartilage rather than bone, an asymmetrical tail, bony plates covering the head, and diamond-shaped scales. With these characteristics, the sturgeon reminds one of a shark, which is a primitive fish of the oceans. The comparison is further enhanced by the location of the two species' mouths on the underside of their heads — the sturgeon uses it for "vacuuming" food from the lake bottom, however, rather than attacking large prey.

The sturgeon, once an important food for the Indians in Vermont and New York, later became a commercially valuable catch for white settlers. In those early years it probably lived in both the St. Lawrence and Connecticut rivers, in addition to Lake Champlain. But since it must enter main, unspoiled tributaries for spawning, it has suffered under the subsequent damming of those rivers, as well as the siltation from farmland runoff, and now it is scarce enough to be the only fish on Vermont's endangered-species list. It is so infrequently caught, and then quite by accident, that startled fisherman often do not know what it is.

Patriarchs like the sturgeon, but with more sizable populations, are the bowfin and the long-nosed gar. Their primitive body characteristics are similar to the sturgeon's, but in addition they have an air bladder that acts like a lung, through which they can actually breathe air directly, much in the manner of African lungfish. This allows them to stay for extended times in oxygen-poor waters, such as in a marsh or muddy shallows, where they swim near the surface and gulp air. Both are voracious feeders, and a turmoil witnessed at the surface of a Champlain marsh or shoreline may well involve one of these fish in action.

Of all the lakes in Vermont, Champlain alone has these ancient species. It is likely that over a long period of time its size has provided the only habitat safisfactory for the needs of such large, specialized fish. Following the glacier's retreat they probably lived in many other big lakes in the north, but as the waters receded they were unable to sustain themselves: the lakes' shrinking produced increasingly specialized local conditions that impinged on the fish more and more.

Other fish in Lake Champlain also remind us of its onetime tie, at the close of the Wisconsin glaciation, to the Atlantic Ocean through the St. Lawrence River. The fleshy, almost eellike ling is a freshwater codfish whose ancestors are thought to have come from the sea, entered the basin during the era of the Champlain Sea, and been subsequently cut off from egress to the ocean. They adapted totally to life in fresh water, have since evolved in that setting, and have even moved into many rivers adjoining the lake. The sheepshead, socalled for the appearance of its blunt head, has a similar history, as we believe does the smelt, a cold-water species that normally migrates from salt to fresh water to spawn, like the salmon or shad. Smelt have been taken by people to many other lakes in Vermont, where for the most part they have evidently done very well.

Birds

On Vermont lakes in summer, especially the large ones, the "sea gulls" are ever-present in greater or lesser numbers. The ring-billed gull is the species seen most often in the state now, as it also feeds in the smaller lakes, swarms around town dumps, and follows the plow in many a farmer's field. It is interesting to note that it had not even been sighted in Vermont until the 1940s, at which time its population exploded everywhere in the East and moved inland. It even outnumbers the herring gull on Lakes Champlain and Memphremagog, and may, in fact, be driving that gull out. The competition focuses on the shared breeding sites: both species nest on islands in Lake Champlain, some of which are really no more than rocky emergences from the lake. Here ringbills form large colonies and the herring gulls smaller, more isolated groups on the fringes of the ringbills', where they seem barely able to hang on. On one of the Four Brothers Islands more than 12,000 ringbills now nest each year. Elsewhere on the lake small colonies of them are also scattered, occasionally sharing the sites with colonies of the common tern.

The Four Brothers Islands, technically in New York but owned by the University of Vermont, is a preservation area, home to other interesting birds, some not strictly "water" or lake birds at all. There the black-crowned night heron has a rookery of 30 to 35 individuals that nest and roost in scraggly cedar trees growing over the island. As their name implies, these herons are busy mostly at night, sleeping during the day. In summer evenings you may hear their hoarse "wok-wok" as they fly with slow wings to feed in outlying marshes and swamps. The cattle egret, closely related to the herons, is an interesting newcomer to the Four Brothers, in fact, to the United States. It made its first appearance in the Western Hemisphere sometime between 1920 and 1930 in South America, having wandered or been blown in a storm from its native home, Africa. From South America, it got to the West Indies, thence to Florida, where the first breeding was recorded for this country in the 1950s. Since then it has moved north, breeding on the Four Brothers Islands for the first time in 1973. More recently it has been seen in other areas, occasionally a good distance from Lake Champlain. This white egret is a bird of the open fields, where it follows cattle and other farm animals here as it does wild animals in Africa, picking up insects and worms that their hooves stir up.

With the summer days' shortening and blending into fall,

the lakes and ponds of Vermont begin to reveal new birds, the migrants on their way south. As mentioned earlier, Lake Champlain, an important branch of the Atlantic Flyway, attracts the greatest variety and numbers, while the other main branch, the Connecticut River, draws fewer birds. Most of the larger lakes, however, have something to offer the bird-watcher at this time of year.

Earliest to appear are the shorebirds, the sandpipers and stubbier-billed plovers, as they begin passing through as early as mid-July. Shorebirds migrate over bodies of water, yet stop to rest and feed along the exposed edges, where they are most often seen. Low-water years bring down many new species, those that would normally fly over Vermont to marshes and shores elsewhere but which come down to take advantage of newly exposed flats in marshes, rivers, or lakesides. For example, an artificial drawdown in 1974 of the Dead Creek Waterfowl Area near Addison attracted great numbers of shorebirds, including species rarely, if ever, seen in Vermont.

Ducks and geese arrive in October and November, the dabblers working the perimeters and marshes, the divers heading for more open water. The geese split the difference, moving at the edges and into fields to feed, but spending much resting time in the open-water areas.

The most regularly seen diving ducks at this time are the common goldeneye, the smaller bufflehead ("butterball"), the ring-necked duck, the greater and lesser scaups ("bluebills"), three species of ocean-bound scoter, and the common merganser. A few other birds more oriented to oceans and saltwater bays appear sporadically, such as the oldsquaw, the red-breasted merganser, and the horned grebe. The duck so prized by hunters of the prairie states, the canvasback, is sometimes seen, but its formerly more common look-alike cousin, the redhead, is now a rarity. Both are victims in the Midwest of the draining of marshlands, potholes, and other bodies of water for conversion to farmland.

Some water birds stay longer than others in the fall, being ever more squeezed into the ice-free areas of the lakes. Several even overwinter where the water remains open, such as at the base of hydroelectric dams, the mouths of fast-moving rivers, or, as at one spot in Burlington harbor, where heat from an electrical generating plant keeps warm water circulating.

At the other end of the season's pendulum, spring soothes us out of the grip of ice and the waterfowl mellow the evenings as we see and hear them heading north. They keep pace with the thaw, moving to breeding grounds in the Canadian tundra and prairies, or perhaps farther west. Only a few diving ducks remain in Vermont to breed: the mergansers (some of which have stayed the entire winter) and common goldeneyes in tree cavities and the marsh-nesting ring-necked ducks. The rest keep going to lands far away, which they reach by May.

One large diving bird comes early and some of its kind remain in Vermont to nest, but precious few. This is the common loon, whose eerie, trembling "laugh" evokes the solitude of the unspoiled lakes of the northern wilderness. The loon was at one time fairly common to the state and New England as a whole. But it has retreated from civilization, as it requires freedom from disturbance to ensure successful nesting. Lakeside cottages, motorboats, increased tourism, and the camp-following raccoon, which preys on loon eggs and young, have driven the loon out of most of the East, and soon it will have left the entire

The Common Loon. "The diver with the necklace," as the French have called it. The loon's heavy body (its bones are not hollow, as in most flying birds) and powerful legs located far back on the body allow it to dive deeply after fish— occasionally as much as 200 feet. Formerly an abundant bird breeding on most fair- to large-sized lakes in New England, the loon is now reduced to one or two breeding pairs in southern New England, a handful in Vermont, and greater but declining numbers in New Hampshire and Maine.

Northeast. A 1979 survey in Vermont yielded sobering results: 18 pairs of loons attempted to nest in the state in spring and summer, with only 12 successful nestings, which produced but 14 young. However, this is good compared with Massachusetts and Connecticut, each having only one nesting pair.

Over the ice-free seasons, and by most smaller lakes and ponds, other birds are active in their daily pursuits. Early in spring one sees tree swallows practically everywhere, twisting and turning on their wings as they snap up insects close to the water surface. Later, bank swallows return to ponds and lakes with sandy banks, where they dig their nesting burrows, often bunching in huge colonies that riddle the banks with holes. A solitary sandpiper, true to its name, may appear as a lone migrant along streamsides, ponds, and lakes. Until very recently none had ever been reported to breed in the continental United States, but in the summer of 1976 breeding of the species was confirmed at a pond near Groton State Forest. So now Vermont boasts a first for the country!

Other Animals

As we turn to other animals we realize that in many ways the area of Vermont west of the Green Mountains has more biological affinity with the Midwest than it does with the rest of the state or the East, as has been seen with some plants. In theory, the height of the mountain range and different climates and soil types on either side have been deterrents to uniform distribution of many plants and animals, and this is especially so with some reptiles and amphibians. For instance, the eastern spiny softshell turtle is an aquatic animal of the Midwest, but an isolated population exists in Lake Champlain and north in the lower Ottawa River. The map turtle lives in the waters of the Lake Champlain basin, but its main range is through Lake Ontario, Lake Erie, and the Midwest. The mud puppy ("proteus" to earlier naturalists) is a large, external-gilled salamander that lives in Lake Champlain and its larger tributaries, but not farther east. So, for many species, these east-west biological zones are as real and important as the more evident north-south ones.

Other reptiles and amphibians of Vermont are not so restricted, occurring all over the state and in most bodies of water, even though they are only occasionally seen. One has no trouble perceiving the "jug-o-rum" of the bullfrog from almost any pond edge throughout the warm months, but the silent snapping turtle is usually seen only as it moves onto dry land for egg laying in midsummer—otherwise it remains hidden by day in the water depths or within the shoreside vegetation, moving out at night to catch a fish or amphibian, or perhaps sample the plants.

The Eastern Spiny Softshell Turtle. The name of this turtle comes from small spines on the front and back of a shell that is soft at the edges and covered with a leatherlike "skin." A widely distributed reptile in the Midwest, especially the Great Plains, it barely ranges into Vermont: it occurs in the Champlain basin but is not abundant even there. It is usually about a foot in length and is primarily an aquatic animal. Its long snout allows it to breathe in while it is submerged and to uproot mud-dwelling organisms to eat.

In a final look from lake to shore, past marshes and swamps that build to forests, we see everything reflected in the water. In the ripples the wind pushes across, we see the interplay of sun and soil, the merging of land and water. The bass below eats a perch that slid out too far from the underwater marsh. A snapping turtle lumbers out of a pond to the land to lay its eggs. A rainbow trout labors far upstream to spawn. With the ending day, a ring-necked duck coasts in from the open lake to its marshland nest, while a wood duck rises out of the marsh for the trees. And the spring peeper that greets our spring at the edge of water will be looking from the forest as we make our way through another summer.

IV   Openings

And as I was green and carefree, famous among the barns
About the happy yard and singing as the farm was home,
  In the sun that is young once only,
    Time let me play and be
    Golden in the mercy of his means. . . .

All the sun long it was running, it was lovely, the hay
Fields high as the house, the tunes from the chimneys, it
  was air
And playing, lovely and watery
    And fire green as grass.

—Dylan Thomas, *Fern Hill* (1945)

14

Fields, Farms, and Towns

We have come quite a way down from mountains, through forests of evergreens and broad-leaved trees, through mystical coves of bogs, down rivers to lakes and past the vital marshes.

But before we leave this adventure we should step into the fields of rural Vermont, the small woodlots, or even villages. They are still much of what the state is all about—under cultivation, in pastures, managed for local wood supplies or maple syrup, cleared for houses and other buildings, or left on their own to let Nature decide.

One often hears of Vermont that it is the most rural state in the Union, meaning that it has the greatest percentage of its citizens living "in the country." This way of life leaves its personal mark on the landscape and in many ways helps make Vermont

An Old Farm. Lone elm trees and a weathered barn stand like monuments in a Vermont pasture.

181

an attractive state from the tourists' point of view. It means there is a nice variety of scenery, a healthy blend of village, farm, field, and forest. Vermont is never monotonous, and the work of people often relates directly to the land.

Being basically a forested state, Vermont does not come easily by its open spaces. It takes work to maintain a field here. A clearing will not long remain if untended, for the natural momentum is toward building the forest, following the various paths of succession: field to shrubs to forest is a continuous evolution, set back only by fire, flood, wind, mowing by man, and grazing by animals, or else the replacement of the earth with concrete and steel.

For our various needs in life, we have chosen to try to stop this succession at several places along the way. In a society that is forever looking for more and more things to come out of the land, for increasing numbers of people—lumber, crops, acreage for houses, fuel, recreation—the provision for and management of the open and forested spaces are critical considerations. The maintenance of a natural diversity becomes the prevention of a deadly sameness in our environment.

Plants

Plants of the earliest field stages must be able to tolerate the full sun and wind—the drying effects of these forces during the growing season. They must endure widely fluctuating temperatures from day to night and from season to season. They must have the means to survive the months of ice and snow, and they must have ways to reach and colonize new openings quickly.

Field plants have met those demands in many ways. The first to appear on bare soil are the annuals, growing rapidly from seed to flower in one season and releasing multitudes of seeds the same fall or winter. Fireweed is one of these, a hardy plant whose name belies its role as a colonizer of burned-over areas, but which also grows prolifically along roadsides.

Following the groundbreaking of the annuals are the biennials, which take two years to flower, then the perennials, living many years and flowering each year after reaching maturity. These two groups usually have deeper root systems than the annuals and a variety of means to retain water and endure desiccating conditions. Perennial grasses are clumped and bunched into water-holding mats and have narrow bladelike leaves with tough outer coats. The milkweeds store water in the milky sap of leaves and stems, and the fine coat of hairs covering the common mullein reflect light rays, thereby lowering leaf temperatures and evaporation rates.

These plants have effective methods of reaching new territories, and once there, of spreading rapidly. Structures attached to the seeds of milkweeds, dandelions, goldenrods, thistles, and many grasses—usually in the form of little "parachutes"—allow them to be carried away by the wind. The tough, indigestible seeds of many fruits—raspberries and blackberries, for example—are eaten by birds and mammals and then deposited elsewhere in their excrement. Other seeds, such as those of burdock and beggarticks, hitchhike by sticking to fur, feathers, or clothing.

The perennials have extensive subterranean rootstocks, from which the colony quickly expands. Above ground, the sensitive growing tips of the stems often are protected under a shield of leaves or buried in the tangle of a vegetative mat. The

The Shepherd's Purse. A nonnative species now very common in the United States, this field plant is well equipped for life in the often-dry open by virtue of its deep taproot, which pulls moisture and nutrients from far underground. In addition, the basal rosette of leaves can overwinter and thus initiate plant growth quickly in the spring.

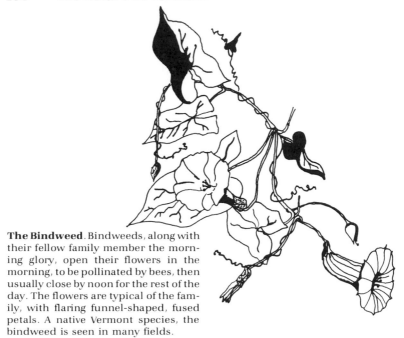

The Bindweed. Bindweeds, along with their fellow family member the morning glory, open their flowers in the morning, to be pollinated by bees, then usually close by noon for the rest of the day. The flowers are typical of the family, with flaring funnel-shaped, fused petals. A native Vermont species, the bindweed is seen in many fields.

basal growth of grasses and the rosette of winter cress well illustrate these forms of protection.

Summer and early fall are the time for the field flowers to show their riches. The names and hues seem to come without end: the clovers and cinquefoils, a yellow snapdragon called butter-and-eggs and the sweet-smelling milkweeds, birdfoot trefoil, chickory, bedstraws, the aggressive purple loosestrife, black-eyed Susans, Queen Anne's lace, yarrow, the many goldenrods, asters, and thistles.

Ironically, most of the pioneer plants of the fields and meadows are not native to the United States. They have come from other countries, mostly European, in the plant food for human beings or livestock, in clothing or fur, by ship or plane. Or sometimes they have been introduced intentionally, as food crops and pasturage, or simply out of a person's nostalgia for his or her homeland. The Vermont state flower, red clover, was brought over from England in 1747, for use as cattle fodder and a soil enricher; burdock and devil's paintbrush (orange hawkweed), so prevalent along almost any summer roadside, are both originally from Europe. Once early Europeans in this country had incorporated their methods of farming and way of life here, these species and many others of the field found the newly cutover eastern America similar to their original environment and much to their liking, so that, thus encouraged by the re-creation of their former habitats, they easily outcompeted the American natives, which were more at home in the woodlands.

As succession advances beyond the fields, shrubs and brambles appear, such as meadowsweet, steeplebush, alternate-leaved dogwood, blackberries, and raspberries. Small trees soon follow—staghorn sumac with its clumps of velvet red seeds, hawthorns, pin cherry, beaked hazelnut, and shadbush. In areas that have been burned, the pioneer trees may sidestep this sequence: quaking aspen and paper birch may grow from bare ground directly into the mature forest and, where white pine grows nearby, it may enter the fields early and quickly take over from the herbaceous plants.

This shrub stage, intermediate between open field and closed forest, is a habitat all its own, a productive mixing zone usually classified by ecologists as an "edge," connoting a place of great diversity and wildlife activity. Animals such as the white-tailed deer, wild turkey, and even some birds of the deeper forest come to the edge to feed. Certain birds move from the forest to openings for their territorial displays and mating—the ruffed grouse and woodcock, for example. And the edge is a home for a whole group of living things, especially birds, that neither venture far out into the open nor drop back deep into the woods.

Finally, beneath the shrubs and the rapidly growing pioneer trees, the seedlings of a new forest appear, protected in the shade of the older growth, awaiting their turn for dominance. For most of Vermont, it is young sugar maples, beeches, ashes, and others of the northern hardwoods that make up this vigorous understory and one day will be the mature forest of the region (if the landowner lets the process to go that far).

Today's fields, thickets, and smaller woodlots of the Vermont hillsides and valleys still largely owe their existence and character to the farmer. Though farming has dwindled greatly in the past few decades—down from when it was the most important industry in Vermont to now, when many homesteads are falling into abandonment or being converted to country houses for people employed elsewhere—agriculture is still a substantial part of Vermont's economy. Nearly 6,000 farms continue in opera-tion, and farming as a business ranks third, behind manufactur-ing and tourism. Dairy farming, based on mixed-grain croplands and pasturage, accounts for 90 percent of all agriculture in the state: it is the natural form of farming in the Vermont terrain, with its rocky soils and short growing season. Most are small farms, averaging less than 300 acres and supporting a variety of side activities to supplement the primary work, including the cultiva-tion of honey, the supplying of firewood and lumber, and the production of something for which Vermont is world-famous — maple syrup.

The woodlot is a special kind of forest, usually small and closely tended, for whatever uses the owner puts it to. For the forester, who likes to deal with big tracts, managing trees on a large scale, the home woodlot may present problems. With the general pattern in Vermont of small parcels of land owned by individuals (many of whom live out of state), one woodlot might be highly managed for lumber production and its neighbor left completely untouched. Such "piecemealing" of the land among the privately owned woodlots, though it makes for scenic variety,

The Edges. White-tailed deer in early spring come out of the forest to its edges to scratch for and feed on mosses and other ground plants. The cold months are a difficult season for these mammals, as they spend most of their time confined to small coniferous "yards," depending on an ever decreasing supply of needles, twigs, and buds. As spring comes they move out into the fields and hardwood forests in search of the emerging growth.

is a continual source of frustration to the professional forester, who sees these woodlots as untapped potential, a renewable resource that's not being managed. Foresters have long recognized that not only is Vermont wasting its wood resources, but this lack of management is also reducing the quality of the state's forests.

The picture may be changing. With the energy crises of the 1970s, particularly the high cost of home-heating fuels, Vermonters have been increasingly looking to their forests for firewood. Now more than 60 percent of the state's residents use wood as their primary or secondary source of heat, and the number is rising. Stores selling woodstoves and supplies have blossomed overnight, and dry firewood is each year becoming harder to buy. More than ever woodlot owners are turning to foresters for information on putting their land into production for their own wood supplies. Even the scope of wood for energy is expanding: a few industrial plants in the state now use wood

Maple Sugaring. Gathering sap in spring is still a strong ritual in the rural areas of Vermont. Traditional methods involving spouts, buckets, wood fires for boiling down, and horse-drawn sleds are still very much in evidence despite the introduction of laborsaving machinery employing plastic tubing and oil burners. Vermont ranks first in the nation in maple-syrup production.

chips instead of coal or oil to generate electricity, and proposals are in the works for larger operations of this nature in the future.

The movement toward wood for energy raises many questions: how much can the woodlots produce?, what are the long-term effects of continually taking too many "cull" trees?, and so forth. But for now, the possibilities of wood for energy have meant not only a cheaper and more local source of fuel for Vermonters, but also a way for forestry to become visible—to show its purpose and improve the state's woodlands.

In addition to supplying firewood and lumber, many of Vermont's woodlots have been used for generations for the production of maple syrup. Vermont is now the country's leading maple-syrup producer, having in 1979 boiled down 465,000 gallons, compared with New York's next-best output of 315,000. The tradition here is still strong, though ever more difficult to maintain from an economic standpoint, despite modern, labor-saving innovations. Nevertheless, maple-sugaring time in March and April remains a cherished rite of a new season, which will not soon be allowed to disappear, for it means much more than money to those involved in it.

Birds

The spring and summer fields are places of busy bird activity in Vermont. But though many species visit the fields for hunting or picking at seeds and fruits, few actually nest there, for the open space affords limited protection, and there is a lack of plant diversity and only a few "levels" of vegetation here.

The killdeer is one of the most widely recognized of the birds that do succeed in raising a brood under these conditions. It is one of the earliest migrants to return after winter, often arriving when snow is still on the ground. This plover (the family of short-billed shorebirds) lays its eggs in completely exposed areas—plowed fields, gravel parking lots, grassy knolls, and the like. To deter predation, its eggs are nearly invisible, as they blend perfectly with the background. In addition, its young are able to run and fend for themselves soon after they hatch, and when predators are near the parents can call them to cover or else distract the enemy by ostentatiously pretending to be injured. Predators and human activity in the spring do take their toll on this bird, but the killdeer seems nonetheless to be doing very well as a Vermont species.

Out of the mountains, in grassy pastures, hay fields, and the flatlands of river valleys and lakes, bobolinks and meadowlarks nest, the males of which have pleasant bubbling territorial songs in the spring. The Savannah sparrow is one of the most common sparrows that nest within the grasses of our western lowlands. A much rarer open-field bird is the upland sandpiper, its decline over the years probably owing to the gradual replacement of fields by forests and the haying earlier in the year of the places it uses to nest.

Many of the birds that hunt over the fields nest and spend their inactive hours in a nearby forest, forest edge, or tree cavity. From above, the red-tailed hawk winds high, ready to descend upon its prey, which is working through the grasses below. The more agile and darting kestrel ("sparrow hawk"), a kind of falcon, comes in low like a boomerang for insects or small birds, or hovers over a crouching mouse. The tilting and gliding turkey vulture — once rare in Vermont but now seen regularly over many fields in the southern half of the state — looks for dead animals in the open, but retires to the seclusion of cliffs, swamps, or deep forests for nesting and roosting. (The first record of the turkey vulture's breeding in Vermont came in 1979, when mating and young were observed on a cliff in a forest near Rutland.)

With night a great horned owl or a screech owl may soar out from the trees, where it has spent the day, and on silent wings directed by great, staring eyes and large, sensitive ears, glide toward its prey. In the mornings and evenings of a fall, winter, or early spring, the short-eared owl is seen once in a while, especially in the broad valley of the Lake Champlain basin. This visitor from the north is the most open-oriented of owls seen in Vermont, frequenting the fields for both hunting and nesting (although nesting has not yet been documented in Vermont).

Several smaller birds require the fields they hunt in to be near the shrub thickets or forest edges in which they nest. The bluebird, one welcome early sign for us that spring has really arrived, is one of these, eating the insects of the field but nesting in the cavities of trees nearby. In addition to fields, it is especially fond of orchards, where it finds an abundance of insects to eat.

The bluebird is Vermont's smallest species of thrush, and though popular with people it has gone through difficult periods in its history here, as well as in other places in the country. It became scarce early in this century for lack of suitable cavity-bearing trees for nesting and owing to its inability to deal with the house sparrow and the starling. The latter two were brought to the United States — the house sparrow in 1850 and the starling in 1890 — by well-intentioned people, but the consequences have been disastrous. These two aliens have moved into every state in the Union, traveling east to west, and have driven the bluebird from its nest sites, preempting them for their own broods. The decline of the bluebird population reached a low in the 1960s, perhaps at that time aggravated by the use of the pesticide DDT, but with the construction of nest boxes, the leveling off of sparrow and starling numbers, and the cessation of the use of DDT bluebirds have struggled to a minor comeback.

Other small birds are busy in the shrubs that border the fields, but they often come out where they can be easily seen. The male indigo bunting, looking much like a bluebird but without the brown breast, is a common songster that perches high (telephone wires are a favorite stakeout), although the less brilliantly colored female stays down near the nest she has built in blackberries, raspberries, or other thick low shrubs. The yellow warbler, one of the most widespread of all warblers, lives in bushy areas, streamsides, river bottomlands, and other semiopen habitats in Vermont, as it does throughout North America. Its counterpart in wetter areas is the handsome common yellowthroat. The nests of both warblers are targets of the brown-headed cowbird, a "brood parasite" that lays its eggs in the nests of others, leaving the eggs to be incubated and the young cared for by the foster parents. The cowbird is often seen following in the footsteps of cows, picking up insects stirred up by the hooves, much as they did, it is thought, when bison and other large wild mammals roamed the plains of this country.

Several bird species spend most of their time in the shrubs and small trees of the forest edge, coming out into the open only infrequently; they are nevertheless familiar in the fields through their songs. The song sparrow flits about from shrub to shrub, and the rufous-sided towhee scratches in the dead leaves, singing its "drink-your-TEEE," or sharply warning "chee-wink." There are also the "mimic thrushes," a family of birds that resemble thrushes and have the ability to imitate the songs of many birds. The two most common mimics are the catbird and the brown thrasher, but the best imitator is also the rarest in Vermont, being a bird of Southern origin: the mockingbird, of residential areas, farms, and orchards of the milder lowlands, sings more than 35 different songs of other species, repeating each phrase several times and continuing at length without a pause. This species, once restricted to the South and southern Midwest, has moved North within the last 10 to 20 years. The first breeding in Vermont occurred in 1973, in Pownal, near the Massachusetts line, and since then it has progressed steadily northward, now spending summers beyond midstate.

The mockingbird is but one of several "rural" species that only recently have moved into northern territories. The cardinal is another—heretofore a very common bird in almost every Eastern and Midwest state outside northern New England. It is being seen more and more regularly in Vermont, especially in its new range of the northern half of the state, and now even overwinters two-thirds the way up the state. The reasons for its range expansion are not entirely clear, but a combination of factors seems responsible: the proliferation of bird feeders, the planting of ornamental and shade trees that offer an abundance of seeds and fruits, and an absence of major predators in their favored rural or urban environments.

In the protection of the less dense woodlands, in tall trees at the forest edge, or even in urban situations, live many of Vermont's attractive and vocal birds. The male rose-breasted grosbeak has a striking coloration and a long whistle-warble song. Though one of the finches, normally vegetarians, it feeds extensively on beetles and other insects, a reason we see it near gardens, orchards, and other open areas. In fact, one of its favorite foods is the Colorado potato beetle, and by eating it the bird provides a valuable service to farmer and home gardener, whose plants are attacked by the beetle. Most people know of the northern oriole (formerly called the Baltimore oriole), dressed in vibrant orange-on-black, whistling loud and clear, and constructing intricate nests high in elms and other trees. The nest is truly a work of art, finely woven, shaped like a gourd, and featuring a side entrance.

The breeding activity of small birds continues in the weedy fields, forest edges, and thickets throughout the spring and sometimes into summer. A late-nesting field species is the common goldfinch, the "wild canary" that seems to time its nesting to the maturation of the seeds it feeds its young and the appearance of the thistledown with which it lines its nest. The handsome cedar waxwing, crested and buff-colored, is one of the latest in the season to nest, even though it arrives in Vermont early or sometimes stays here throughout the winter. The young waxwings are fed regurgitated fruit (cherries, berries, and so forth) that have ripened in the summer. When the young have fledged and begin to be on their own, one becomes more conscious of the waxwings, as they flock in sizable numbers and move quickly overhead, stripping the trees and bushes of their fruits.

As winter layers its cold and snow over the fields, sealing them off, and as the winds rattle the stalks of goldenrod and sumac, the birds of summer give way to those that will manage an existence off the meager remaining food supplies. Although they stay, some species, such as the goldfinch (the males of which have now molted to a plainer color), move more to the open woods and thickets, where seeds are still to be found on the trees, and they join forces with other finches—the redpolls, purple finches, and pine siskins that have come down from farther north. These and other northern visitors appear unpredictably from year to year: flocks of snow buntings, like flecks of

white on white, swirl along roads or farmyards, searching ma-
nure piles for seeds; tree sparrows and dark-eyed juncos hop
from shrubs or woodland margins for leftover grains, or visit bird
feeders for their offering; and the ever-present blue jays canvass
the areas for just about anything to eat—seeds, hibernating
insects, buds, or the remains of dead animals.

The bugle call of the jay warns other birds in the open areas
that a northern shrike is near, and to be watched. The shrike is a
bird about the size of a robin, but pound for pound one of the
toughest of all predators, eating other birds, as well as small
mammals (shrews, deer mice). Shrikes—the northern and the
rarer summer visitor, the loggerhead—are called butcher-birds
for their macabre habit of hanging up prey they have killed on
thorns, barbed wire, or other sharp objects, apparently to store
them for future use. The northern shrike is usually unable to kill
its victim in the air, so it pulls the prey to the ground, where it
batters the animal to death with its heavy hooked bill.

The Northern Shrike. A usual perch of this winter visitor is at the top of a tree,
on a telephone wire, or at some other high vantage point where it can keep an
eye out for small birds and mammals of the open country. The northern shrike
is one of the most skillful fliers in tight spaces. It kills prey with its heavy bill
and may hang the victim on a thorn or similar sharp object, apparently to store
it. The bird nests in the spruce forests of Canada.

We human beings have created most of the fields we see, have made the edges that lead us into forest, and Nature has responded to what we have done: our work has discouraged some species and encouraged others. At the time of the virgin forests edges and fields were uncommon, and so were the birds of those habitats—the chestnut-sided warbler, for example, one of the most familiar birds of shrubby areas today, but very rare in the early years of Vermont settlement. On the other hand, the untouched forest was ideal for the passenger pigeon, a species long since gone to extinction but once probably the most abundant bird on the North American continent. The bobwhite quail that now thrives on small grains of Midwestern grasslands no longer lives wild in predominantly forested Vermont, but it came to the state in the mid-1800's, after the woods had been cutover. Today this quail is "replaced" by its more woodland relative, the wild turkey, an early native that became extinct and then was brought back. What changes we bring to our future landscapes will surely be reflected in the birds that use them.

Mammals

Except for a few species of bats that fly over in search of insects, or some large mammals, such as deer, that wander in to graze or hunt, most of the mammals residing in the open areas, thickets, and woodlots are small and remain within the shelter of the vegetation, or else go below ground.

The meadow vole is a little vegetarian rodent with sunken eyes, short tail, small ears, and a loose skin—all of which allow it to move freely and quickly in its tight runways through the grasses. The short-tailed shrew hunts the field for ground insects, worms, grubs, or even small mammals in an endless search to satisfy its burning hunger; this little insectivore is busy all year, and its winding tunnels through the snow seem to be everywhere. Another field insectivore, the hairy-tailed mole, uses its spadelike front paws to excavate its way through the soil. Like the shrew, it has an extremely high metabolism and must eat constantly to fuel its body; in winter the mole moves deeper into the soil, below the line of frozen ground, to hunt a variety of organisms. This species is one of only two moles in Vermont, the other being the peculiar star-nosed mole (so called for the fleshy projections on its snout) of wetter and more forested habitats.

Some mammals live completely within the bounds of a field, others combine the fields and forest edges as home or feeding ground. Many, because of their catholic preferences, are often the unwanted companions of human beings, and may in certain situations become pests. The nighttime foraging of the raccoon and the striped skunk, Vermont's only skunk species, are all too well known to campers and homeowners of every corner of the state. Deer mice may move into country or village houses in the winter, and actually supplant the house mouse of more urban areas. Mice, chipmunks, and red squirrels have become a problem in sugar bushes that employ the relatively new method of plastic tubing to collect sap—the rodents eat into the tubing, whether to taste the sap or merely sharpen their teeth, causing considerable loss of time, money, and effort of those working the trees in the spring. And to many gardeners trying to raise vegetables, the woodchucks, deer, mice, voles, raccoons, skunks, and rabbits are an ever-present threat, the source of much annoyance.

In summer nights, bats take to the air over towns, fields, and other open areas, such as marshes, rivers, and lakes. They are out to catch their meals of insects, which they locate with the sensitive "sonar" equipment of their mouths and ears, and capture in the webs between their legs. All the bats in Vermont are insect-eating, and for all the loathing heaped on them because of their appearance, their nocturnal activities, and their reputation as carriers of rabies, in reality bats do a great service by consuming vast quantities of insects. Estimates run as high as a single bat's consuming half its weight in mosquitoes each night; one researcher found that 100 little brown bats ate 42 pounds of insects over a summer.

Most bats in Vermont are nonmigratory, roosting and hibernating here in often large groups in barns, attics, and caves. The big and little brown bats are two of the most common hibernating species, and are usually the subject of most concern when they congregate by the hundreds in people's attics for their winter dormancy. A few species, such as the red bat, are more solitary and roost by day in trees, then migrate out of state as the fall and freezing temperatures approach. One species, the Indiana bat, is of particular interest. It spends summer out of state but in winter moves to Vermont, where it hibernates in only one or two caves. Such a "reversed" migration, up from more southern states in New England, departs from the normal pattern. However, its migratory habits are not the only reason for interest in this species. Inexplicably, it is becoming scarcer over all its natural range, from the East Coast to the Midwest, so much so that it has been placed on the federal endangered-species list and is the subject of much research and rehabilitation work. The Indiana bat is likewise on the endangered-species list of Vermont, where its presence is further threatened by much vandalism of its primary place of hibernation while the animal is in residence.

Winter for most field or forest-edge mammals means retirement to semi- or total hibernation underground or in other protected places, or else removal from the exposed open spaces. True hibernation is experienced in Vermont only by the woodchuck, woodland and meadow jumping mice, and some bats — whether in underground chambers, as in the case of the woodchuck and mouse, or in the colonial "dormitories" or caves of bats. Others Vermont mammals, such as the skunk, raccoon, and squirrels, move into nests or dens, where they fall into deep slumber but are able to wake in winter's warmer spells, to venture out to scrounge for food.

A few field animals will move into the winter shelter of the shrubs and trees, from where they will occasionally steal out to the open, snowswept spaces for foraging or to get from place to place. The New England cottontail, conspicuous in its brown coat against the white background, must remain close to shrubs and brambles, and only carefully moves out in the evenings and nights to chew on buds and twigs. It and other smaller rodents scurrying around on top of the snow become the winter targets of hungry mammals, especially the red fox and weasels, in addition to the hawks and owls. The short-tailed and long-tailed weasels are perhaps the most deadly of these predators, small but extremely efficient, able to kill animals much larger than themselves. They are called ermine in winter, when they have changed their coats from brown to white.

The winter is long and bitter for Vermont's mammals, and it is the time of greatest mortality, be they predators or prey. But when the spring finally comes and the fields rise up with new

The Weasel. Vermont has both the long-tailed and the short-tailed weasel, the first being larger and living more in the forests, the second inhabiting the forest edges and openings. In winter both change into coats of white, except for the black tips of their tails, at which time they are called ermine. Young are born in the spring, after about nine months of gestation. Weasels are very energetic hunters, as one can easily see from their zigzag prints in the snow.

foods and homes, many of the mammals will have already mated, and the young will be brought forth in the welcoming season in preparation for their own winters.

Insects

Insects play an enormous role—both positive and negative—in the workings of the field and forest. Whether in their pollination of the myriad wild flowers or in their attacks on valuable timber trees, we can measure the effect of insects in economic terms. These small organisms may go unnoticed in many instances, but their presence is of great importance. And they are literally everywhere.

The display of wild flowers, pretty and perfumed as it is, is intended for eyes and "noses" other than ours. It is for the insects that have also blossomed in summer. The flowers' colors and smells attract the insects, the agents of their pollination, thus providing for the plants' posterity. The insects, in turn, find in the flowers food for themselves and their newly hatched young, or secure places in which to lay eggs. Butterflies float by day over the fields, probing blossoms with their long, extensible tubelike tongues, while moths perform similar functions on flowers that open in the evening and night, such as white campion and evening primrose.

The mourning cloak butterfly is one of the earliest in Vermont to emerge from hibernation, appearing in April with its yellow-bordered brown wings—sometimes it even rouses from dormancy during a particularly warm interval in winter and flickers out over the snow! The mourning cloak spends a good deal of time in the fields and open forests; its caterpillar feeds on tree leaves. A common later butterfly, the white admiral (or "banded purple"), flocks sometimes by the hundreds to flowers, dead insects and animals, and animal droppings. In July one often sees this attractive species by the roadside, feeding on animals or insects killed by cars.

One of the most familiar yet remarkable butterflies is the monarch, or milkweed, butterfly, which performs a unique migration. The species lives in Vermont all summer long, but individuals that emerge from metamorphosis late in the season make an epic journey to Mexico and elsewhere in Central America. Migration begins here in August and September—earlier in Canada—as they glide and kite their way south from high in the mountains to the expanses over Lake Champlain and other lakes. At night they congregate in trees or on rock ledges—the same places from year to year, though these individuals have never been there before. They take flight again by day. After thousands of miles of travel they arrive at the same wintering grounds their

ancestors have always used. Here they mate. Months later with
the spring they drift north again, although without the massed
push of the autumn migration. Most do not make it all the way
back to where they hatched the preceding year, but stop along
the way to lay eggs and die. The new butterflies from these eggs
complete their parents' trip north and they, in turn, mate and lay
eggs late the same summer. The population of monarchs from
this last hatch repeats the extraordinary cycle. It is interesting to
speculate on the origin of—the "need" for—this migration, and
on the mysterious mechanisms that allow the insects to find
their way to places they have never seen before.

When one mentions pollination, one automatically thinks of
bees. Bees are some of the most prevalent and important insects
as far as human beings are concerned, having played key roles
throughout history, besides being critical to the success of many
plants. Though most people equate *bee* with *honeybee* and
bumblebee these are only two among many thousands of kinds
worldwide and hundreds in this part of the continent. But because the honeybee has for so long been linked with the lives of
human beings, it has attracted the most attention and garnered
the most laurels: it was sacred to the ancient Babylonians, the
Incas, the Egyptians, and others. Until sugar cane was brought to
Europe from the Near East, honey was the sole sweetener on that
continent and the main fermenting agent in liquors. Just recently the honeybee became "sacred" to Vermont, also. In 1978 it
was proclaimed the state insect, owing to its value as a producer
of honey and as a pollinator of apple trees, many farm crops, and
countless other plants that have less commercial importance
but are aesthetically important as wild flowers.

The honeybee was first transported to this country in 1638,
from Europe, by the Massachusetts Bay Colony. Since then it and
all its later imported strains have spread across every state in the
Union, working the flowers of the fields, gathering pollen and
nectar for hives in the hollows of trees and other places. The

The Honeybee. The Vermont state
insect. The colony is highly organized, with one queen laying all the
eggs, drones (males) fertilizing the
eggs, and workers (sterile females)
carrying out the work of the hive—
gathering pollen and nectar, building the comb, feeding the young
and queen, and defending the hive.

honeybee has been one of our most welcome and productive immigrants.

Like the honeybee, the Vermont bumblebee is a social insect—this habit is rare, however, among bees in general. The bumblebee's nest is usually underground, whereas the hive of the honeybee is above ground; but unlike the latter, the bumblebee colony does not live through the winter. Except for new queens hatched late in summer, the entire bumblebee colony dies in autumn. These queens, having earlier mated with drones, move to subterranean seclusion to spend the winter. Though impregnated, the queens are able to delay egg laying until the following spring, at which time they emerge—often very early—to gather pollen and nectar to make into honey, which will be stored in wax cells they have just constructed. The queens then lay a few eggs in the wax cells, and when these larvae hatch they eat the stored food. Later these young bees take over tending the new young hatched from eggs the queen has laid throughout the rest of the spring and summer. Thus, the survival of the bumblebee as a species depends upon a relatively few individuals', the queens', making it through the long winter.

The bumblebee has played a decisive part in the fertilization of the nonnative clovers in this country—the ordinary white and red clovers, in particular. It performs the same function here that the various European species of bumblebee do for clover overseas, in that it is one of the few insects with tongues long enough to reach into the deep recesses of clover flowers and thereby insure pollination. Without the bumblebee the clover could not be pollinated, and thus would not have become the highly important agricultural plant it is today in the United States.

Besides such helpful behavior on the part of insects there is activity that is "neutral," though fascinating, as well as activity that harms the environment—from our point of view. The caterpillars of moths and butterflies have mouth parts designed for chewing leaves (the adults have only sucking mouth parts). Ahead of one's footsteps in the summer grass jump the short-horned grasshoppers, insects that also graze on vegetation and later inject their eggs into plant stems to hatch. In the evenings of late summer one hears the steady buzzing of a green long-horned grasshopper—the katydid ("long-horned" and "short-horned" refer to the length of their antennae). The larvae of the spittlebug ("froghopper" similar to the leafhopper) feed on the juices of goldenrod and other plants, producing as a by-product a frothy protective envelope, from which they acquire their name. Ground beetles scurry among grasses in search of other insects to eat, which they grab with large pincers and devour with strong, sharp jaws.

The leaf-chewing caterpillars of some moths, butterflies, and sawflies have become serious pests for the Vermont woodlot owner, the maple-syrup producer, and even the average small landowner. In a few cases, when they have reached epidemic proportions, they have menaced the state's forests.

Two of the most serious current infestations are by the forest tent caterpillar and the gypsy moth. The larvae (caterpillars) of both species feed on the leaves of many deciduous trees, but

The Eastern Tent Caterpillar. Two tent caterpillars live in Vermont. The eastern tent caterpillar, shown here, concentrates on apple and other fruit trees, eating the leaves and laying eggs in a varnished brown case near the end of a twig. The young caterpillars emerge from small cells in the case, eat their way down the twig, and finally weave a "tent" in which they pupate before changing into adult moths.

The other species, the forest tent caterpillar (not shown) eats leaves of a variety of commercially important deciduous trees. Unlike the eastern tent caterpillar, this one does not spin a web tent. It is called a tent caterpillar because of its other characteristics and life cycle, which resemble those of the eastern tent.

because the sugar maple is the most prized species—often the biggest moneymaker—the people are most concerned about the effects the insects are having on this tree, which is so prevalent in Vermont. Statewide, these insects together defoliated more than 110,000 acres of hardwoods in 1978; the forest tent caterpillar has the wider range, the gypsy moth staying mostly in the milder lowlands, especially around the Champlain basin. This defoliation has been so severe that the trees are stripped bare by early summer and thus are forced to put out a new set of leaves to stay alive. Repeated over a few summers this can reduce a tree's vitality, make it prone to disease, and in the case of the sugar maple, severely reduce its sap production. Additionally, it becomes a costly and unsightly problem in towns and backyards, and over the long run could have an adverse impact on the forest and tourism industries of the state.

The forest tent caterpillar is a native insect of North America, and large outbreaks of it may be seen as part of a natural cycle of 10 to 15 years here. But the gypsy moth is not part of our original fauna. A tussock moth, it was brought over from Europe in 1869 by a researcher who was attempting to produce silk from its cocoon-weaving caterpillar. Several moths escaped and 20 years later the population of moths had exploded across New England, the larvae defoliating hundreds of thousands of acres in their advance. This range extension is apparently still going on, even after millions of dollars have been spent in attempting to check it. Vermont is on the edge of its advance north, and places such as Maryland are on its southern limit.

It seems probable that the natural cycle of the forest tent caterpillar will soon reach its peak and then descend to acceptable levels. It is not so clear what will happen to the gypsy moth, whether it will continue to run rampant for some time to come or else soon reach saturation and be brought under control by disease or new predators or artificial methods.

Reptiles and Amphibians

As many parents can attest, small children find a treasury of wild creatures in the fields and woodlots near their homes. From the many insects that go into collections, to the amphibians placed in terraria, to the reptiles that are occasionally stumbled upon in a child's room, the animals of these areas are a never-ending source of fascination.

Vermont's field snakes, all harmless to people, slide through the grasses, sensing their way toward insects or other small animals to eat. The smooth green snake (usually wrongly called "grass snake") is between 1 foot and 2 feet long, but because it is so perfectly camouflaged it is rarely seen. It is sometimes found crawling out on the branches of shrubs, where it has gone after insects or is seeking warmth from the sun. The smaller red-bellied snake prefers the security of fallen logs and woodpiles; people often discover these snakes curled up in the warm spaces between logs, or find their shed skins draped over the bark. The red-bellied snake usually eats small "game"—insects, slugs, earthworms, and the like. The larger and much more common garter snake, undoubtedly the most widespread and abundant snake in the United States, goes after rodents. Known to almost everyone, it is especially remembered by those who have grabbed it—from the foul-smelling oil it leaves on the hands.

Also quite common is the milk snake, a medium-sized reptile of wide distribution in forests, forest edges, meadows, and the lawns of rural houses. It has the local name checkered adder, "checkered" for its skin pattern and "adder" for the false fancy that it is poisonous. Even the common name milk snake is misleading, for it alludes to the myth that the snake slithers into barns and milks cows with its mouth. However, its presence around barns and houses should be encouraged rather than feared, since the snake is in fact there to capture mice and rats.

The Milk Snake. This medium-sized snake lives in many natural habitats and is also often seen around houses and farm buildings, where it eats rodents. Despite a bad reputation as the "checkered adder," it is harmless to human beings (and does not milk cows), and in fact makes a good pet.

Several amphibians are field dwellers in the summer. The leopard frog is probably the most obvious as it leaps out from underfoot, in some areas seemingly with every step. It is the most land-bound of the large frogs in Vermont, a fact noted in its other common name, meadow frog. But like the other amphibians, it requires to some extent a moist environment and wet areas for egg laying in the spring. In late summer one may easily see hundreds of leopard frogs in the fields and crossing the roads, along with many other species, such as treefrogs and American toads, as they work their way inexorably toward water, where they will dig down into the muds to spend the winter.

And when winter comes the snakes and other cold-blooded animals of these regions will have gone into hibernation. The small snakes often take up communal residence in underground dens, apparently to pool their slight body heat. The amphibians are buried in the muds underground, underwater, or under logs. Some, such as the spotted salamanders, have moved into the foundations or basements of houses, to spend a secure and slightly warmer winter.

This time of quiet will last until some signal, unknown to us, tells the animals of spring outside. From out of the muds, from under the trees and rocks will come these lives brought over from darkness. No sooner out of that darkness they will create, with the sounds we associate with rising spring or else silence, the new lives to carry on.

V ENDING

I could not hope
to touch the sky
with my two arms

—Sappho
Greek poem (ca. 550 B.C.)

As we walk from that final field perhaps we can see the crusting of the first frost upon the mountain. Or in another season, the touch and ripple of a swallow's wing upon the water. Or hear the deep-February bark of foxes. Or smell the spring come out of violets.

These are all part of this time and place, Vermont's own place, fixed for our lives on earth, but hardly more than an illusion in the timeless memory of shifting continents. We have no recollection of Vermont as an ocean bottom heaving up into Green Mountains, only the evidence of it. We see our time in its passing, but we also see its accumulation, whether in the ribboned rocks or the thin trees sprouting up from cellar holes.

It is all so simple. Change is our continuum, and how different the land is from when it was next to Africa, and the Atlantic Ocean but a trickling stream between them. How different from when the glacier smoothed down this valley, and laid it open for the first human beings. How different from when the last passenger pigeon flew away from the forests, forever. How different now that tracks of skis cross roads and melt within the settlement of houses.

The natural world of Vermont does not stop with borders. But borders let us comprehend this one part of our world a little better.

Our arrival to this day makes sense only when we try to imagine years by the millions. The changes over days will mount to years, then to eons. There will be a future time when mountains are worn to plains and lakes are dried to land. Yet mountains will then come to other places, the rivers will cut new ways to other lakes. One hundred million years may make another earth.

And for the moment, the sun will set beyond Lake Champlain tonight and be born again to Mansfield in the morning. The brook will glaze the rocks before it slides under the snow. A bird will be ready for daybreak. May will come as it always has.

And some lives will always awaken to it.

Appendices

Appendix I — Areas to Visit

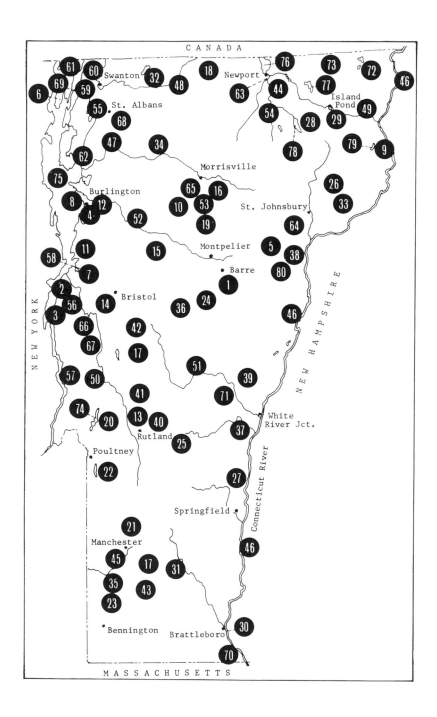

The areas are listed numerically, corresponding to their initial entries in the following section: refer to the page number in parentheses for descriptions of sites. The map is to be used in conjunction with the official Vermont state map, published by the Vermont Agency of Transportation and Agency of Development and Community Affairs, Montpelier, Vermont 05602. It is available at many locations throughout the state.

Descriptions of Areas to Visit

The areas listed below are illustrative of what is discussed in the text. In some cases they are among the best examples of these natural features, in others merely representative of many such places in Vermont. Locations are not pinpointed, but are generally indicated by large dots on the map on page 208. In the case of small or delicate environments, the interested reader will have to go to some effort to find them.

Most of the areas listed are publically owned and open at all times of the year. Maps and other descriptive material are available through state or federal agencies that administer the areas in question. A list of these agencies is included in Appendix II. For information on state parks and forests, contact the Vermont Department of Forests, Parks, and Recreation; for wildlife-management and waterfowl areas, contact the Vermont Fish and Game Department. The addresses of these departments are given in Appendix II.

Certain critical areas, such as some waterfowl-management refuges and breeding-bird islands, are closed to the public at particular times of the year or in certain sections (for example, during the nesting period or in special study areas). The reason for this is that human visitation could jeopardize breeding or interfere with scientific research. These areas are specified. Permission from the refuge manager or other appropriate authority is absolutely required for entry.

Many excellent natural areas are in private ownership, and out of respect for the owners are not listed here. For those who wish to go farther afield in search of such areas, research of the literature will lead them in the proper direction. But before attempting to enter new regions, everyone should be mindful of the rights and wishes of the landowner. The privately owned sites where visitors are welcome are listed here, with sources for additional information on them.

A special note of *caution.* Alpine areas and bogs are among the state's most fragile natural communities and need to be treated with respect. When you visit such an area please be aware of your presence and actions. As explained in the chapters on these environments, the picking of plants or careless footsteps may destroy valuable components of the communities or even change their composition permanently. Many of the plants are endangered and are protected by state and, in some cases, federal laws. Furthermore, it is illegal to pick or uproot any plant on state property without a permit. But beyond its illegality, taking from these unique areas for selfish reasons robs both ourselves and our children of a beautiful, priceless, rightful inheritance.

Chapter I. To Move the World

Barre Granite Quarries (1)*. The Rock of Ages quarry is the largest granite quarry in the world, extracting this important igneous rock down to 350 feet. The granite here is older than most found in the Northeastern Highlands or the White Mountains, and of special quality.

---

*The number in parentheses following each entry refers to the dot on the map.

The quarry may be viewed from an observation platform or on a short train ride. Literature and other information on the rock, its geology and uses, and the industry based upon it are available. For more information contact the Rock of Ages Corporation, Barre, Vermont 05641.

Button Bay State Park (2). 225 acres. Fossilized corals, snails, and other prehistoric animals are present in the limestone of Button Island Natural Area and on the mainland shore. The nature center (open summer only) has exhibits of many geological items and formations. The name Button Bay comes from the peculiar button-shaped rocks formed in the clays of the area.

D.A.R. State Park (3). 183 acres. Fossil trilobites, brachiopods, and bryozoans can be seen in the beach limestones, along with good examples of shale.

East Woods Natural Area (4). 100 acres. This is an important research and education site, used primarily by the University of Vermont as an example of a mature northern-hardwood forest, but the area is actually composed of great sand dunes that once were on the shore of the Champlain Sea. Owned by the University of Vermont. No large groups

Groton State Forest. A view from Owl's Head toward Kettle Pond, showing the Piedmont peaks, the smooth valleys that the glacier helped to shape, and the long ponds so prevalent in east-central Vermont.

permitted. For more information contact the Environmental Program, University of Vermont, Burlington, Vermont 05405.

Groton State Forest (5). 26,132 acres. This large forest contains abundant evidence of the glaciers: north-south elongated ponds and lakes, till, erratics, blocked drainages giving rise to wetlands, U-shaped valleys, and rounded peaks. *Noyes Pond (Seyon Ranch Fishing Area,* 4,000 acres) is an excellent example of the work of a valley glacier, active after the continental glacier left the area. Such features as the cirque (carved basin), tarn (lake at the bottom of the basin—dammed and modified by man in this case), and outwash plain are all evident.

Isle La Motte (6). One of the most important geological areas of the state, containing the oldest fossil coral reef in the world. This 500-million-year-old reef can be seen from the island roads, as it outcrops smoothly in the fields. All the areas are on private property, and permission to enter is required. Inquire at the Town Clerk's Office, Isle La Motte, Vermont 05463.

Kingsland Bay State Park (7). 128 acres. Fossils occur in the limestone ledges along the shore. The park is at present undeveloped and has no facilities.

Lone Rock Point (8). 100 acres. One of the best views of thrust-fault formations in the eastern United States is at this site. Here the Champlain Thrust Fault outcrops into the lake, showing the older dolostone lying on top of the younger shale. The best panoramas are from the lake. The land is owned by the Vermont Episcopal diocese and visitors are requested to obtain prior approval before entering the property. Write the Episcopal Diocesan Center, Rock Point, Burlington, Vermont 05401.

Maidstone State Forest (9). 471 acres. This heavily glaciated area has a great deal of deposition, owing to the activity of the last glacier. An unsorted collection of boulders, gravel, sand, and erratics are everywhere in evidence.

Mount Mansfield State Forest (10). 33,692 acres. This very large state forest comprises many interesting features. *Little River Campground* sits atop a large, sandy delta formed in a glacial lake. *Nebraska Valley,* some of it in private ownership, contains fine examples of the work of a valley glacier that existed here after the continental glacier left. The cirque and associated features are from a geologist's point of view among the best in the entire United States. The large delta, kame terrace, lateral and terminal moraines (formed by the valley glacier), tarn (Lake Mansfield, privately owned), and the beautifully sculpted cirque basin can be seen in large part on a drive up the valley road. On *Mount Mansfield* itself, the glacier left evidence that it reached that high: the large erratic "Drift Rock" perched alone on the summit, deep scratches (striae) in the bedrock where rocks were dragged over the surface, and the different topographies of the two exposures—the smoothly sloping west flank, where the glacier passed over, and the steep cliffs of the east side, where it plucked rocks away. Scenic *Smugglers Notch* is a unique sinuous way through the Green Mountain range, carved by now defunct rivers that once flowed down either side in a series of complicated postglacial events. Most of these areas are owned by the Vermont Department of Forests, Parks, and Recreation, but the summit of Mount Mansfield is owned by the University of Vermont.

Mount Philo State Park (11). 172 acres. This "mountain" is actually an isolated part of the Champlain Thrust Fault, with older quartzite and dolostone pushed over and on top of younger shales. Evidence of the Champlain Sea is in the marine-beach gravels just west of the park, and of Lake Vermont in lake-beach gravels on both east and west sides of the mountain. These features indicate that Mount Philo in prehistoric times was an island, with waves lapping its shores. Excellent views of the Champlain basin can be seen from the summit, reached via a toll road.

Redstone Quarry Natural Area (12). 3 acres. This unused quarry within the city limits of Burlington is now an education and research site owned by the University of Vermont. The red quartzite once quarried here for building material, along with the lighter-colored dolostone, represents the time 400 to 500 million years ago when this area was a seashore beach or estuary, then the bottom of a shallow sea. The rocks exposed in some places show pits, ripples, and holes where rain once fell, the currents passed, and worms lived. No large groups permitted. For further information contact the Environmental Program, University of Vermont, Burlington, Vermont 05405.

Miller Brook Cirque, Nebraska Valley. The beautiful carved basin of Lake Mansfield and related features are geologically some of the most important areas in Vermont. See the text for discussion of these features.

Vermont Marble Exhibit (13). Displays of both local and foreign marble can be seen here, with information given on the rock's formation, uses, and Vermont's industry based on it. Marble is the important rock of this region of Vermont, along with slate. Operated by the Vermont Marble Company. For more information contact the company in Proctor, Vermont 05765.

Weybridge Cave Natural Area (14). 97 acres. The large cave in this undeveloped state park was formed by the dissolving of limestone bedrock. Interesting geological formations are associated with the cave, and it is possible (we don't know for certain) that this is an important roosting and hibernating place for bats. *Caution:* This cave is suitable for exploration only by expert spelunkers, as no provisions for public access have been made; it is deep and very dangerous. Owned by the Vermont Department of Forests, Parks, and Recreation.

Chapter 2. Physiographic Regions of Vermont

The Green Mountains

The entire length of the Green Mountains may be traveled on Route 100,

Camel's Hump State Park. This 17,000-acre park has many faces. The forest below 2500 feet is managed for multiple uses, while above that elevation it is preserved as a natural area. The 10-acre tundra summit, containing many rare arctic-plant species, is patrolled by ranger-naturalists.

with many fine views along the way. In addition, on the western side of the range Routes 7 and 116 offer similar vistas.

Camel's Hump State Park (15). 17,356 acres. This important segment of the Green Mountain range contains Camel's Hump, the fourth-highest peak in Vermont, and provides excellent views of the state. Many hiking trails to the summit, including the Long Trail.

Elmore State Park (16). 709 acres. This park is at the north end of the Worcester range, an important subrange of the Green Mountains. From the summit of Mount Elmore are good views of this range, more of the Green Mountains, and the White Mountains of New Hampshire.

Green Mountain National Forest (17). 250,000 acres. This extensive forest encompasses much of the southern half of the Green Mountain range. The Long Trail runs its entire length and the Appalachian Trail goes as far north as Route 4. Many interesting natural features occur along its length.

Jay State Forest (18). 1,400 acres. The northernmost state forest in this range through which the Long Trail passes.

The Worcester Range. This range east of the main line of the Green Mountains is seen here from the west, near Waterbury. Putnam State Forest occupies most of the Waterbury area.

Mount Mansfield State Forest (10). 33,692 acres. Many hiking trails in this region go to the summit of Mount Mansfield and give overviews of the state. The toll road and privately run gondola operate in the summer, taking visitors on a scenic ride to the summit and near it. Summit owned by the University of Vermont, Burlington, Vermont 05405, but open to the public.

Putnam State Forest (19). 12,260 acres. A hiking trail to Mount Hunger and White Rocks leads to excellent views of other parts of Vermont, including the wide glacier-carved valley between the Worcesters and Green Mountains.

The Taconic Mountains

Bomoseen and Half Moon State Parks (20). 2,739 acres. Situated at the extreme northern end of the Taconics, these parks provide views of the gentle old mountains and of the abandoned slate quarries so extensive in the region.

Emerald Lake State Park (21). 430 acres. The western portion of the park is in the Taconics, and Dorset Peak, the highest in that range, can be seen nearby.

Lake St. Catherine State Park (22). 117 acres. The park offers good views of the mountains.

The Valley of Vermont

The Valley of Vermont can be traveled in its entirety along Route 7.

Emerald Lake State Park (21). 430 acres. This park is situated at the narrowest place in the valley, where the Green Mountains and Taconics rise sharply within a few hundred yards of each other.

Shaftsbury State Park (23). 88 acres. This park lies within the Valley of Vermont, and the calcium-based rocks of the area are reflected in the kinds of vegetation growing, which can be well observed along a pleasant nature trail that goes around the lake.

The Champlain Lowlands

Many state parks and other public property display the low relief and topography of this region. Most are within or near the agricultural lands the area is known for, featuring its heavy clayey soils. For other parks in the region, consult the various guides and maps.

Mount Philo State Park (11). 172 acres. This park probably gives the best overall view of the lowlands, reached by way of a toll road.

The Vermont Piedmont

Allis State Park (24). 487 acres. An excellent panorama of the Piedmont can be seen from the summit of Bear Mountain, within the park, where a fire tower stands.

Calvin Coolidge State Forest (25). 17,949 acres. This large forest area shows typical Piedmont characteristics, with smaller monadnocks, worn relief, and valleys filled in with glacial till. The forest is within easy reach of the asbestos, talc, garnet, and other igneous-mineral deposits that are found in the Piedmont.

Darling State Park (26). 2,029 acres. Burke Mountain, within the park, is a granitic monadnock of 3,244-foot elevation, up which a privately maintained toll road runs. This road and the mountain's many hiking trails offer good views north to the gouged basin of Lake Willoughby. Although state owned, the park is leased to a private company, Burke Mountain Recreation, Inc., East Burke, Vermont 05832.

Groton State Forest (5). 26,132 acres. The views from Owl's Head (reached via a dirt road and a short, easy trail) and other peaks within

The Champlain Lowlands. A view of land-use patterns and, in the distance (top right), of Snake Mountain, from Bristol Cliffs. Snake Mountain is part of the Champlain Thrust Fault, the line of which can be seen running south here (to the left).

this area show many of the Piedmont features—worn hills and mountains, numerous small ponds and lakes, and so on.

Mount Ascutney State Park (27). 1,984 acres. The mountain itself is a fine example of an igneous monadnock, 3,144 feet high. A toll road and hiking trails take the visitor to fine views of the surrounding countryside and the Connecticut River Valley.

The Northeastern Highlands

Vermont Route 105 passes through the scenic beauty of these lands.

Brighton State Park (29). 152 acres. One of two state parks in the region, Brighton shows kettles and other works of glaciation, and one can see the granite hills of the surrounding area.

Maidstone State Forest (9). 471 acres. More remote than Brighton State Park, this forest offers ample evidence of the structure and formation of the "Granite Hills" of Vermont.

Willoughby State Forest (28). 7,125 acres. Trails to the summit of Mount Pisgah on the east side of Lake Willoughby offer outstanding views of the area and show typical Highland structures in a more northern environment.

Chapter 3. Before We Came

This chapter sets the stage for what is to follow in greater detail in subsequent chapters. Virgin forests mentioned in the text are listed under the coniferous and hardwood categories in the material accompanying chapters six and seven.

Chapter 4. People Arrive in Vermont

Most Indian sites in the state have vanished and are known only through the evidence uncovered by archaeological excavations or the occasional discovery of artifacts; the digs are not suitable for the casual visitor. Later Vermont civilization, especially as it relates to impacts on the natural resources, can be studied largely by "reading the landscape." Many areas have noteworthy local histories. Community historical societies as well as the Vermont Historical Society, in Montpelier, are most helpful holders of this information.

Brighton State Park (29). 152 acres. Spectacle Pond, within the park, apparently was the site of the council fires of the Iroquois Five Nations and was part of the migration route of the St. Francis Indians, traveling from Canada to the Atlantic coast. Logging of the great white pines is evident here in the huge stumps standing throughout the park.

Fort Dummer State Park (30). 217 acres. This was the site of the first permanent white settlement in Vermont in 1724. The fort was built to protect what was then a Massachusetts colony from invasion by the French and Indians.

Groton State Forest (5). 26,132 acres. Old mill sites, railroad beds, and other remnants of an earlier time show the extent of a great logging industry here. A brief account of its history, along with some spots to visit, are contained in a self-guiding booklet available at the various campgrounds in the forest.

Jamaica State Park (31). 42 acres. Archaeological evidence of Indian settlements.

Lake Carmi State Park (32). 482 acres. There is evidence of Indian settlements near the lake, and an old railroad bed in the park indicates a former route to Canada. Some of the land in this park is private.

Mount Mansfield State Forest (10). 33,692 acres. The *Little River Block* especially (the southern portion, off the campground) has many old stone walls, foundations of farmhouses and barns, cemeteries, and other indications of the past uses of this forestland. An extensive self-guiding trail from Little River Campground visits some of the farm sites, which are now grown to woodland.

Victory Basin Wildlife Management Area (33). 4,790 acres. Evidence is plentiful here of an extensive old logging operation, as seen in the extant railroad beds, camps, and mill sites.

Lake Willoughby. The cliffs of Mount Pisgah rise on the left, those of Mount Hor on the right. This view is from the northern end of the lake, looking south.

Chapter 5. Alpine Communities

Caution: As stated earlier, to protect these environments all visitors should exercise good judgment and extreme care. You are asked to stay on the rock trails, off the vegetation, and to disturb no living thing. Only this way can the plants have a chance to survive.

Camel's Hump State Park (15). 17,356 acres. The Camel's Hump summit of only 10 acres contains the second-largest area of tundra in Vermont, one of only two. Access is by hiking trails only.

Mount Mansfield Summit (within Mount Mansfield State Forest, 10). 250 acres. This highest peak in Vermont holds the largest tract of tundra in the state. It can be reached by hiking trails, a toll-road, or, part way, by gondola (the last two means are privately operated). Owned by the University of Vermont, Burlington, Vermont 05405 but open to the public.

Mount Pisgah (within Willoughby State Forest, 28). 500 acres. The cliffs here harbor many alpine plants. No trails lead directly to this area, but a hiking trail to the top of the cliffs allows for a view of the habitat, as well as spectacular surrounding scenery.

Smugglers Notch (within Mount Mansfield State Forest, 10). 20 acres. This part of the state forest is home to many rare alpine plants and is a great tourist attraction. No trail access, but many pull-offs along the road offer views. Most of the cliffs are owned by the Vermont Department of Forests, Parks, and Recreation.

Chapter 6. Coniferous Forests

Brighton State Park (29). 152 acres. The huge stumps in the park are evidence of a virgin white-pine forest that existed until 1900. An excellent stand of red pine is located on the sandy east side of Spectacle Pond. The area north and east of the park—most of it owned by pulp and paper companies—is the most extensive spruce-fir forest of lower elevations in Vermont.

Calvin Coolidge State Forest (25). 17,949 acres. In this predominantly hardwood forest *Tinker Brook Natural Area* is a 15-acre virgin stand of red spruce and hemlock, growing on the banks of the brook ravine.

Cambridge State Forest (34). 25 acres. This small area contains a splendid stand of virgin white pine and hemlock on both sides of a stream, where the banks are deep and drop off sharply.

Canfield-Fisher White Pine Forest (35). 13 acres. Another fine virgin stand of white pine, on a slope. This area was the retreat of the well-known Vermont writer Dorothy Canfield Fisher. Owned by the Vermont Department of Forests, Parks, and Recreation.

Granville Gulf Reservation (36). 1,171 acres. A small section of 6 acres here supports a virgin, or near-virgin, stand of red spruce and hemlock, located on the cool, steep eastern slopes. Owned by the Vermont Department of Forests, Parks, and Recreation.

Quechee Gorge (37). 10 acres. A portion of the gorge contains untouched mixed forest, with many boreal species of plants growing below it or on the near-vertical ledges. Owned by the U. S. Army Corps of Engineers, regional office in North Springfield, Vermont 05150.

Roy Mountain Wildlife Area (38). 1,187 acres. A fine 57-acre stand of native red pine is located within this fish-and-game land, and is a registered natural area of the Society of American Foresters, as well as a state natural area.

Victory Basin Wildlife Management Area (33). 4,790 acres. This is a region of wild swamps, forests, and a few boglike sections. It is one of Vermont's best, most extensive boreal-forest realms.

The alpine boreal forest is well developed and in many cases along mountain ranges has not been touched by human beings. It can be seen particularly well at *Mount Mansfield State Forest* (10), *Camel's Hump State Park* (15), *Putnam State Forest* (19), and *Willoughby State Forest* (28), as well as in other forests in the state.

Chapter 7. The Northern Hardwoods

The bulk of state and national forests in Vermont are of the hemlock—northern-hardwood association, or hardwoods and softwoods mixed. Hence a visit to areas mentioned previously as well as many others will reveal the ecology and natural history of these environments. The places listed below have some special attributes beyond the "generalized" forest, most being undisturbed virgin-forest tracts.

Bomoseen and Half Moon State Parks (22). 2,739 acres. Sections on the hills within the parks have stands of oak-hickory climax, with elsewhere much red cedar, common juniper, and the more standard northern hardwoods.

Downer State Forest (39). 800 acres. Though small this is an operating model for forest management, with plantations (mostly in softwoods), timber-stand improvement, research projects, and the demonstration of various silvicultural techniques.

Gifford Woods State Park (40). 114 acres. A 5-acre parcel on the east side of Route 100 has a stand of virgin hardwoods, including sugar maple, white ash, yellow birch, American beech, and many others. This is one of the very few such stands left in the state, and it has been designated a National Natural Landmark by the National Park Service.

Green Mountain National Forest (17). 250,000 acres. Forests of many characters are comprised in this large, complex system, and much of it is managed for multiple use. *Lookoff Mountain Maple-Beech Forest* (41) is a 100-acre tract within it that has been registered as a state natural area; old hardwoods grow on the west slope of the mountain. Though not strictly virgin, two forests here have been designated wilderness areas, to be left untouched except for hiking, backwoods camping, hunting, fishing, cross-country skiing, and other compatible recreational uses: *Bristol Cliffs* (42), 4,495 acres in the northern section, and *Lye Brook* (43), 14,300 acres in the southern. A permit to use these areas is mandatory and may be obtained from the U.S. Forest Service offices listed in Appendix II.

Groton State Forest (5). 26,132 acres. Part of this forest is an isolated 25-acre tract on Lord's Hill, where impressive virgin hardwoods and some conifers exist—one of the best stands in the Northeast. Access to this area is by logging road only.

Chapters 8 and 9. Brooks and Streams; Rivers

It is impossible here to list all the significant waterways of Vermont, so just the most noteworthy appear. In addition, some waterfalls and gorges are pointed out, for their beauty and because they serve to indicate youthful streams and rivers. *Caution*, however: these features are dangerous areas for climbing—visitors should not attempt to hike up or beside the falls. For a thorough delineation of the distribution of the state's fish species, the reader may refer to the Vermont Fish and Game Department's map "Vermont Guide to Fishing," which shows all the rivers and streams and their fish. All navigable waters are state owned, though access to them may be restricted by private ownership of the surrounding land.

Arrowhead Mountain Reservoir. This impoundment accentuates the sinuous curves of an old-age section of the Lamoille River, not far from Lake Champlain. The sands and silts deposited by the river collect on the inner curve, building large flats that are exposed when the reservoir is drawn down. Such exposed areas are good places to see migrating shorebirds in the late summer and early fall. The "knobs" of mountains in the near background show the line of the Hinesburg Thrust Fault, running from near Bristol, Vermont, north into Canada. See the text for descriptions of thrust faults.

Barton River (44), running north-south, is a major tributary of Lake Memphremagog, having important wetlands associated with it as it enters the lake.

Batten Kill (45) in southern Vermont is famous for trout fishing. It is a subsequent river for part of its course, and superimposed through the Taconic Mountains.

Connecticut River (46). This is the largest, longest river associated with Vermont, but it is actually controlled by New Hampshire. It has been a major waterway for transportation to and through Vermont throughout human history, with the state's first white settlers from the south inhabiting its shores. It is geologically significant for the glacial record it has kept.

Lamoille River (47) is another major river on the west side of the state. It is superimposed on the Green Mountains. Marshes and swamps at the Sand Bar Waterfowl Area occupy the site of old river-delta deposits into Lake Champlain. It is used by some overwintering ducks where the waters stay open.

Missisquoi River (48). This superimposed river in the northern reaches of the Green Mountains is especially important for the large delta formed at its mouth, which supports an extensive wetland area. It is also the principal spawning ground in the northern part of the state for muskellunge and walleye.

Nulhegan River (49). A northern tributary of the Connecticut River, the Nulhegan and the smaller streams that drain into it from the north are integral to the moist, boggy, swampy areas of boreal forest in the region. This is the river the famous Rogers' Rangers traveled down in their escape from the St. Francis Indians, before Vermont was settled by whites.

Otter Creek (50) is the longest river within Vermont's borders, known by early Indians as one of the best fishing areas in the state. It was also an important Indian passageway and a transportation route for early white trappers. The present river was preceded by an ancient one before glaciation, which left great deltas near Brandon. The modern Otter Creek is a meandering subsequent river with major wetlands at its lower end, near Lake Champlain.

White River (51) is a long, winding river that flows east from the Green Mountains to the Connecticut River. Its valley was once a long arm of the post glacial Lake Upham.

Winooski River (52). Indians considered this an excellent river for fishing and a major way into the interior of Vermont. (They called it Winooski, meaning "onion," supposedly because of the great numbers of wild leeks growing on its rich banks.) It is a splendid example both of a superimposed river and of a U-shaped valley that was re-formed by the continental glacier. Valuable and extensive wetlands lie at its mouth as it enters Lake Champlain, where some ducks and other water birds remain in winter. Much of the area of Colchester sits on a massive delta formed when the river dumped its sands into Lake Vermont and the

Champlain Sea. Interstate Route 89 travels through this valley, affording good views of the river.

Granville Gulf Reservation (36). 1,171 acres. *Moss Glen Falls* can be seen here, on the west side of Route 100, cascading down the sheer rock face. Owned by the Vermont Department of Forests, Parks, and Recreation.

Green Mountain National Forest (17). 250,000 acres. The *Falls of Lana* are long, sinuous, and precipitous; they can be reached by trails from Silver Lake and Branbury State Park, near Lake Dunmore. *Texas Falls* is another scenic attraction, also in the northern sector of the National Forest.

Quechee Gorge, of the Ottauquechee River. View of the bridge over the gorge.

Moss Glen Falls (53). Near Stowe, this is a newly acquired access to the long, picturesque series of falls through a forested region. The falls are now part of *Putnam State Forest* (19).

Quechee Gorge (37). The gorge is an outstanding example of a river's (the Ottauquechee) cutting its way through metamorphic bedrock (schist), making a spectacular steep-walled valley more than 160 feet deep. Owned by the U.S. Army Corps of Engineers, regional office in North Springfield, Vermont 05150.

Willoughby Falls Wildlife Management Area (54). 130 acres. The Willoughby River in this section, owned and managed by the Vermont Fish and Game Department, is where the spectacular spawning runs of the steelhead rainbow trout may be observed and fished in early spring.

Chapter 10. *Marshes*

Visitors to marshes should keep two things in mind: the need to be well prepared for the special physical conditions, and the necessity of not disturbing the birds during their nesting season. The first requirement includes equipping oneself with information about the area, maps, and a canoe (essential in many marshes), and learning of any special precautions to take. Observing the second requirement is simple, since spring and summer are the critical times for nesting and the rearing of young birds—it is then that care should be taken when visiting, for human traffic can disrupt breeding cycles, even causing the failure of birds to breed.

The Vermont Fish and Game Department owns and manages 17 waterfowl areas, mostly marshes, comprising more than 8,000 acres. The U.S. Fish and Wildlife Service has one area in the state, of 5,661 acres.

Most marshes of substantial acreage are attractive to bird-watchers and waterfowl hunters. For more information on species and good areas for birding, consult *Birds of Vermont* (See Appendix III); for rules and regulations regarding hunting, contact the Vermont Fish and Game Department and the Missisquoi National Wildlife Refuge.

Black Creek Waterfowl Area (55). 158 acres. A relatively small marsh, located near St. Albans Bay State Park, accessible only by water.

Dead Creek Wildlife Management Area (56). 2,630 acres. The lengthy impoundments are maintained, regulated, and managed by the Fish and Game Department, and part of the river is free-flowing. The marsh complexes are among the most important in the state for waterfowl of many kinds and other species. Numerous access points are available by water, but most of the area can be seen from lookout stations and roadside pull-offs at several places. Part of the area requires permission from the year-round manager for visitation. There is also a controlled goose-hunting area near the headquarters. Office: R.F.D.#1, Box 130, Vergennes, Vermont 05491.

East Creek Waterfowl Area (57). 398 acres. This shallow marsh is visible from several locations along roads, and portions are boatable by canoe only.

Little Otter Creek Marsh (58). 1,048 acres. This highly valued area is one of the most extensive unspoiled marshes in Vermont. Many species of waterfowl and water-based birds nest here, including the black tern. The marsh can be well explored only by boat or canoe, though it can be reached via fishing-access areas or through private fields. Much of the marsh is owned by the Vermont Fish and Game Department, but some of it is in private holdings.

Maquam Bay Waterfowl Area (59). 391 acres. A medium-sized marsh adjacent to the Missisquoi National Wildlife Refuge, it augments the marshlands of this northern area. It is accessible by boat or canoe only.

Missisquoi National Wildlife Refuge (60). 5,561 acres. This refuge contains great expanses of marsh and swamp associated with Lake Champlain, the Missisquoi River, and its delta. Large numbers of migratory and nesting birds have been recorded here. Most of the refuge is accessible only by boat or canoe, and visitors must have permission from the refuge manager before entering. (R.F.D. #2, Swanton, Vermont 05091). Some of the marshland is private property, but most of it is federally owned.

Dead Creek Waterfowl Area. This area, adjacent to Lake Champlain (at top of photograph), is one of the state's most important for migratory and nesting birds, both waterfowl and others. See the text, page 225, discussion.

Mud Creek Waterfowl Area (61). 1,019 acres. An important impound-ment on Mud Creek has created a good habitat for waterfowl and other birds. It can be reached on foot as well as by canoe.

Sand Bar Waterfowl Area (62). 1,668 acres. One of the state's most important refuges for nesting waterfowl and other birds, as well as for migrating species. The marshes are only part of the whole wetland area. Some of the area can be viewed from Route 2, which travels through the refuge, although canoeing provides the best observations. Visitors must obtain permission to enter from the refuge manager, R.D., Sand Bar, Milton, Vermont 05468.

South Bay Wildlife Management Area (63). 1,545 acres. The large Coventry Marsh occupies the mouth of the Barton River where it empties into South Bay of Lake Memphremagog. The marshlands are best seen from the water but a road that parallels the marsh on the east side and railroad tracks through the area offer excellent hiking possibili-ties. One of the finest marshes outside the Lake Champlain region, it features many boggy characteristics.

Chapter 11. Bogs

Bogs are some of the most interesting yet delicate of our natural areas. Visitors are therefore implored to remember the fragility and irreplaceable beauty there, and leave everything as it lives. *Caution:* because of the floating mat, many bogs present tough going for hikers — people have trouble getting through the thick tangle of shrubs or may sink down into the mat and find it difficult to walk. In view of this, it is a good idea not to go alone into bogs and when there to watch one's footing at all time.

Green Mountain National Forest (17). 250,000 acres. *Lost Pond Bog* is a 10-acre bog within the national forest, near the Long Trail, and has a quaking sphagnum-moss mat and some open water.

Groton State Forest (5). 26,132 acres. 200-acre *Peacham Bog* is one of the more extensive treed bog systems in the state, where black spruce and tamarack dominate, with shrubs underneath. Trail access is from the nature center in the forest.

Lake Carmi State Park (32). 482 acres. *Lake Carmi Black Spruce–Tamarack Bog* covers more than 200 acres; much of it is on private land but a portion of it is part of the state park, through which a road passes. This is a mature bog with abundant tree cover in black spruce and tamarack, many shrubs, and typical bog plants.

Lucy M. Bugbee Bog (64). 12 acres. The limestone-bearing bedrock makes this bog less acid than many other bogs, encouraging a different type of bog flora. The trees are mostly tamarack and white cedar, with a rich understory. No open water in the bog, and no trail access. Named after a champion of wild-flower protection in Vermont. Owned by the Vermont Department of Forests, Parks, and Recreation.

Morrisville Bog (65). 30 acres. This is a predominantly black-spruce bog with a sphagnum mat, Labrador tea, pitcher plants, and other bog plants. No trail access. Owned by the Vermont Department of Forests, Parks, and Recreation.

Snake Mountain Wildlife Management Area (66). 999 acres. The 10-acre *Cranberry Bog* sits within this high-elevation area, near the summit of Snake Mountain. A more or less typical kettle bog, with no open water but trail access from the base of the mountain.

Chapter 12. Swamps

The same words of warning apply here as in marshes: know where you are going, be prepared for adverse conditions, and do not disturb breeding birds in season. In addition, most swamps are without trail systems, so it is easy to become disoriented and even lost. A compass and map are good tools to take along.

Cornwall Swamp Wildlife Management Area (67). 1,380 acres. This wild-red-maple and cedar swamp along Otter Creek has best access by foot, off a road that passes east-west through the forest. The large swamp lacks well-defined trails.

Fairfield Swamp Wildlife Management Area (68). 1,153 acres. This extensive swamp was created by a dam impoundment and is composed mostly of white cedar. It is a good area for herons and ducks. Best access is by canoe, but Route 36 crosses it from east to west.

Lake Carmi State Park (32). 482 acres. A hemlock–red-maple–tamarack swamp lies within the park, adjacent to the bog. It can be seen easily and "dryly" from the abandoned railroad bed that runs its entire length. Although situated in a state park, much of the swamp is privately owned.

Missisquoi National Wildlife Refuge (60). 5,561 acres. A fine silver-maple–swamp-white-oak swamp grows at the edges of the marshes and in the impoundments where they are subject to seasonal flooding. The swamp is alive in summer with wood and numerous other ducks, black-crowned night herons, great blue herons, and countless songbirds. Permission from the refuge manager (R.F.D. #2, Swanton, Vermont 05091) is required for entry, and the best views are taken by boat or canoe. A nature trail near the headquarters leads visitors through a small sample of the forest.

North Hero State Park (69). 399 acres. Part of the park near Lake Champlain contains a silver-maple–swamp-white-oak swamp that can be reached by a hiking trail.

Sand Bar Waterfowl Area (62). 1,668 acres. Another excellent silver-maple–swamp-white-oak swamp grows in conjunction with the Lamoille River, its delta, and the marshes of the waterfowl area. This important area for a great many birds and mammals can be seen best from a boat or canoe, but the general lay of the land can be gathered from the road. Permission from the refuge manager is necessary for entry: R.F.D., Sand Bar, Milton, Vermont 05468.

Vernon Black Gum Swamps (70). 60 acres. A series of four black-gum swamps are the best stands in the state, containing aged specimens of the black gum and other more southern species of plants. The swamps are owned by the town of Vernon and maintained as a natural area; no large groups are permitted, and visitors are asked to inquire of the Vernon town clerk for directions to swamps: Town Clerk's Office, Vernon, Vermont 05354.

Victory Basin Wildlife Management Area (33). 4,790 acres. Within this area are extensive tracts of spruce fir tamarack red-maple swamps, mixed with more upland forest types, boggy areas, and some marshlands.

Chapter 13. Ponds and Lakes

As in the case of rivers, the important ponds and lakes in Vermont are simply too numerous to mention in their entirety here. Again, consult the "Vermont Guide to Fishing" for the spectrum of bodies of water and the species of fish living in them. All navigable waters are owned by the state, but often access to them is privately controlled, except where the state has purchased or been granted right-of-way.

Amity Pond Natural Area (71). 182 acres. This very small pond and surrounding land have been designated a natural area of the Vermont Department of Forests, Parks, and Recreation, which owns it.

Green Mountain National Forest (17). 250,000 acres. The forest contains several natural and unspoiled lakes and ponds, many of which are within close hiking distance of the Long Trail. Several are high-elevation ponds with boglike characteristics and shore vegetation. *Wallingford Pond* (81 acres), *Bourn Pond* (65 acres), *Fifield Pond* (20 acres), *Griffith Lake* (18 acres), and *Branch Pond* (53 acres) are all splendid natural areas here.

Great Averill Pond (72). 847 acres. This and its close companion, *Little Averill Pond* (482 acres), are important deep-water lakes of the Northeastern Highlands, containing lake trout and other cold-water species. State-owned fishing access.

Groton State Forest (5). 26,132 acres. The state forest contains several nice undeveloped lakes (called ponds): *Marshfield Pond, Kettle Pond,* and *Osmore Pond.*

Hurricane Brook Wildlife Management Area (73). 9,386 acres. This large area encompasses many ecosystems and provides important habitat for black bear and other animals. Included are fine examples of unspoiled ponds and lakes, some officially designated prime natural areas of Vermont. *Beaver Pond, Duck Pond, Round Pond,* and *Turtle Pond* are all small (40 acres or less), in the northern sector of the management area.

Lake Bomoseen (74). 2,364 acres. The largest lake wholly within Vermont, Bomoseen contains both warm- and cold-water species of fish, including pike, large and smallmouth bass, and rainbow trout. State-owned accesses, including Bomoseen State Park.

Lake Champlain (75). 172,032 acres. An extremely important body of water for many reasons, not only because of its biological features, but also owing to its richness of geological information. Vermont shares it politically with New York and Canada. People interested in pursuing its history are directed to the references in Appendix III.

Several islands in the lake are noteworthy for the birds that nest on them in summer. The *Four Brothers Islands*, across from Shelburne Bay, (technically in New York) are a natural area owned by the University of Vermont, and are used by ring-billed and herring gulls, black-crowned night herons, cattle egrets, ducks, and other birds for nesting. West of Grand Isle is *Young Island*, a 10-acre site for nesting gulls and common terns (owned by the Vermont Fish and Game Department). North of St. Albans Bay is *Popasquash Island*, a 1-acre rocky emergence where common terns—which are actually uncommon in Vermont—nest annually (owned by the Vermont Fish and Game Department). Several other public and private islands and rock outcrops serve as breeding places in Champlain for these colonial species.

Caution: because of the small size of these islands and their critical

The Four Brothers Islands. These islands make up an important natural area in Lake Champlain, particularly for birds. Although within New York, the islands belong to the University of Vermont. See above for discussion.

importance to the nesting birds, people should not visit them in summer. Good observation may be made from a distance.

The book *Birds of Vermont* (see references, Appendix III) lists principal areas on the lake for birds and what may be expected there at various times of the year. The "Vermont Guide to Fishing" shows the distribution of game fish in the lake.

Lake Memphremagog (76). 6,317 acres. This is the second-largest lake with which Vermont has contact (it is shared with Canada). It is a major area for various species of gull and tern, with other waterfowl and many land birds living in the wetlands at the southern end. It may be viewed well from South Bay and from paved roads that run along much of its perimeter. There are several state-owned access points.

Lake Seymour (77). 1,732 acres. This is the second-largest lake entirely within Vermont. It possesses fine populations of lake trout and smelt. State-owned access areas.

Lake Willoughby (78). 1,692 acres. One often hears this lake referred to as the Lake Lucerne of Vermont, and indeed it is a uniquely beautiful area. Spectacular views of this deep, long body of water are reached by the hiking trail in *Willoughby State Forest* (28) or by road (Route 5A). It is one of the deepest lakes in New England, having been carved by the glacier in a preexisting valley. It contains a large variety of cold-water fish. A few state-owned accesses.

Maidstone Lake (79). 748 acres. Home of lake trout, landlocked salmon,

Lake Seymour. This large lake in northeastern Vermont borders on the boreal-forest realm of the state.

and smelt, this deep lake also supports loons, an occasional moose coming in to drink, and other, wilder animals. State-owned accesses, including Maidstone State Park.

Mount Mansfield State Forest (10). 33,692 acres. The high-elevation ponds are of interest as glacial relicts and for the plant life within them. They are small, shallow, and eutrophic. The largest is *Sterling Pond*, in the section of the forest north of Route 108. South of the road, nearer Mount Mansfield's summit, are *Bear Pond* and *Lake of the Clouds. Goose Pond* is in the southern portion of the forest, off the main trail. The rest of the ponds are reached by the Long Trail or other hiking trails.

Pine Mountain Wildlife Management Area (80). 2,187 acres. Within this land are two undeveloped connecting ponds, totaling 70 acres. Trail access on state-owned property.

Chapter 14. Fields, Farms, and Towns

The plants and wildlife of meadows, woodlots, woodland edges, and urban areas can be observed the length and breadth of the state, for the human presence, which created these spaces, is felt throughout. Most clearings for agriculture occur in the Champlain Valley, the Valley of Vermont, and the Connecticut River Valley, and there we expect to find the greatest array of field flora and fauna; in addition, the milder climates of these areas encourage more southerly species to infiltrate, both plants and animals.

Many of the state's farms and their operations can be viewed by the public, with prior arrangements. The Vermont Department of Community Affairs supplies brochures on these and related places and events. A sample of the selections includes "Red Clover Trail" (operating farms), "Maple Sugar Houses Open to Visitors," "Morgan Horse Farm of the University of Vermont," and "Vermont Agricultural Fairs and Field Days." For more information, contact either the Department of Community Affairs or the Vermont Department of Agriculture, both listed in Appendix II.

Appendix II

Conservation and Environmental-Education Organizations

The following are the major organizations in Vermont for conservation, land management, environmental education, and resources protection. (Organizations that deal more with local issues or that are professional scientific societies are not listed.) A few out-of-state and national organizations that have close ties to Vermont are included.

Maps, literature, checklists of plants, birds, and mammals, special-use permits, special services, and other aids for many of the public areas listed in Appendix I are available upon request from the appropriate agency below.

Audubon Societies

Several regional Vermont chapters are affiliated with the National Audubon Society. They have regular programs, conservation activities, field trips, educational services, and newsletters.

Audubon Council, c/o Vermont Institute of Natural Science, Woodstock, Vermont 05091. Composed of representatives of all Vermont chapters of Audubon. Conducts conservation, research, and educational projects on a volunteer basis, and issues public-information statements.

Ascutney Mountain Audubon Society, P.O. Box 191, Springfield, Vermont 05156.

Central Vermont Audubon Society, P.O. Box 1122, Montpelier, Vermont 05602.

Green Mountain Audubon Society, P.O. Box 33, Burlington, Vermont 05401. Owns the *Green Mountain Audubon Nature Center*, Huntington, Vermont 05462, a 250-acre establishment including headquarters, museum, trails, blinds, and library, and conducting a variety of year-round educational programs. Literature available.

Northeast Kingdom Audubon Society, c/o Fairbanks Museum, St. Johnsbury, Vermont 05819.

Otter Creek Audubon Society, P.O. Box 482, Middlebury, Vermont 05753.

Rutland County Audubon Society, P.O. Box 524, Rutland, Vermont 05701.

Southeastern Vermont Audubon Society, c/o Albert S. Watson, R.F.D. #2, Box 180, West Brattleboro, Vermont 05301.

Center for Northern Studies, Wolcott, Vermont 05680.

Concerned with scientific research and education, specializing in arctic and boreal environments. Owns 200-acre Bear Swamp and headquarters building, in which various classes and field studies are conducted.

Conservation Society of Southern Vermont, Townshend, Vermont 05353.

Legal involvement in conservation and historic-preservation matters in southern Vermont. Operates summer nature center and educational programs.

Discovery Museum, Essex Junction, Vermont 05452.

A museum geared to children, with hands-on exhibits, including animals that may be picked up. Regular programs, outdoor aviary, and short nature trails. Gift and book shop.

Ducks Unlimited, P.O. Box 66300, Chicago, Illinois 60666 (main office). Private organization dedicated to conservation of wetlands and waterfowl, with a few chapters in Vermont, promotion of wise use of this natural resource. Literature, conservation programs, meetings. For status of local chapters, contact the main office.

Fairbanks Museum, St. Johnsbury, Vermont 05818.

Exhibits, lectures, and year-round programs, for adults and schools, on a variety of natural and physical sciences. Planetarium, outdoor aviary, gift shop and bookstore.

Federated Garden Clubs of Vermont, Newfane, Vermont 05345.

Representatives of all Vermont garden clubs. Meetings, reports, conservation projects, especially as related to wild-flower preservation and promotion.

Federation of Sportsmen's Clubs, c/o Henry Ross, Randolph, Vermont 05060.

Representatives of Vermont sportsmen's clubs, sponsoring many hunter-safety programs, conservation projects, meetings, talks. Takes stands on issues.

Green Mountain Club, Inc., 43 State Street, Montpelier, Vermont 05602.

Concerned with hiking in Vermont, maintenance of the Long Trail and side trails, lodges, hiker education and safety, conservation, and public education. Runs a cooperative program with Vermont Department of Forests, Parks, and Recreation and other groups supporting the ranger-naturalists on Mount Mansfield and Camel's Hump. *Long Trail Guide*, books, and other literature available. Programs on request.

Hulbert Outdoor Education Center, Fairlee, Vermont 05405.

Year-round operation, accommodating 200 students in summer, 50 to 60 in winter: main facility, meeting rooms, tenting area on a 1,000-acre site. Conducts a variety of educational programs for schools and adults.

Keewaydin Environmental Education Center, Salisbury, Vermont 05769.

Educational camps for groups, teacher training, conservation workshops. The center has facilities for extended stays. Located on Lake Dunmore.

Lake Champlain Basin Study, The Ice House, 177 Battery Street, Burlington, Vermont 05401.

A New York–Vermont organization of the New England River Basins Commission. Addresses and recommends solutions to major water- and land-resources problems associated with Lake Champlain. Maps, educational literature available.

Lake Champlain Committee, Merchants Bank Building, South Hero, Vermont 05486.

A citizens' group involved in the protection, management, and proper use of Lake Champlain and its tributaries. Sponsors scientific study, educational approaches, and legal means to achieve its ends.

Lake Champlain Islands Trust, c/o Vermont Natural Resources Council, 7 Main Street, Montpelier, Vermont 05602.

Established in 1978, the Trust works to protect the scenic beauty, wildlife habitat, and recreational opportunities of Lake Champlain, especially its islands. Organized through voluntary agreements with island and shoreline owners and some land acquisition. Newsletter.

Merck Forest Foundation, West Rupert, Vermont 05776.

An educational center with a managed forest, natural area, demonstration area, lodgings for small groups, cross-country-ski trails. Specializes in forestry and outdoor recreation. Year-round programs.

Montshire Museum, 45 Lyme Road, Hanover, New Hampshire 03755.

A natural-history museum with collections of birds, shells, insects, minerals, reptiles, amphibians, and others. Focuses on conservation education. Year-round programs for adults and schools.

National Wildlife Federation, c/o Warner Shedd, Regional Executive, East Calais, Vermont 05650.

Northeastern chapter, including Vermont, New Hampshire, and Maine. Coordination with the national organization, conservation action on regional issues, public education. State affiliate is Vermont Natural Resources Council (see below).

Nature Conservancy, 7 Main Street, Montpelier, Vermont 05602.

Focuses on the acquisition and management of important natural areas, including forests and other valuable tracts, for scientific, educational, and preservation purposes. Newsletter, coordination with national organization.

Pember Museum, Granville, New York 12832.

Natural-history museum with large bird-egg collection, mounted birds, and related exhibits. Year-round programs for schools and the community; field trips throughout the East; nature trail in Vermont. Newsletter.

Shelburne Farms Resources, Inc., Shelburne, Vermont 05482.

An educational organization with interdisciplinary programs in agriculture, environmental education, and the arts. Operates out of a large barn, house, and coach house. Prearranged tours of the farm (June–September), teacher workshops, seminars, concerts, and other cultural events.

Sierra Club, 530 Bush Street, San Francisco, California 94108 (main office).

Two Vermont chapters in operation. Conservation action on a variety of issues, outdoor activities, field trips. For information on the status of local chapters, contact the national organization.

Society of American Foresters, Green Mountain Chapter, Room 216, Hills Science Building, University of Vermont, Burlington, Vermont 05405.

Professional organization dedicated to the advancement of forestry in many areas: education, technology, research, and application.

Trout Unlimited, 4260 East Evans Avenue, Denver, Colorado 80222 (main office).

A national organization concerned with conservation and promotion of trout species in North America, including the restoration of habitat and sound management practices. For information on the Vermont chapter, contact the main office.

University of Vermont, Burlington, Vermont 05405.

Owns and manages several important natural areas in the state; maintains a geology museum; conducts year-round programs for the community. In addition, the UVM Extension Service, Morrill Hall, offers many public-information and education programs, specializing in forest management, insect-pest control, horticulture, maple-sugaring, gardening, tree pruning, and other applied sciences; much literature available; field workshops.

U.S. Department of Agriculture

Forest Service

> *Green Mountain National Forest,* Federal Building, Rutland, Vermont 05701.
>
> Controls, administers, and manages the large National Forest in Vermont, including allied education and recreation work. For maps and literature, rules and regulations, and wilderness permits, contact the main office or one of four regional offices, located at: Catamount National Bank Building, Manchester Center, Vermont 05255; Rochester Company Building, Rochester, Vermont 05767; P.O. Box 568, Middlebury, Vermont 05753; Hector Land Use Area, Rural-Urban Center, Montour Falls, New York 14865.
>
> *Northeastern Forest Experiment Station,* 705 South Spear Street, Burlington, Vermont 05401.
>
> Conducts forest-related research in New England, specializing in sugar maples and sap production.
>
> *Soil Conservation Service,* 1 Burlington Square, Burlington, Vermont 05401 (main office).
>
> Conservation information and assistance to landowners with regard to soils, water, and land use. Maps, old land-survey records, literature available.

U.S. Department of the Interior

Fish and Wildlife Service

> *Missisquoi National Wildlife Refuge,* R.D. # 2, Swanton, Vermont 05091.
>
> Refuge established mainly for migratory waterfowl, but many other resident and migratory wildlife are also cared for. Nature trail and other areas to visit, with permission of manager. Programs, literature available.

Geological Survey, Water Resources Division, 8 East State Street, Montpelier, Vermont 05602.

Concerned with federal projects in Vermont as they relate to the quality of water and other resources. Literature, personal assistance.

Vermont Botanical and Bird Club, c/o Fred Taylor, 38 East Terrace Street, South Burlington, Vermont 05401.

Scientific interest in plants and birds. Newsletter, annual meeting, field trips. Maintains records of their proceedings.

Vermont Institute of Natural Science, Woodstock, Vermont 05091.

Private organization with educational programs year round for all age groups, school programs, workshops, field trips, and special lectures. Includes nature preserve with trails, headquarters, library, auditorium, photograph collection, exhibits. Research projects. Maintains complete records of Vermont birds. Sponsors annual Vermont Bird Conference. Publishes a newsletter monthly and *Vermont Natural History* magazine annually.

Vermont Natural Resources Council, 7 Main Street, Montpelier, Vermont 05602.

A statewide private organization affiliated with the National Wildlife Federation, promoting wise use and management of Vermont's natural resources, focusing on land-based issues. Public education, legal services, and literature available. Regional workshops in forest management and other topics. Field trips at annual meeting. Publishes a bimonthly newsletter.

Vermont Public Interest Research Group, 26 State Street, Montpelier, Vermont 05602.

Statewide private organization that researches environmental issues and problems, and works through legal means and legislative channels to address them.

Vermont, State of, main offices in Montpelier, Vermont 05602.

Agency of Development and Community Affairs

Distributes information on state events, places to visit, agricultural field days; historic preservation; promotes archaeology and cultural heritage; publication of books, periodicals, and other literature. Includes: Department of Community Affairs, Historic Preservation Division, State Archaeologist, *Vermont Life* magazine, Vermont Travel Division.

Agency of Environmental Conservation

Responsible for the administration and management of almost 230,000 acres of public lands, including state natural areas, hunting and fishing areas, state parks and forests, waterfowl areas, navigable waters, ski areas, and others. Legal and technical information. Provides services for education of public, recreation, and management of natural resources, as carried out by county foresters, park naturalists, wildlife biologists, water-resource specialists, and others. Also responsible for protection and management of Vermont's endangered species of flora and fauna. Films, special programs, and much literature available. Includes: Department of Fish and Game; Department of Forests, Parks, and Recreation; Department of Water Resources; Divisions of Environmental Engineering and Protection; State Geologist; and State Naturalist.

Regional offices:

R.F.D., North Springfield, Vermont 05150.

P.O. Box 129, Rutland, Vermont 05701.

111 West Street, Essex Junction, Vermont 05452.

R.F.D. #1, Morrisville, Vermont 05661.

P.O. Box 586, Waterbury, Vermont 05676.

180 Portland Street, St. Johnsbury, Vermont 05819.

Department of Agriculture

Concerned with the maintenance and promotion of Vermont's farming community. Technical assistance, landowner consultation, administration of federal-state programs. Literature and special programs available.

Department of Education

Includes an environmental-science coordinator, who works with schools, state agencies, and other groups to enhance environmental education in all schools in Vermont.

State Energy Office

Concerned with the wise use and conservation of energy in the state. Promotes alternate energy sources (wood energy in many cases), provides homeowner assistance and energy audits, administers federal grants, conducts special programs and educational projects, and publishes a variety of literature.

State Planning Office

Planning for land use, involving statewide conservation considerations and population projections. Maps and other literature available.

Vermont Historical Society

Deals with Vermont history from ancient geological times to the present, focusing on period soon after white settlement. Many exhibits, artifacts, films, and slide show. Extensive library. Gift shop and bookstore.

Appendix III

References
Background, General

Graham, Frank, Jr. 1971. *Man's Dominion: The Story of Conservation in America.* M. Evans and Company, New York.

Matthiessen, Peter. 1959. *Wildlife in America,* The Viking Press, New York.

Newman, Walter S., and Salwen, Bert. 1977. *Amerinds and their Paleo-environments in Northeastern North America.* Annals of the New York Academy of Science. Volume 288.

Odum, Eugene P. 1971. *Fundamentals of Ecology* (third ed.). W. B. Saunders Company, Philadelphia.

Oosting, Henry J. 1956. *The Study of Plant Communities.* W. H. Freeman and Company, San Francisco.

Press, Frank, and Siever, Raymond. 1974. *Earth.* W. H. Freeman and Company, San Francisco.

Ritchie, William A. 1965. *The Archaeology of New York State.* The Natural History Press, Garden City, N.Y.

———. 1973. *Aboriginal Settlement Patterns in the Northeast.* New York State Museum and Science Service. Memoir 20.

Russell, Howard S. 1976. *A Long, Deep Furrow: Three Centuries of Farming in New England.* University Press of New England, Hanover, N.H.

Smith, Robert L. 1966. *Ecology and Field Biology.* Harper & Row, New York.

Snow, Dean R. 1968. "Wabanaki Family Hunting Territories." *American Anthropologist* 70 (6):1143–1151.

Thomas, Peter A. 1976. "Contrastive Subsistence Strategies and Land Use as Factors for Understanding Indian-White Relations in New England." *Ethnohistory* 23 (1):1–18.

Udall, Stewart. 1963. *The Quiet Crisis.* Avon Books, New York.

Willey, Gordon R. 1966. *An Introduction to American Archaeology, Volume I: North and Middle America.* Prentice-Hall, Englewood Cliffs, N.J.

Background, Vermont

Allen, Ira. 1798. *The Natural and Political History of the State of Vermont.* J. W. Meyers, London.

Daniels, Thomas E. 1963. *Vermont Indians.* Journal Press, Poultney, Vt.

Day, Gordon M. 1971. "The Eastern Boundary of Iroquoia: Abenaki Evidence." *Man in the Northeast,* Amherst, Mass. 1:7-13.

Hagermann, Robert L. 1975 (second ed.). *Mansfield: The Story of Vermont's Loftiest Mountain.* Phoenix Publishing, Canaan, N.H.

Haviland, William A. 1970. "Archaeological Sites of the Champlain Valley." *Lake Champlain Basin Studies,* number 8. Department of Resource Economics, University of Vermont, Burlington, Vt.

Hill, Ralph Nading. 1976. *Lake Champlain: Key to Liberty.* Countryman Press and Burlington Free Press, Taftsville and Burlington, Vt.

Huden, John C. (ed.). 1971. *Archaeology in Vermont.* Charles E. Tuttle Company, Rutland, Vt.

Lake Champlain Basin Study. 1978. *Lake Champlain Atlas: Water Quality and Shoreland Use.* Sponsored by the State of New York, State of Vermont, and the New England River Basins Commission.

Marsh, George Perkins. 1864. *Man and Nature.* Scribner's, New York.

Ritchie, William A. 1953. "A Probable Paleo-Indian Site in Vermont." *American Antiquity* 18 (3):249-258.

U.S. Army Corps of Engineers. 1973. *Environmental Reconnaissance Inventory of the State of Vermont.* Engineer Agency for Resources Inventories, Washington, D.C.

Vermont Agency of Environmental Conservation. 1974. *Vermont Guide Plan for Water and Related Land Resources.* Technical Services, New England River Basins Commission, Monpelier, Vt.

Vermont Department of Budget and Management. 1975. *Vermont Facts and Figures.* State of Vermont, Department of Budget and Management, Office of Statistical Coordination, Montpelier, Vt.

Vermont State Planning Office. 1974. *Vermont Land Capability.* Vermont State Planning Office, Montpelier, Vt.

Williams, Samuel. 1794. *The Natural and Civil History of Vermont.* (n.p.), Walpole, N. H.

Works Progress Administration for the State of Vermont. 1937. *Vermont: A Guide to the Green Mountain State.* Houghton Mifflin Company, Boston.

Natural History, General

Farb, Peter. 1963. *Face of North America: The Natural History of a Continent.* Harper & Row, New York.

Jorgensen, Neil. 1977. *A Guide to New England's Landscape.* Pequot Press, Chester, Conn.

———. 1978. *A Sierra Club Naturalist's Guide to Southern New England.* Sierra Club Books, San Francisco.

Lull, Howard W. 1968. *A Forest Atlas of the Northeast.* Northeastern Forest Experiment Station, Forest Service, U. S. Department of Agriculture, Upper Darby, Pa.

Palmer, E. Laurence, and Fowler, H. Seymour. 1975. *Fieldbook of Natural History* (second ed.). McGraw-Hill Book Company, New York.

Society of American Foresters. 1954 (reprinted 1975). *Forest Cover Types of North America.* Society of American Foresters, Bethesda, Md.

Thomson, Betty F. 1958. *The Changing Face of New England.* Macmillan Company, New York.

Trippensee, Reuben E. 1948. *Wildlife Management* (2 vols.). McGraw-Hill Book Company, New York.

Watts, May Theilgaard. 1957. *Reading the Landscape.* Macmillan Company, New York.

Natural History, Vermont

Borie, Louis. 1977. *University of Vermont Natural Areas.* Environmental Program, University of Vermont, Burlington, Vt.

Foote, Leonard E. 1946. *A History of Wild Game in Vermont.* Vermont Fish and Game Service Bulletin, Montpelier, Vt.

Hard, Walter R., Jr. (ed.). 1967. *Vermont Life Book of Nature.* The Stephen Greene Press, Brattleboro, Vt.

Klein, Robert. 1976. *Technical Report: Vermont Natural Areas Project (Phase II).* Vermont Natural Resources Council, Montpelier, Vt.

Perry, Florence J. 1964. *Progress Report of the Vermont Fish and Game Department.* Montpelier, Vt.

Thompson, Zadock. 1853. *Natural History of Vermont.* Originally published by the author, 1853. Reprinted in 1972 by Charles E. Tuttle Company, Rutland, Vt.

Vermont Institute of Natural Science. 1973–79. *Vermont Natural History* (magazine). VINS, Woodstock, Vt.

Vermont, State of. 1975. "Endangered Species List." Agency of Environmental Conservation, Montpelier, Vt.

Vogelmann, Hubert W. 1964 (reprinted 1971). *Natural Areas in Vermont: Some Ecological Sites of Public Importance.* Report 1. Vermont Agricultural Experiment Station, University of Vermont, Burlington, Vt.

———. 1969. *Vermont Natural Areas.* Report 2. Central Planning Office and Interagency Committee on Natural Resources, Montpelier, Vt.

Young, Augustus. 1856. *Preliminary Report on the Natural History of the State of Vermont.* Chauncy Goodrich, Burlington, Vt.

Geology

Christman, Robert A. 1956. *The Geology of Mt. Mansfield State Forest.* Vermont Geological Survey, Vermont Development Commission, Montpelier, Vt.

———. 1956. *The Geology of Groton State Forest.* Vermont Geological Survey, Vermont Development Commission, Montpelier, Vt.

Dewey, John F. 1972. "Plate Tectonics." *Scientific American* 226 (5):56–68.

Dietz, Robert S. 1972. "Geosynclines, Mountains and Continent Building." *Scientific American* 226 (3):30–38.

Dodge, Harry W., Jr. 1959. *The Geology of Calvin Coolidge State Forest Park.* Vermont Geological Survey, Vermont Development Commission, Montpelier, Vt.

———. 1962. *The Geology of Button Bay State Park.* Vermont Geological Survey, Vermont Development Commission, Montpelier, Vt.

———. 1967. *The Geology of Darling State Park.* Vermont Geological Survey, Montpelier, Vt.

———. 1969. *The Geology of D.A.R. State Park, Mt. Philo State Park and Sand Bar State Park.* Vermont Geological Survey, Montpelier, Vt.

Doll, Charles G. (ed.). 1961. *Centennial Geologic Map of Vermont.* Vermont Geological Survey, Vermont Development Department, Montpelier, Vt.

———. 1970. *Surficial Geologic Map of Vermont.* Vermont Geological Survey, Department of Water Resources, Montpelier, Vt.

Jacobs, Elbridge Churchill. 1950 (reprinted 1969). *The Physical Features of Vermont.* Vermont Geological Survey, Vermont Development Department, Montpelier, Vt.

Mills, John Ross. 1951. *A Study of Lakes in Northeastern Vermont*. Vermont Geological Survey, Vermont Development Commission, Montpelier, Vt.

Stewart, David P. 1961. *The Glacial Geology of Vermont*. Vermont Geological Survey, Vermont Development Commission, Montpelier, Vt.

Welby, Charles W. 1962. *Paleontology of the Champlain Basin in Vermont*. Vermont Geological Survey, Vermont Development Department, Montpelier, Vt.

Plants

Appalachian Mountain Club. 1964. *Mountain Flowers of New England*. Appalachian Mountain Club, Boston.

Boelter, D. H., and Verry, E. S. 1977. *Peatland and Water in the Northern Lake States*. North Central Forest Experiment Station, U.S.D.A. Forest Service General Technology. Reference NC-31.

Burns, G. P., and Otis, C. H. 1916 (reprinted 1979). *The Trees of Vermont*. Originally published by Free Press Printing Company, Burlington, Vt. Reprinted by Charles E. Tuttle Company, Rutland, Vt.

Clark, Anna M. 1899. *Trees of Vermont*. Free Press Association, Burlington, Vt.

Cobb, Boughton. 1963. *A Field Guide to the Ferns*. Peterson Field Guide Series. Houghton Mifflin Company, Boston.

Harlow, William M. 1957. *Trees of the Eastern and Central United States and Canada*. Dover Publications, New York.

Harper, Roland M. 1918. "Changes in Forest Area of New England in Three Centuries." *Journal of Forestry* 16:442–452.

Jones, L. R., and Rand, F. V. 1909 (reprinted 1979). *Vermont Shrubs and Woody Vines*. Originally published by Vermont Agricultural Experiment Station, Burlington, Vt. Reprinted by Charles E. Tuttle Company, Rutland, Vt.

Korling, Torkel. 1973. *Wild Plants in Flower, Volume II: The Boreal Forest and Borders*. Published by the author, Dundee, Ill.

Mackenzie, Katherine. 1973. *Wildflowers of the North Country*. Tundra Books of Northern New York, Plattsburgh, N.Y.

Newcomb, Lawrence. 1977. *Newcomb's Wildflower Guide*. Little, Brown, and Company, Boston.

Peterson, Roger Tory, and McKenny, Margaret. 1968. *A Field Guide to Wildflowers of Northeastern and North-central North America*. Peterson Field Guide Series. Houghton Mifflin Company, Boston.

Seymour, Frank C. 1969. *The Flora of Vermont*. Bulletin 660, Vermont Agricultural Experiment Station, University of Vermont, Burlington, Vt.

Siccama, Thomas G. 1971. "Presettlement and Present Forest Vegetation in Northern Vermont, with Special Reference to Chittenden County." Reprint from *American Midland Naturalist* 85 (1):153–172.

———. 1974. "Vegetation, Soil, and Climate on the Green Mountains of Vermont." *Ecological Monographs* 44:325–349.

Steele, Frederic L., and Hodgdon, Albion R. 1971. *Trees and Shrubs of Northern New England* (second ed.). Society for the Protection of New Hampshire Forests, Concord, N.H.

Westveld, Marinus, et al. 1956. "Natural Forest Vegetation Zones of New England." *Journal of Forestry* 54 (5):332−338.

Mammals

Allen, Joel A. 1876. "Former Range of New England Mammals."*American Naturalist* 10 (12):708−715.

Burt, William H., and Grossenheider, Richard P. 1964. *A Field Guide to the Mammals*. Peterson Field Guide Series. Houghton Mifflin Company, Boston.

Coppinger, Raymond P., Sands, Michael, and Groves, Emily. 1973. "Meet New England's New Wolf."*Vermont Natural History* 1 (2 and 3):21−23.

Dickinson, Nathaniel R., and Garland, Lawrence E. 1974. *The White-Tailed Deer Resource of Vermont*. Vermont Fish and Game Department, Agency of Environmental Conservation, Montpelier, Vt.

Godin, Alfred J. 1977.*Wild Mammals of New England*. The Johns Hopkins University Press, Baltimore.

Osgood, Frederick R. 1938. "Mammals of Vermont."*Journal of Mammalogy* 19 (4):435−441.

Smith, Peter. 1970. "Seasonal Distribution of Several Small Species of Mammals of Camel's Hump, Vermont." Ph.D. thesis, University of Vermont, Burlington, Vt.

Spargo, John. 1950.*The Catamount in Vermont*. Published by the author, Bennington, Vt.

Titcomb, J. W. 1901. "Animal Life in Vermont." *The Vermonter* 6 (11):197−215.

Vermont Fish and Game Department. (N.d.) "Vermont Fact Sheets: Eastern Bobcat, Eastern Coyote, Fisher, Wild Mammals of Vermont." Vermont Fish and Game Department, Agency of Environmental Conservation, Montpelier, Vt.

—— 1973-1975. *Vermont's Game Annuals*. Bulletin 73-2 through 75-2. Vermont Fish and Game Department, Agency of Environmental Conservation, Montpelier, Vt.

Willey, Charles H. 1978. *The Vermont Black Bear*. Vermont Fish and Game Department, Montpelier, Vt.

Birds

Bent, Arthur C. 1919−58 (reprinted 1961−68). *Life Histories of North American Birds*. Originally published as a 21-part series of bulletins by the United States National Museum. Reprinted as a 26-volume set by Dover Publications, New York.

Brett, James. 1973. *Feathers in the Wind: The Mountain and the Migration*. Hawk Mountain Sanctuary Association, Kempton, Pa.

Bull, John, and Farrand, John, Jr. 1977.*The Audubon Society Field Guide to North American Birds (Eastern Region)*. Alfred A. Knopf, New York.

Farrar, Richard B., Jr. 1973. *Birds of East-Central Vermont*. Vermont Institute of Natural Science, Woodstock, Vt.

Forbush, Edward H., and May, John B. 1939. *A Natural History of American Birds of Eastern and Central North America*. Houghton Mifflin Company, Boston.

Harrison, Hal H. 1975. *A Field Guide to Birds' Nests*. Peterson Field Guide Series. Houghton Mifflin Company, Boston.

McElroy, Thomas P., Jr. 1974. *The Habitat Guide to Birding*. Alfred A. Knopf, New York.

Peterson, Roger Tory. 1966. *A Field Guide to the Birds*. Peterson Field Guide Series. Houghton Mifflin Company, Boston.

Spear, Robert N., Jr. 1976. *Birds of Vermont* (third ed.). Green Mountain Audubon Society, Burlington, Vt.

Vermont Department of Forests, Parks, and Recreation and Vermont Fish and Game Department. 1979. "Vermont Fact Sheet: Status of the Common Loon in Vermont." Vermont Departments of Forests, Parks, and Recreation and Fish and Game, Agency of Environmental Conservation, Montpelier, Vt.

Vermont Institute of Natural Science. 1973–79. "Records of Vermont Birds." Seasonal Records published by Vermont Institute of Natural Science, Woodstock, Vt.

———. 1976–79. "Vermont Breeding Bird Atlas Project." Continuing study of breeding birds from 1976 to 1981. List published by Vermont Institute of Natural Science, Woodstock, Vt.

Fish

Coker, Robert E. 1954. *Streams, Lakes, Ponds*. The University of North Carolina Press, Chapel Hill, N.C.

Eddy, Samuel. 1969. *The Freshwater Fishes* (second ed.). William C. Brown Company, Dubuque, Iowa.

Everhart, W. Harry. 1958. *Fishes of Maine*. Maine Department of Inland Fisheries and Game, Augusta, Me.

Halnon, Leonard C. 1963. *Historical Survey of Lake Champlain's Fishery*. Vermont Fish and Game Department, Montpelier, Vt.

Hubbs, Carl L., and Lagler, Karl F. 1949. *Fisheries of the Great Lakes Region*. Bulletin 26. Cranbrook Institute of Science, Bloomfield, Mich.

Scarola, John. 1973. *Freshwater Fishes of New Hampshire*. New Hampshire Fish and Game Department, Concord, N.H.

Technical Committee for Fisheries Management of the Connecticut River Basin. 1971. *Connecticut River Atlantic Salmon Restoration Program*. (No publisher named, n.p.)

Van Oosten, John. ca. 1938. "Resume of the History of the Atlantic Salmon in the United States with Special Reference to its Reestablishment in Lake Champlain." Mimeographed paper, Vermont Fish and Game Department. Agency of Environmental Conservation, Montpelier, Vt.

Vermont Fish and Game Department. 1973–75. *Vermont's Fisheries Annuals*. Bulletins 73-1 through 75-1. Vermont Fish and Game Department, Agency of Environmental Conservation, Montpelier, Vt.

———. (N.d.) "Vermont Guide to Fishing" (map). Vermont Fish and Game Department, Agency of Environmental Conservation, Montpelier, Vt.

———. (N.d.) "Vermont Fact Sheet: Connecticut River Salmon and Shad Program." Vermont Fish and Game Department, Agency of Environmental Conservation, Montpelier, Vt.

Reptiles and Amphibians

Babcock, Harold L. 1971. *Turtles of the Northeastern United States*. Dover Publications, New York.

Conant, Roger. 1975. *A Field Guide to Reptiles and Amphibians of Eastern and Central North America* (second ed.). Peterson Field Guide Series. Houghton Mifflin Company, Boston.

Countryman, William D. 1976. "Checklist of Recent Amphibia of Vermont." Mimeographed sheet.

———. 1979. "Checklist of Recent Reptilia of Vermont." Mimeographed sheet.

Gemmill, Dennis. 1976. "The Snakes of Vermont." *Vermont Natural History* 4:1–5.

Oliver, James A. 1955. *The Natural History of North American Amphibians and Reptiles*. P. Van Nostrand Company, Princeton, N.J.

Porter, George. 1967. *The World of the Frog and the Toad*. J. B. Lippincott Company, Philadelphia.

Vermont Fish and Game Department. (N.d.) "Vermont Fact Sheet: Amphibians of Vermont." Vermont Fish and Game Department, Agency of Environmental Conservation, Montpelier, Vt.

Insects

Borror, Donald J., and DeLong, Dwight M. 1964. *An Introduction to the Study of Insects*. Holt, Rinehart and Winston, New York.

Frost, S. W. 1959. *Insect Life and Insect Natural History*. Dover Publications, New York.

Headstrom, Richard. 1977. "The Butterflies of Vermont." *Vermont Natural History* 5:1–6.

Lutz, F. E. 1935. *Fieldbook of Insects*. G. P. Putnam's Sons, New York.

Swain, Ralph. 1948. *The Insect Guide*. Doubleday and Company, Garden City, N.Y.

Appendix IV

Common and Scientific Names of Plants and Animals in the Text

Plants, Flowering

Arbutus, trailing—*Epigaea repens*
Arethusa (Dragon's mouth)—*Arethusa bulbosa*
Arrowhead, common (Duck potato)—*Sagittaria latifolia*
Arrowhead—*Sagittaria spp.*
Aster, white wood—*Aster divaricatus*
Aster, whorled—*Aster acuminatus*
Bedstraws—*Galium spp.*
Beggarticks—*Bidens frondosa*
Bilberry, alpine (bog)—*Vaccinium uliginosum*
Bindweed—*Convolvulus spp.*
Black-eyed Susans—*Rudbeckia serotina*
Bladderwort, horned—*Utricularia cornuta*
Bloodroot—*Sanguinaria canadensis*
Blue flag (Iris)—*Iris versicolor*
Bunchberry—*Cornus canadensis*
Burdock—*Arctium minus*
Burreed—*Sparganium spp.*
Butter-and-eggs—*Linaria vulgaris*
Butterwort—*Pinguicula vulgaris*
Calopogon (Grass-pink)—*Calopogon pulchellus*
Campion, white—*Lychnis alba*
Catchfly, night-flowering—*Silene noctiflora*
Cattail, common—*Typha latifolia*
Chestnut, water—*Trapa natans*
Chickory—*Cichorium intybus*
Cinquefoil, three-toothed—*Potentilla tridentata*
Cinquefoils—*Potentilla spp.*
Clintonia (Bead lily)—*Clintonia borealis*
Clover, red—*Trifolium pratense*
Clover, white—*Trifolium repens*
Cotton grass—*Eriophorum spp.*
Cranberry, large—*Vaccinium macrocarpon*
Cranberry, mountain—*Vaccinium vitis-idaea*
Cranberry, small—*Vaccinium oxycoccus*
Crowberry, black—*Empetrum nigrum*
Daisy, ox-eye—*Chrysanthemum leucanthemum*
Dandelion, common—*Taraxacum officinale*
Devil's paintbrush (Hawkweed)—*Hieracium aurantiacum*

Duckweeds—*Lemnaceae* (family)
Dutchman's-breeches—*Dicentra cucullaria*
Elodea (Waterweed)—*Anacharis canadensis*
Evening primrose, common—*Oenothera biennis*
Fireweed—*Epilobium angustifolium*
Foamflower—*Tiarella cordifolia*
Gentian, bottle (closed)—*Gentiana clausa*
Ginger, wild—*Asarum canadense*
Goldenrods—*Solidago spp.*
Goldthread—*Coptis groenlandica*
Grasses—*Poaceae* (family)
Hepatica, round-lobed—*Hepatica americana*
Indian pipe—*Monotropa uniflora*
Jack-in-the-pulpit—*Arisaema atrorubens*
Jewelweeds—*Impatiens spp.*
Lady's-slipper, pink—*Cypripedium acaule*
Lady's-slipper, showy—*Cypripedium reginae*
Lady's-slipper, yellow—*Cypripedium calceolus*
Lady's-tresses—*Spiranthes spp.*
Leek, wild—*Allium tricoccum*
Loosestrife, purple—*Lythrum salicaria*
Marigold, marsh—*Caltha palustris*
Milfoil, water—*Myriophyllum spp.*
Milkweed, common—*Asclepias syriaca*
Morning glory—*Ipomoea spp.*
Moss, Spanish—*Tillandsia usneoides*
Mullein, common—*Verbascum thapsus*
Nettles—*Urtica spp.*
Orchids—*Orchidaceae* (family)
Orchis, showy—*Orchis spectabilis*
Orchis, white bog—*Habenaria dilatata*
Partridgeberry—*Mitchella repens*
Pickerelweed—*Pontederia cordata*
Pitcher plant—*Sarracenia purpurea*
Pogonia, rose—*Pogonia ophioglossoides*
Pond lily, yellow—*Nuphar variegatum*
Pondweeds—*Potamogeton spp.*
Primrose, bird's eye—*Primula mistassinica*
Queen Anne's lace—*Daucus carota*
Rattlesnake plantains—*Goodyera spp.*
Rice, wild—*Zizania aquatica*
Rushes—*Juncaceae* (family)
Sandwort, mountain—*Arenaria groenlandica*

Sarsaparilla, wild—*Aralia nudicaulis*
Saxifrage, purple mountain—*Saxifraga oppositifolia*
Sedge, Bigelow's—*Carex Bigelowii*
Sedges—*Cyperaceae* (family)
Shepherd's purse—*Capsella bursa-pastoris*
Shinleaf—*Pyrola elliptica*
Smartweeds—*Polygonum spp.*
Spatterdock (Yellow pond lily)—*Nuphar variegatum*
Starflower—*Trientalis borealis*
Sundews—*Drosera spp.*
Sunflowers—*Helianthus spp.*
Tea, Labrador—*Ledum groenlandicum*
Thistles—*Cirsium spp.*
Trefoil, birdfoot—*Lotus corniculatus*
Trillium, painted—*Trillium undulatum*
Trillium, red—*Trillium erectum*
Trillium, white—*Trillium grandiflorum*
Turtlehead—*Chelone glabra*
Twayblades—*Liparis* and *Listera spp.*
Twinflower—*Linnaea borealis*
Violet, dogtooth (Trout lily)—*Erythronium americanum*
Violets—*Viola spp.*
Water lilies—*Nymphaea spp.*
Windflower (Wood anemone)—*Anemone quinquefolia*
Winter cress—*Barbarea spp.*
Wintergreen—*Gaultheria procumbens*
Yarrow—*Achillea millefolium*

Trees and Shrubs
Alder, speckled—*Alnus rugosa*
Arrow-wood—*Viburnum dentatum*
Ash, black—*Fraxinus nigra*
Ash, white—*Fraxinus americana*
Aspen, big-tooth—*Populus grandidentata*
Aspen, quaking—*Populus tremuloides*
Basswood (Linden)—*Tilia americana*
Bayberry—*Myrica cerifera*
Bayberry family—*Myricaceae* (family)
Beech, American—*Fagus grandifolia*
Birch, gray—*Betula populifolia*
Birch, heart-leaved paper—*Betula papyrifera v. cordifolia*
Birch, paper (white)—*Betula papyrifera*
Birch, yellow—*Betula lenta*

Blackberry—*Rubus allegheniensis*
Blueberries—*Vaccinium spp.*
Box-elder (Ash-leaved maple)—*Acer negundo*
Butternut—*Juglans cinerea*
Cedar, northern white—*Thuja occidentalis*
Cedar, red—*Juniperus virginiana*
Cherry, black—*Prunus serotina*
Cherry, choke—*Prunus virginiana*
Cherry, pin (fire)—*Prunus pensylvanica*
Chestnut, American—*Castanea dentata*
Cottonwood, eastern—*Populus deltoides*
Dogwood, alternate-leaved—*Cornus alternifolia*
Dogwood, flowering—*Cornus florida*
Elm, American—*Ulmus americana*
Fir, balsam—*Abies balsamea*
Fir, Frasier—*Abies Fraseri*
Gale, sweet—*Myrica gale*
Gum, black (Tupelo)—*Nyssa sylvatica*
Hawthorns—*Crataegus spp.*
Hazelnut, beaked—*Corylus cornuta*
Heath, beach—*Hudsonia tomentosa*
Heaths—*Ericaceae* (family)
Hemlock, eastern—*Tsuga canadensis*
Hickory, shagbark—*Carya ovata*
Hobblebush (Witch-hobble)—*Viburnum alnifolium*
Holly, mountain—*Nemopanthus mucronata*
Juniper, common—*Juniperus communis*
Laurel, bog (pale)—*Kalmia polifolia*
Laurel, great—*Rhododendron maximum*
Laurel, mountain—*Kalmia latifolia*
Laurel, sheep—*Kalmia angustifolia*
Leatherleaf—*Chamaedaphne calyculata*
Meadowsweet—*Spirea latifolia*
Maple, mountain—*Acer spicatum*
Maple, red (soft)—*Acer rubrum*
Maple, silver—*Acer saccharinum*
Maple, striped—*Acer pensylvanicum*
Maple, sugar (hard or rock)—*Acer saccharum*
Mountain ash—*Pyrus americana*
Nannyberry—*Viburnum lentago*
Oak, black—*Quercus velutina*
Oak, bur (mossy-cup)—*Quercus macrocarpa*
Oak, chestnut—*Quercus prinus*

Oak, red—*Quercus rubra*
Oak, scarlet—*Quercus coccinea*
Oak, swamp white—*Quercus bicolor*
Oak, white—*Quercus alba*
Pine, jack—*Pinus Banksiana*
Pine, pitch—*Pinus rigida*
Pine, red (Norway)—*Pinus resinosa*
Pine, white—*Pinus strobus*
Poplar, balsam—*Populus balsamifera*
Poplar, tulip—*Liriodendron tulipifera*
Raspberries—*Rubus spp.*
Redbud—*Cercis canadensis*
Rosemary, bog—*Andromeda glaucophylla*
Sassafras—*Sassafras albidum*
Shadbush (Serviceberry)—*Amelanchier arborea*
Spruce, black—*Picea mariana*
Spruce, red—*Picea rubens*
Spruce, white—*Picea glauca*
Steeplebush—*Spirea tomentosa*
Sumac, staghorn—*Rhus typhina*
Sycamore—*Plantanus occidentalis*
Tamarack (American larch)—*Larix laricina*
Viburnums—*Viburnum spp.*
Walnut, black—*Juglans nigra*
Willows—*Salix spp.*
Winterberry (Black alder)—*Ilex verticillata*
Witherod (Wild raisin)—*Viburnum cassinoides*

Plants, Nonflowering
Algae, green—*Chlorophyceae* (family)
Chanterelles—*Cantherellus spp.*
Cliffbrake, slender—*Cryptogramma Stelleri*
Club moss, bristly—*Lycopodium annotinum*
Club moss, fir—*Lycopodium Selago*
Diatoms—*Diatomaceae* (family)
Fern, cinnamon—*Osmunda cinnamomea*
Fern, crested shield—*Dryopteris cristata*
Fern, hayscented—*Dennstaedtia punctilobula*
Fern, interrupted—*Osmunda Claytoniana*
Fern, lady—*Athyrium Filix-femina*
Fern, male—*Dryopteris Filix-mas*
Fern, marsh—*Thelypteris palustris*
Fern, New York—*Thelypteris noveboracensis*
Fern, ostrich—*Matteuccia Struthiopteris*

Fern, royal—*Osmunda regalis*
Fungi—*Fungi* (subdivision)
Horsetails—*Equisetum spp.*
Moss, sphagnum—*Sphagnum spp.*
Mosses—*Bryophyta* (division)
Old-man's beard—*Usnea barbata*
Spleenwort, green—*Asplenium viride*
Spleenwort, narrow-leaved—*Athyrium pycnocarpon*
Spleenwort, silvery—*Athyrium thelypteroides*
Wall rue—*Asplenium Ruta-muraria*
Woodfern, marginal—*Dryopteris marginalis*
Woodfern, spinulose—*Dryopteris spinulosa*

Mammals
Bat, big brown—*Eptesicus fuscus*
Bat, Indiana—*Myotis sodalis*
Bat, little brown—*Myotis lucifugus*
Bat, red—*Lasiurus borealis*
Bear, black—*Ursus americanus*
Beaver—*Castor canadensis*
Bison—*Bison bison*
Bobcat—*Lynx rufus*
Caribou, woodland—*Rangifer caribou*
Catamount (Mountain lion)—*Felis concolor*
Chipmunk, eastern—*Tamias striatus*
Cottontail, eastern—*Sylvilagus floridanus*
Cottontail, New England—*Sylvilagus transitionalis*
Coyote, eastern—*Canis latrans*
Deer, white-tailed—*Odocoileus virginianus*
Elk (Wapiti)—*Cervus canadensis*
Fisher—*Martes pennanti*
Fox, gray—*Urocyon cinereoargenteus*
Fox, red—*Vulpes fulva*
Hare, snowshoe (varying)—*Lepus americanus*
Lemming, southern bog—*Synaptomys cooperi*
Lynx, Canada—*Lynx canadensis*
Mammoth, woolly—*Elephas primigenius*
Marten, pine—*Martes americana*
Mastodon—*Mastodon americanus*
Mink—*Mustela vison*
Mole, hairy-tailed—*Parascalops breweri*
Mole, star-nosed—*Condylura cristata*
Moose—*Alces alces*
Mouse, deer—*Peromyscus maniculatus*

Mouse, house—*Mus musculus*
Mouse, meadow jumping—*Zapus hudsonius*
Mouse, white-footed—*Peromyscus leucopus*
Mouse, woodland jumping—*Napaeozapus insignis*
Muskrat—*Ondatra zibethica*
Opossum—*Didelphis marsupialis*
Otter, river—*Lutra canadensis*
Pipistrel, eastern—*Pipistrellus subflavus*
Porcupine—*Erethizon dorsatum*
Raccoon—*Procyon lotor*
Shrew, masked—*Sorex cinereus*
Shrew, northern water—*Sorex palustris*
Shrew, pygmy—*Microsorex hoyi*
Shrew, short-tailed—*Blarina brevicauda*
Skunk, striped—*Mephitis mephitis*
Squirrel, black—*Sciurus carolinensis*
Squirrel, gray—*Sciurus carolinensis*
Squirrel, northern flying—*Glaucomys sabrinus*
Squirrel, red—*Tamiasciurus hudsonicus*
Vole, boreal red-backed—*Clethrionomys gapperi*
Vole, meadow—*Microtus pennsylvanicus*
Weasel, long-tailed—*Mustela frenata*
Weasel, short-tailed—*Mustela erminea*
Wolf, timber (gray)—*Canis lupus*
Wolverine—*Gulo luscus*
Woodchuck (Groundhog)—*Marmota monax*

Birds
Bittern, American—*Botaurus lentiginosus*
Blackbird, red-winged—*Agelaius phoeniceus*
Blackbird, rusty—*Euphagus carolinus*
Bluebird, eastern—*Sialia sialis*
Bobolink—*Dolichonyx oryzivorus*
Bobwhite, common (Quail)—*Colinus virginianus*
Bufflehead—*Bucephala albeola*
Bunting, indigo—*Passerina cyanea*
Bunting, snow—*Plectrophenax nivalis*
Canvasback—*Aythya valisineria*
Cardinal—*Cardinalis cardinalis*
Catbird, gray—*Dumetella carolinensis*
Chickadee, black-capped—*Parus atricapillus*
Chickadee, boreal—*Parus hudsonicus*
Cowbird, brown-headed—*Molothrus ater*
Crossbill, red—*Loxia curvirostra*

Crossbill, white-winged—*Loxia leucoptera*
Crow, American—*Corvus brachyrhynchos*
Duck, black—*Anas rubripes*
Duck, mallard—*Anas platyrhynchos*
Duck, ring-necked—*Aythya collaris*
Duck, wood—*Aix sponsa*
Eagle, bald—*Haliaeetus leucocephalus*
Egret, cattle—*Bubulus ibis*
Falcon, peregrine—*Falco peregrinus*
Finch, purple—*Carpodacus purpureus*
Finches—*Fringillidae* (family)
Flicker, common—*Colaptes auratus*
Flycatcher, alder—*Empidonax alnorum*
Flycatcher, great crested—*Myiarchus crinitus*
Flycatcher, least—*Empidonax minimus*
Flycatcher, olive-sided—*Nuttallornis borealis*
Flycatcher, yellow-bellied—*Empidonax flaviventris*
Gadwall—*Anas strepera*
Gallinule, common—*Gallinula chloropus*
Goldeneye, common—*Bucephala clangula*
Goldfinch, American—*Carduelis tristis*
Goose, Canada—*Branta canadensis*
Goose, snow—*Chen caerulescens*
Goshawk—*Accipiter gentilis*
Grebe, horned—*Podiceps auritus*
Grebe, pied-billed—*Podilymbus podiceps*
Grosbeak, evening—*Hesperiphona vespertina*
Grosbeak, pine—*Pinicola enucleator*
Grosbeak, rose-breasted—*Pheucticus ludovicianus*
Grouse, ruffed (Partridge)—*Bonasa umbellus*
Grouse, spruce—*Canachites canadensis*
Gull, herring—*Larus argentatus*
Gull, ring-billed—*Larus delawarensis*
Gyrfalcon—*Falco rusticolus*
Harrier, northern (Marsh hawk)—*Circus cyaneus*
Hawk, board-winged—*Buteo platypterus*
Hawk, Cooper's—*Accipiter cooperii*
Hawk, red-shouldered—*Buteo lineatus*
Hawk, red-tailed—*Buteo jamaicensis*
Hawk, rough-legged—*Buteo lagopus*
Hawk, sharp-shinned—*Accipiter striatus*
Heron, black-crowned night—*Nycticorax nycticorax*
Heron, great blue—*Ardea herodias*

Heron, green—*Butorides striatus*
Jay, blue—*Cyanocitta cristata*
Jay, gray (Canada)—*Perisoreus canadensis*
Junco, dark-eyed—*Junco hyemalis*
Kestrel (Sparrow hawk)—*Falco sparverius*
Killdeer—*Charadrius vociferus*
Kingfisher, belted—*Megaceryle alcyon*
Kinglet, ruby-crowned—*Regulus calendula*
Loon, common—*Gavia immer*
Meadowlark, eastern—*Sturnella magna*
Merganser, common—*Mergus merganser*
Merganser, hooded—*Lophodytes cucullatus*
Merganser, red-breasted—*Mergus serrator*
Mockingbird—*Mimus polyglottos*
Nuthatch, red-breasted—*Sitta canadensis*
Nuthatch, white-breasted—*Sitta carolinensis*
Oldsquaw—*Clangula hyemalis*
Oriole, northern (Baltimore)—*Icterus galbula*
Osprey—*Pandion haliaetus*
Ovenbird—*Seiurus aurocapillus*
Owl, barred—*Strix varia*
Owl, great horned—*Bubo virginianus*
Owl, hawk—*Surnia ulula*
Owl, long-eared—*Asio otus*
Owl, saw-whet—*Aegolius acadicus*
Owl, screech—*Otus asio*
Owl, short-eared—*Asio flammeus*
Owl, snowy—*Nyctea scandiaca*
Parula, northern—*Parula americana*
Pewee, eastern wood—*Contopus virens*
Phoebe, eastern—*Sayornis phoebe*
Pigeon, passenger—*Ectopistes migratorius*
Pintail—*Anas acuta*
Plovers—*Charadriidae* (family)
Quail, bobwhite—*Colinus virginianus*
Rail, Virginia—*Rallus limicola*
Raven, common—*Corvus corax*
Redhead—*Aythya americana*
Redpoll, common—*Carduelis flammea*
Redstart, American—*Setophaga ruticilla*
Robin, American—*Turdus migratorius*
Sandpiper, solitary—*Tringa solitaria*
Sandpiper, spotted—*Actitis macularia*

Sandpiper, upland—*Bartramia longicauda*
Sapsucker, yellow-bellied—*Sphyrapicus varius*
Scaup, greater—*Aythya marila*
Scaup, lesser—*Aythya affinis*
Scoters—*Melanitta spp.*
Shoveler—*Anas clypeata*
Shrike, loggerhead—*Lanius ludovicianus*
Shrike, northern—*Lanius excubitor*
Siskin, pine—*Carduelis pinus*
Snipe, common—*Capella gallinago*
Sparrow, house—*Passer domesticus*
Sparrow, Lincoln's—*Melospiza lincolnii*
Sparrow, Savannah—*Passerculus sandwichensis*
Sparrow, song—*Melospiza melodia*
Sparrow, swamp—*Melospiza georgiana*
Sparrow, tree—*Spizella arborea*
Sparrow, white-throated—*Zonotrichia albicollis*
Starling—*Sturnus vulgaris*
Swallow, bank—*Riparia riparia*
Swallow, tree—*Iridoprocene bicolor*
Tanager, scarlet—*Piranga olivacea*
Teal, blue-winged—*Anas discors*
Teal, green-winged—*Anas crecca*
Tern, black—*Chlidonias nigra*
Tern, common—*Sterna hirundo*
Thrasher, brown—*Toxostoma rufum*
Thrush, gray-cheeked—*Catharus minimus*
Thrush, hermit—*Catharus guttatus*
Thrush, Swainson's—*Catharus ustulatus*
Thrush, wood—*Hylocichla mustelina*
Towhee, rufous-sided—*Pipilo erythrophthalmus*
Turkey, wild (common)—*Meleagris gallopavo*
Veery—*Catharus fuscescens*
Vireo, red-eyed—*Vireo olivaceus*
Vireo, solitary—*Vireo solitarius*
Vulture, turkey—*Cathartes aura*
Warbler, bay-breasted—*Dendroica castanea*
Warbler, black-and-white—*Mniotilta varia*
Warbler, blackpoll—*Dendroica striata*
Warble, black-throated blue—*Dendroica caerulescens*
Warbler, black-throated green—*Dendroica virens*
Warbler, Cape May—*Dendroica tigrina*
Warbler, chestnut-sided—*Dendroica pensylvanica*

Warbler, magnolia—*Dendroica magnolia*
Warbler, Nashville—*Vermivora ruficapilla*
Warbler, palm—*Dendroica palmarum*
Warbler, pine—*Dendroica pinus*
Warbler, Wilson's—*Wilsonia pusilla*
Warbler, yellow—*Dendroica petechia*
Warbler, yellow-rumped (Myrtle)—*Dendroica coronata*
Waterthrush, northern—*Seiurus noveboracensis*
Waxwing, cedar—*Bombycilla cedrorum*
Wigeon—*Anas americana*
Woodcock, American—*Philohela minor*
Woodpecker, black-backed three-toed—*Picoides arcticus*
Woodpecker, downy—*Picoides pubescens*
Woodpecker, hairy—*Picoides villosus*
Woodpecker, northern three-toed (ladder-backed)—*Picoides tridactylus*
Woodpecker, pileated—*Dryocopus pileatus*
Wren, long-billed marsh—*Cistothorus palustris*
Wren, short-billed marsh—*Cistothorus platensis*
Wren, winter—*Troglodytes troglodytes*
Yellowthroat, common—*Geothlypis trichas*

Reptiles and Amphibians

Bullfrog—*Rana catesbeiana*
Cottonmouth, eastern (Water moccasin)—*Agkistrodon piscivorus piscivorus*
Frog, leopard (meadow)—*Rana pipiens*
Frog, mink—*Rana septentrionalis*
Frog, pickerel—*Rana palustris*
Frog, wood—*Rana sylvatica*
Mud puppy—*Necturus maculosus*
Newt, red-spotted (Red eft)—*Notophthalamus viridescens viridescens*
Peeper, spring—*Hyla crucifer*
Rattlesnake, timber—*Crotalus horridus horridus*
Salamander, four-toed—*Hemidactylium scutatum*
Salamander, Jefferson—*Ambystoma jeffersonianum*
Salamander, northern dusky—*Desmognathus fuscus fuscus*
Salamander, northern two-lined—*Eurycea bislineata bislineata*
Salamander, red-backed—*Plethodon cinereus cinereus*
Salamander, spotted—*Ambystoma maculatum*
Salamander, two-lined—*Eurycea bislineata*
Snake, black rat (pilot)—*Elaphne obsoleta obsoleta*
Snake, eastern milk—*Lampropeltis triangulum triangulum*

Snake, eastern garter—*Thamnophis sirtalis*
Snake, northern ring-necked—*Diadophis punctatus edwardsi*
Snake, northern water—*Natrix sipedon sipedon*
Snake, red-bellied—*Storeria occipitomaculata*
Snake, smooth green—*Opheodrys vernalis*
Toad, American—*Bufo americanus*
Toad, Fowler's—*Bufo woodhousei fowleri*
Treefrog, gray—*Hyla versicolor*
Turtle, bog—*Clemmys muhlenbergi*
Turtle, eastern painted—*Chrysemys picta picta*
Turtle, eastern spiny softshell—*Trionyx spiniferus spiniferus*
Turtle, map—*Graptemys geographica*
Turtle, snapping—*Chelydra serpentina*
Turtle, wood—*Clemmys insculpta*

Fish

Bass, largemouth—*Micropterus salmoides*
Bass, smallmouth—*Micropterus dolomieui*
Bowfin—*Amia calva*
Bullhead, brown—*Ictalurus nebulosus*
Crappie, black—*Pomoxis nigromaculatus*
Eel, American—*Anguilla rostrata*
Gar, long-nosed—*Lepisosteus osseus*
Lamprey, sea—*Petromyzon marinus*
Ling—*Lota lota*
Lungfish, African—*Protopterus spp.*
Muskellunge—*Esox masquinongy*
Perch, yellow—*Perca flavescens*
Pickerel, chain—*Esox niger*
Pike, northern—*Esox lucius*
Pumpkinseed (Sunfish)—*Lepomis gibbosus*
Salmon, Atlantic—*Salmo salar*
Salmon, landlocked (Sebago)—*Salmo salar*
Shad, American—*Alosa sapidissima*
Sheepshead—*Aplodinotus grunniens*
Smelt rainbow—*Osmerus mordax*
Sturgeon, lake—*Acipenser fulvescens*
Sucker, common—*Catostomus commersonnii*
Sunfish (Pumpkinseed)—*Lepomis gibbosus*
Trout, brook—*Salvelinus fontinalis*
Trout, brown—*Salmo trutta*
Trout, lake—*Salvelinus namaycush*

Trout, rainbow—*Salmo gairdnerii*
Walleye (Pike perch)—*Stizostedion vitreum*
Whitefish—*Coregonus clupeaformis*

Invertebrates

Ant, carpenter—*Camponotus herculeanus pennsylvanicus*
Backswimmers—*Notonectidae* (family)
Beetle, Colorado potato—*Leptinotarsa decimlineata*
Beetle, Arctic ground—*Nebria suturalis*
Beetles, ground—*Carabidae* (family)
Beetles, predaceous diving—*Dytiscidae* (family)
Beetles, whirligig—*Dineutes spp.*
Boatman, water—*Corixidae* (family)
Budworm, spruce—*Choristoneura fumiferana*
Bumblebee—*Bombus spp.*
Butterfly, monarch (milkweed)—*Danaus plexippus*
Butterfly, mourning cloak—*Nymphalis antiopa*
Butterfly, white admiral—*Limenitis arthemis*
Caddisflies—*Trichoptera* (order)
Clam, freshwater—*Sphaerium spp.*
Crayfish—*Cambarus bartoni*
Damselflies—*Zygoptera* (suborder)
Dragonflies—*Anisoptera* (suborder)
Earthworm—*Lumbricus terrestris*
Flatworms—*Turbellaria* (class)
Fly, black—*Simulium spp.*
Froghoppers (Spittlebugs)—*Cercopidae* (family)
Grasshoppers, long-horned—*Tettigoniidae* (family)
Grasshoppers, short-horned—*Acrididae* (family)
Honeybee—*Apis mellifera*
Katydid—*Scudderia furcata*
Leafhoppers—*Cicadellidae* (family)
Mayflies—*Ephemeroptera* (order)
Mosquitoes—*Culicidae* (family)
Moth, gypsy—*Porthetria dispar*
Sawflies—*Tenthredinidae* (family)
Snail, land—*Succinea ovalis*
Snails, pond—*Lymnaeidae* (family)
Stoneflies—*Plecoptera* (order)
Tent caterpillar, eastern—*Malacosoma americanum*
Tent caterpillar, forest—*Malacosoma disstria*
Water bugs, giant—*Belostomatidae* (family)
Water striders—*Gerridae* (family)

Index

Only common names of plants and animals are given in the index. Scientific equivalents for these names are listed in Appendix IV, beginning on page 246. *Indicates pages on which illustrations occur.

Illustration Credits

Joseph Artman: 110
Robert Candy: 62. 94, 130, 204, 226, 230
Courtesy William Gove: 65
John Hall: xii, 69, 90, 96, 102, 120, 121, 139, 170, 217
Courtesy Harvard University Forest, Petersham, Mass.: 45-47
Courtesy Norman Hudson: 50
Charles Johnson: 5, 6, 28, 29, 31, 34, 146, 150, 211, 213
Warren Lavery: 222
Thomas Meyers: 154, 156
Eric Nuse: 71
Ann Pesiri: 66, 74, 83, 85, 105, 113, 129, 132, 138, 142, 158, 160, 161, 164-165, 177, 183, 184, 192, 195, 197, 199, 201
Courtesy Rock of Ages Corporation, Barre, Vt.: 25
William Sladyck: 76
Edgar Strobridge: 109
Jack Swedberg: 175
Courtesy Vermont Historical Society, Montpelier, Vt.: 88
Courtesy Vermont Travel Division, Montpelier, Vt.: ii, vi, x, 2, 56, 59, 118, 162, 181, 186, 187, 214, 215, 219, 224, 231
Jean Vissering: 8-9 (adapted from "Plate Tectonics" by J. F. Dewey. Copyright May 1972 by Scientific American, Inc. All rights reserved), 11 (adapted from "The Breakup of Pangaea" by R. S. Dietz and J. C. Holden. Copyright October 1970 by Scientific American, Inc. All rights reserved), 13 (adapted from "Geosynclines, Mountains, and Continent Building" by R. S. Dietz. Copyright March 1972 by Scientific American, Inc. All rights reserved), 16 (adapted from Flint, R. F., 1971. *Glacial and Quaternary Geology*. John Wiley & Sons, New York. Copyright 1971 by John Wiley & Sons. Reprinted by permission), 17 (adapted from "Surficial Geologic Map of Vermont, Vermont Geological Survey. Reprinted by permission), 22 (adapted from Jacobs, E. C. 1950. *The Physical Features of Vermont*. Vermont Geological Survey, Montpelier, Vt.), 37
Charles Willey: v, 98
Ian Worley: 135

Library of Congress Cataloging in Publication Data
Johnson, Charles W., 1943 –
   The nature of Vermont.

   Bibliography: p. 239
   Includes index.
   1. Natural history — Vermont. I. Title.
QH105.V7J63   574.5'09743   79-56774
ISBN 0-87451-182-8
ISBN 0-87451-183-6 (pbk.)